Heritage Dynamics

Heritage Dynamics

Understanding and adapting to change in diverse heritage contexts

Kalliopi Fouseki

UCLPRESS

First published in 2022 by
UCL Press
University College London
Gower Street
London WC1E 6BT

Available to download free: www.uclpress.co.uk

A CIP catalogue record for this book is available from The British Library.

ISBN: 978-1-78735-835-5 (Hbk)
ISBN: 978-1-78735-834-8 (Pbk)
ISBN: 978-1-78735-833-1 (PDF)
ISBN: 978-1-78735-836-2 (epub)
DOI: https://doi.org/10.14324111.9781787358331

Contents

This book is dedicated to all female academics who demonstrated resilience while juggling their increased teaching, research and caring responsibilities during the pandemic.

List of figures

All figures © the author.

List of tables

Acknowledgements

The list of people I would like to thank in writing this book is immense. As the book offers a meta-interpretation of work that I have been conducting since I started my doctoral research 18 years ago, I have engaged in inspirational conversations with numerous individuals (colleagues and students), all of which have shaped my way of thinking *of* and *around* heritage. Listing specific individuals entails the risk of omitting the significant contribution of others. I would thus like to express a collective thanks to colleagues at the UCL Institute of Archaeology, where I completed my PhD; the University of York, where I engaged with the *1807 Commemorated* research project that fostered my work on participatory heritage – especially work with 'socially excluded' museum audiences, which I was then given the chance to exercise in practice at the Science Museum; and, of course, the UCL Institute for Sustainable Heritage which has provided a stimulating, interdisciplinary research environment.

Since the writing of this book coincided with the unprecedented and lengthy lockdowns caused by the Covid-19 pandemic, it was extremely hard to secure the 'time' and 'brain' space needed for such endeavour. With the sudden conversion of face-to-face teaching into the online sphere that led to increased teaching responsibilities, all the while working at home with three young children, the task felt momentarily unfeasible. It only became a feasible task because of the tremendous support and understanding of my family. Although this book may not be as exciting as *Harry Potter* (to the disappointment of my daughters), I hope it offers a new insight into dynamic, systemic, complex and multifaceted heritage.

Introduction

How is heritage created and re-created, shaped and reshaped, formed, reformed and transformed – or even reborn? Heritage in all its forms endures a lengthy and dynamic journey of emergence, transformation, decline and revival. An object displayed within a museum showcase may have travelled through various places and changed uses more than once before acquiring its new function as a museum object. An 'old' building housing a restaurant, cinema or other activities may have performed alternative uses in the past and materially been transformed to accommodate each respective use. An 'old' red bus in the streets of London dedicated for touristic routes may have served millions of everyday commuters in the past. Heritage is thus constantly created, re-created, transformed and reborn. As such, it is a 'renewable resource' subject to constant change, transformation and adaptation.

The materiality of heritage is an important prerequisite for its constant, non-linear, almost 'spiral' life cycles. However, materiality does not always constitute the most influential element in the dynamic transformation of heritage. For example, the empty podiums that once held statues representing slave owners, removed from the public sphere across the UK and beyond as a result of the 'Black Lives Matter' movement, obtained new heritage meanings – and consequently a new 'life' – through the statues' absence. The podiums became symbols of opposition towards and resistance against racism. Their symbolism is enhanced by the absence of materiality (that is, the absence of the statues).

The dynamic transformation of a heritage life cycle is non-linear and multi-dimensional. In essence, heritage transformation is a complex, systemic process that consists of non-linear interconnections of multiple, heterogeneous factors. This proposition underlines this entire book. I will argue that a series of factors such as 'materials', 'values/meanings', 'senses/emotions', 'place/space/environment', 'time', 'resources' and ‘skills/competencies’ are mobilised and interconnected during the transformation of a heritage object, place or practice. I will contend that the continuation and sustainability of a dynamic ‘heritage life cycle’ will depend on the ways in which the aforementioned factors (elements) connect or disconnect. I will then frame this premise as a ‘heritage dynamics’ approach and stress that this framework can enable heritage scholars and heritage professionals to unfold the dynamic nature of heritage conceptually and methodologically in a participatory manner. By doing so, better informed decisions can be made about heritage in the present and future.

Heritage is subject not only to change, transformation and uncertainty, but also to stagnation and permanence. The interactions between ‘materials’, ‘values’, ‘place’, ‘senses’, ‘time’, ‘resources’ and ‘skills’ of the different ‘agents’ involved in heritage making will determine at what points in time heritage emerges, continues, stagnates, disappears or revives. By utilising the framework of ‘heritage dynamics’ in gaining a deep understanding *of* and *for* heritage change, the most critical factors that mobilise change and transformation can be detected.

The proposed ‘heritage dynamics’ framework draws upon complexity theories, assemblage theories, practice theories and systems thinking. In particular, the work of Shove et al. (2012), entitled *The Dynamics of Social Practice*, constitutes a useful departure point. I will thus first introduce their theory on the dynamics of social practice in Chapter 1, according to which the continuation or interruption of a social practice depends on the interconnection of ‘materials’, ‘competencies’ and ‘meanings’. I will expand and refine this proposition by including the additional elements of ‘place/space’, ‘senses/emotions’, ‘time’ and ‘resources’. The expansion of the theory is based on a systematic, in-depth piece of work investigating through the method of system dynamics how residents’ decisions towards thermal comfort, energy efficiency and heritage conservation change over time (Fouseki, Newton et al. 2020). Chapter 3 offers a meta-interpretation of this work which formulated the basis of the suggested ‘heritage dynamics’ approach.

Through this book I intend to bolster and apply the ‘heritage dynamics’ framework in diverse heritage contexts. The range of examples on which the book draws constitutes one of the work’s main strengths. The ‘heritage dynamics’ approach is examined through the lens of historic urban environments with emphasis on urban regeneration, adaptive reuse and retrofitting of ‘historic houses’; exhibition development; participatory approaches to museums and collections management; contested museum and urban heritage spaces and performing arts as heritage using the example of flamenco. Such a wide range of case studies allows us to see heritage in a range of contexts, providing concrete examples of how heritage actually works. By doing so, I seek further to refine and validate the approach of 'heritage dynamics'.

The book is based on a 'meta-interpretation' of extensive research in which I became involved, whether as a single researcher or member of a research team, over the last 18 years. Collectively the case study analysis is based on hundreds (in some cases thousands, such as in Chapter 5) of in-depth interviews, questionnaires, newspaper articles, blogs and social media pages and auto-ethnography. The datasets are thus as diverse as the case studies themselves. Through a process of meta-interpretation the various data can be synthesised, leading to the formulation of new theories and insights.

Meta-interpretation 'focuses on the interpretive synthesis of qualitative research, thus maintaining an interpretive epistemology that is congruent with the majority of primary qualitative research' (Weed 2005). The first step in meta-interpretation is the identification of the subject area in which the synthesis takes place (Weed 2005). In this book, the subject area revolves around 'heritage dynamics'. Prior to synthesising the text, I formulated an initial hypothesis in the context of decision-making between heritage conservation and energy efficiency (Fouseki, Newton et al. 2020). My next step is to explore and refine this initial premise further through the analysis of a diverse range of case studies selected through 'maximum variation sampling' (Weed 2005). A maximum variation sample is 'constructed by identifying key dimensions of variations and then finding cases that vary from each other as much as possible' (Suri 2011, 67). Maximum variation sampling can therefore enable the construction of a 'holistic understanding of the phenomenon by synthesising studies that differ in their study designs on several dimensions' (Suri 2011, 68). Indeed, the case studies upon which this book draws, as well as the methods used in each of the case studies, are divergent, thus widening the breadth and depth of the synthesis. The original methods on which the original analysis was based (especially in Chapters 2, 3, 5 and 7) are divergent because they intended to address a research objective set at the time. However, by using the process of 'meta-interpretation' the original data can be revisited through a new theoretical lens, resulting in new theories and concepts.

The disparate case studies were investigated through a 'concurrent thematic and context analysis' (Weed 2005) offered by the theoretical thread of 'heritage dynamics' developed in Chapter 1. By applying a new theoretical framework, the meta-interpretation dictated areas that had not been researched in the past. Once a 'theoretical saturation point' was reached (Rowlands et al. 2016), no more case studies were included. As a matter of fact, it had already become apparent from the fourth case study that the theory could apply effectively in each case study despite its diversity. In effect I conducted a secondary analysis of qualitative data that I collected individually or as part of a research team (Heaton 2008, 36), the ultimate goal being to contribute new insights into 'heritage dynamics' while consolidating the 'heritage dynamics' framework.

Moreover, 'meta-interpretation sees the location of the researcher in the process as an important and vital part of the synthesis' (Weed 2008, 16). One of the main strengths of this book, in contrast to most meta-interpretation studies, is that the researcher in all case studies is the same person (that is, myself). It is important to note that as meta-interpretation 'features a synthesis of studies that each contain "a truth"' (Weed 2008, 16), meta-interpretation conclusively represents 'an interpretation' rather than 'the interpretation' of these multiple truths' (Weed 2008, 17).

An additional strength of *Heritage Dynamics* is the use of a diverse set of theoretical and methodological 'tools' and approaches, the selection of which was dictated by the nature of each case study. While an overarching 'heritage dynamics' approach underpins all the examples, insights into the particularities of each case study are provided through the application of diverse theoretical lenses such as assemblage theories, complexity theories and urban dynamics (e.g. Chapters 1 and 2), 'functional aesthetics' and 'everyday theories' (Chapter 3), approaches to 'change' and 'lifetime' drawn from heritage science and collections management (Chapter 4), exhibition dynamics and relational theories of affect (Chapter 5), cultural studies on the notion of 'sacredness' and 'nationalism' (Chapter 6) and embodiment theories (Chapter 7).

Methodologically, in Chapters 2, 3, 5 and 7 I illustrate the method of 'system dynamics', a method that allows the mapping of dynamic, cause and effect, non-linear relationships of a 'system' (Sterman 2002). In particular, the visualisation of the dynamic, non-linear interrelationships on the software of Vensim proved useful for gaining a better understanding of the behaviour of the system and the phenomena.

I should note, however, that I did not use 'system dynamics' for developing models, but rather as a 'systems thinking' process, as a thinking tool. Indeed, the method of system dynamics is underpinned by systems thinking theories (see Chapter 1), according to which a phenomenon, event or practice shapes and evolves over time as a result of non-linear interconnections between various elements and parameters (Monat and Gannon 2015). Critical approaches to systems thinking call for commitment to critical self-reflection on chosen methods and an acceptance that all system approaches have a contribution to make (Jackson, 2001). The 'causal loop diagrams' (diagrams that illustrate the dynamic and non-linear cause and effect relationships of multiple factors) depict 'reinforcing' (R) or 'balancing' (B) relationships (Forrester 1987; Randers 1980). The reinforcing relationships indicate growth while the balancing relationships indicate the reverse of growth, decline or stagnation. However, in Chapter 7, which discusses the controversial case of the construction of the New Acropolis Museum, I had to highlight the relationships that are perceived as 'reinforcing' or 'balancing' depending on the approach and perception of each stakeholder.

As mentioned above, the theoretical Chapter 1 is followed by six chapters that consider case studies. In detail, Chapter 2 revolves around the dynamic transformation of historic urban environments through heritage. My geographic focal point is Woolwich, an area in south-east London that has been going through a lengthy – and at times contentious – process of transformation over the last 20 years. This chapter expands the theoretical framework introduced in Chapter 1 by drawing upon urban dynamics. The argument is based on the meta-interpretation of a vast number of collected data (mostly interviews and questionnaires) collected since 2016. This case study is also part of the ongoing European research project 'Deep Cities' (www.deepcities.eu), which aims to develop an 'urban heritage dynamics' model using system dynamics. I conclude with the suggestion of a dynamic hypothesis for 'urban heritage dynamics'.

Chapter 3 is situated in the historic urban context, similarly to the previous chapter, but narrows down the scope on the individual historic (old) building. Here I focus specifically on what I call 'everyday heritage' – that is, the 'everyday' listed or non-listed residential buildings where the ultimate 'managers' are the residents themselves. The chapter examines how residents inhabiting old, traditional houses negotiate their decisions on energy efficiency and heritage conservation. I consider both the 'old house' and the 'decision-making process' to be a social practice. This chapter, like previous ones, offers a meta-interpretation of a unique cross-cultural study published by Fouseki, Newton et al. (2020). The meta-interpretation analysis unveiled how 'heritage values' are highly interconnected and therefore difficult to classify under distinct typologies. In view of this, I will argue in the chapter that heritage values are dynamic, complex systems of meanings and feelings. As a result they are not classifiable. They also require complex methods to be unpacked.

Chapter 4 looks at the dynamic boundaries of 'everyday' and 'official' heritage. The chapter focuses on the emergence and evolution of everyday, functional objects into collection and heritage objects. I utilise the example of the 'old', traditional Maltese buses, which had to be abandoned due to environmental, safety and degradation issues. Their removal from the Maltese urban landscape marked alternative life cycles and futures that their owners might have not considered when they first acquired them. This chapter thus depicts how the traditional Maltese buses evolved from a 'functional', albeit emblematic, object into objects of collection and, later, objects of 'tourist consumption'. This chapter (like Chapter 6) is not based on data collected in the past. I decided to use examples from a dynamic collection (Chapter 4) and 'intangible' heritage (Chapter 6) in order to encompass as much diversity as possible. The data on which this chapter is based derive from personal (auto-ethnographic experience), websites, personal communications and blogs.

Chapter 5 looks at the dynamics unfolded in an exhibition space (that is after the formation and heritagisation of collection described in the previous chapter). The chapter draws on two 'permanent' museum exhibitions on the hidden and dark history of enslavement: the 'London, Sugar and Slavery' exhibition at the Museum of Docklands and the 'Atlantic Worlds' exhibition at the National Maritime Museum, both in London. Chapter 5 unpacks the dynamic mechanisms of each exhibition and explores their impact on visitor experience. Here the exhibition constitutes a social, dynamic practice – the transformation and continuation of which depends on 'internal' and 'external' forces that exist, as will be illustrated, beyond the closed boundaries of the museum's wall.

The chapter offers a meta-interpretation of a vast number of data (including more than 1,490 interviews with visitors at the exhibitions and conversations with community members and museum professionals who became involved in the exhibitions' development). The data were gathered as part of a project funded by the Arts and Humanities Research Council and entitled *1807 Commemorated*. This project coincided with the commemoration of the abolition of the slave trade in 2007 which triggered hundreds of museum exhibitions, both small or larger scale, temporary or permanent. The meta-interpretation allowed the formulation of a dynamic diagram illustrating how the key 'heritage dynamic elements' interact over time while unveiling the critical importance of factors such as trust, negotiation and dialogue.

Chapter 6 unfolds the dissonance of dense, historic urban landscapes through the analysis of one of the world's most controversial museum projects: the New Acropolis Museum in Athens, Greece. This example clearly shows that the relationships formulated between 'dynamic elements' can reinforce or balance, depending on each actor's views.

The elements may be the same but the relationships differ, depending on the angle through which they are examined. The analysis also illustrated the 'fluidity' of elements. A few of these – such as the need visually to connect the new museum with the Parthenon Temple located on the Acropolis Hill – performed the role of a 'sense' element, which then evolved into a 'value' and, ultimately, into a 'material' element.

The final case study in Chapter 7 focuses on the dynamics of what I call 'performing art heritage', looking specifically at flamenco. I intentionally avoid the use of the term 'intangible' heritage where this is possible, although flamenco has been recognised as a form of 'intangible' heritage by UNESCO. I regard the distinction between 'tangible' and 'intangible' particularly problematic as it juxtaposes the very nature of the 'heritage dynamics' framework of the book. *Heritage Dynamics* approaches heritage as a socio-cultural, material and environmental system, the emergence and continuity of which depends on multiple factors, both material and immaterial. Using 'auto-ethnography', I contend how the 'heritage dynamics' elements are embodied through performativity. Deconstructing the dynamics of 'performing art heritage' will hopefully re-orientate our thinking towards heritage more generally by shifting a focus on the 'materiality', 'authenticity' and 'originality' towards 'creativity', 'adaptation' and 'innovation'.

Why, and for whom, is this book important? Firstly, from an academic point of view, the proposition of a 'heritage dynamics' framework, which has been applied in diverse heritage contexts, can galvanise a new way of thinking about heritage: it can lead us beyond problematic divisions such as 'cultural' or 'natural', 'tangible' or 'intangible', 'discursive', 'affective' or 'material' heritage. Moreover, the decision to approach heritage or heritage-related actions as dynamic, complex and systemic processes forces us to rethink the methods employed to understand change and continuity *in* and *for* heritage. The everyday work of heritage professionals is to deal with change. Discerning how change is manifested will thus encourage a more constructive and creative attitude to 'heritage change': one that regards change not as a risk, but rather as a value that needs to be captured, understood and incorporated into heritage management strategies. The method of system dynamics has the potential to be used in an interactive manner at meetings with decision-makers collectively able to decide upon the present and future interventions in a heritage place.

1

Heritage dynamics

Introduction

'Concepts should bring about a new way of seeing something and not simply fix a label to something we think we already know about' (Buchanan 2017, 473). In this chapter I introduce the 'heritage dynamics' approach which will guide the case study analysis in subsequent chapters. In my approach to heritage dynamics I conceptualise heritage as a complex system of dynamic, constantly evolving interactions between 'materials', 'values' (meanings), 'competencies' (skills), 'senses and emotions', 'space/place/environment', 'time' and 'resources' (see also Fouseki, Newton et al. 2020). The underpinning premise of this approach is that heritage is a dynamic and complex socio-cultural practice. In this light, the ways in which heritage as a practice emerges, shifts, transforms, disappears or revives are shaped by how the connections between the aforementioned elements are made, sustained or dissolved. Behind these interactions lie the agents – the various individuals or groups of people who value, use or simply do heritage work. Therefore, although the agents may seem invisible in the systemic conceptualisation of heritage, they are in fact omnipresent.

By framing heritage as a socio-cultural practice, I suggest a 'practice oriented' approach to the fields of heritage studies and heritage management. In my attempt to address heritage as a complex and dynamic system, I do not intend to de-value former theories which focus on the 'material' (e.g. Harrison 2012), 'affective' (e.g. Munroe 2016; Tolia-Kelly et al. 2017) or 'discursive' (e.g. Smith 2006; Waterton et al. 2006) 'turn' to heritage. I have intentionally avoided use of the word 'turn' (such as 'practice-turn') in *Heritage Dynamics*, as this implies a reaction to a predominant assumption, theory, trend, practice or discourse. Before introducing the 'practice-oriented' approach to heritage that regards it as a dynamic social complex, I will review briefly the aforementioned 'turns' through which the field of heritage studies evolved.

Laurajane Smith (2006) pioneered the first, significant 'turn' to heritage studies. In her influential monograph *Uses of Heritage*, she introduced a 'discursive' approach to heritage as a response to the 'material-oriented' paradigms that dominated heritage management in the 1970s, 1980s and 1990s (Smith 2006). Smith coined the term 'authorised heritage discourse' (AHD) to connote the dominant 'Western' ideas and discourses on heritage, which privilege certain attributes as prioritised by heritage experts. Such attributes mostly link to the materiality of heritage (such as aesthetics or monumentality), thus excluding wider communities from heritage practices and from attaching their own intangible meanings to heritage. By doing so, she aimed to problematise the dominant heritage discourse which 'unproblematically' identified heritage as '"old", grand, monumental and aesthetically pleasing sites, buildings, places and artefacts' (Smith 2006, 11).

Smith further argued that 'there is rather a hegemonic discourse about heritage, which acts to constitute the way we think, talk and write about heritage', thus naturalising the 'practice of rounding up the usual suspects to conserve and "pass on" to future generations, and in so doing promotes a certain set of Western elite cultural values as being universally applicable' (2006,11). One of the consequences of AHD, Smith contends, is the exclusion of 'certain social actors and interests from actively engaging with heritage' (2006, 144). According to her, heritage audiences are framed in the authorised heritage discourse as 'passive receptors of the authorised meaning of heritage' who are further prevented from 'active public negotiation about the meaning and nature of heritage, and the social and cultural roles that it may play' (2006, 144).

Smith (2006) and Waterton et al. (2006) have drawn on critical discourse analysis in order to unpack the underpinning, hegemonic ideologies of heritage discourses adopted by those who make decisions on the future of heritage. By using critical discourse analysis the authors unfolded the interconnection between power and the language of heritage. In doing so they demonstrated the ways in which the dominant discourses of heritage shaped by the managers create a particular set of socio-cultural practices which includes certain communities and excludes others.

The discursive approach to heritage evidently signifies that heritage is not just a material 'thing', but also a cultural and social process. As Smith (2006, 144) puts it, heritage is 'what goes on at these sites, and while this does not mean that a sense of physical place is not important for these activities or plays some role in them, the physical place or "site" is not the full story of what heritage may be'. Smith continues by defining heritage as a cultural process

> that engages with acts of remembering that work to create ways to understand and engage with the present, and the sites themselves are cultural tools that can facilitate, but are not necessarily vital for, this process. (Smith 2006, 144)

In view of this, her conceptualisation of heritage encompasses elements of the 'practice-oriented' approach that I would like to introduce in this book.

Harrison (2012) responds to Smith's discursive approach to heritage by advocating a 'material' and 'affective turn'. He is motivated to do so as he argues that

> official practices of heritage and academic heritage studies have actually increasingly distanced themselves from material 'things' and have become dominated by the discourse of heritage. (Harrison 2012, 228)

Although Harrison acknowledges the importance of a 'discursive turn' to heritage – in that it draws 'attention to the knowledge/power effects of heritage and its processes of identification, exhibition and management' (2012, 228) – he also points out that the discursive turn has 'tended to de-privilege the significant affective qualities of material things and the influences the material traces of the past have on people in the contemporary world' (Harrison 2012, 228). To this end, he explores

> not only the ways in which heritage operates as a discursive practice, but also its corporeal influences on the bodies of human and non-human actors, and the ways in which heritage is caught up in the quotidian bodily practices of dwelling, travelling, working and 'being' in the world. (Harrison 2012, 112–13)

He is interested in exploring heritage as a 'strategic socio-technical and/or bio-political assemblage composed of various people, institutions, apparatuses (dispositifs) and the relations between them' (Harrison 2012, 35). As he contends:

> Thinking of heritage in this way not only helps us to understand the way it operates at the level of both material and social relations, but also helps us to focus our attention on the particular constellation of power/knowledge effects that it facilitates, that is, the relationship between heritage and governmentality. (Harrison 2012, 35)

By doing so, Harrison attempts to co-examine the tangible and intangible as well as socio-cultural, natural and material dimensions of heritage, thus fostering a dialogical rather than a separatist model. To do so, he draws on actors network theory which looks at the interconnections of human and non-human agents; by doing so he aspires to challenge the 'modernist impulse to separate "objects" and "humans", "nature" and "culture", "subject" and "object"' (Harrison 2012, 37). He suggests that heritage can be approached as an assemblage in two ways. The first of these, according to Harrison, is 'a conventional way in which heritage is thought of as a series of objects, places or practices that are gathered together in a museum or on a list, register or catalogue of some form' (Harrison 2012, 33). The second is to approach heritage as an assembly of 'specific arrangements of materials, equipment, texts and technologies, both "ancient" and "modern", by which heritage is produced in conversation with them' (Harrison 2012, 35). The 'specific arrangements' to which Harrison refers include the material fabric of heritage sites as well as the 'assortment of artefacts and "scars" that represent its patina of age and authenticity' and 'various technologies of tourism and display by which it is exhibited and made visitable as a heritage site' (Harrison 2012, 35). The sections below examine assemblage theories in greater detail and compare them with system and practice theories, identifying commonalities and differences.

Skrede and Hølleland (2018) are supportive of this argument, contending that:

> 'If Heritage Studies is to become more cross-disciplinary and engage (more) with heritage practitioners, insisting too hard on the intangibility of heritage would probably separate rather than unify different 'camps' in the heritage field. (Skrede and Hølleland 2018, 89)

To achieve this systemic exploration, a combination of approaches and methodological tools may be needed. They make specific reference on how actors network theory complements critical realism and critical discourse analyses, both of which have been previously used in isolation by heritage scholars. The authors acknowledge the insistence of critical realism on laminated systems (Bhaskar 2010), where discourse may constitute one layer or affect another (Skrede and Hølleland 2018, 89), as a promising one for the interdisciplinary field of heritage studies. In conclusion they note that 'we have yet a distance to go before the tangible, intangible, discursive and affective aspects of heritage are succinctly treated as a complementary rather than oppositional' (Skrede and Hølleland 2018, 89).

The 'material' turn in Harrison's work is linked to an 'affective' turn in heritage studies which seems to occur almost simultaneously. The 'affective turn' connotes an ontological shift away from the 'discursive turn' that dominated social sciences (including heritage studies) to the role of affect (Munroe 2016, 116; see also Waterton and Watson 2013). This turn emerged from a concern that the 'discursive turn' was 'writing the body out of theory' (Hemmings, 2005, see also Tolia-Kelly et al. 2017) and attempted to revive the study of the material and physical affects of the world around us (Munroe 2016, 116).

The world was conceptualised by scholars advocating the 'affective' turn as 'dynamic and flowing, full of "potentials", "forces" and "intensities" that can work upon the body and elicit intensely felt experiences that transcend cognitive rationalisation' (Munroe 2016, 116). As a result

> these understandings of affect often decentre or completely relegate analyses of discourse, and obscure historical and social contexts such as the impact gender, race, class and historical frames of reference can have upon how we interact with the world around us. (Munroe 2016, 116)

Yet Wetherell argues that the distinction between affect and emotion is untenable (2013; see also Smith et al. 2018; Lünenborg and Maier 2018, 2). She states that it would be futile to attempt to pull apart the cognitive and bodily processes which spark both affective and emotional reactions as they are inherently intertwined. Burkitt (1999) similarly advocates a relational, social approach to emotions and affects that sees them as knotted together.

Drawing on cultural geography 'more-than-representational' theories on affect, Waterton points out that such approaches allow heritage scholars to conceptualise 'heritage in terms of the body, practice and performativity, together with an insistence that our engagements with it occur through a range of embodied dispositions and interactions' (Waterton 2014, 823). She argues that the turn towards 'practice' in heritage (practice here being defined as the process of engagement, experience and performance), combined with a focus on understanding heritage as a complex and embodied process of meaning- and sense-making that takes into account the 'more-than-human' agents or co-participants/producers of a heritage experience (Harrison 2012), 'means foregrounding notions of "becoming" and "embodiment"' (Waterton 2014, 823). She turns instead to 'more-than-representation' theories because this turn

> pushes beyond the idea of affect as precognitive, and thus unknowable, and simultaneously takes up the notion of intersubjectivity, principally through the concept of contagion. (Waterton 2014, 826; see also Anderson and Harrison 2010)

Waterton adopts a dual approach to affect. For her, affect connotes 'those impulses and nerve firings that sit within bodies, just below mindful consciousness' (2014, 827). It also 'hints at the relational interactions between bodies and places' by looking at what happens inside the body, as well as seeking to understand a little more 'the affective charges of heritage spaces and how those charges circulate and interact' (Waterton 2014, 827; see also Tolia-Kelly et al. 2017).

'Practice theories' and 'heritage dynamics'

I began this chapter by stating that I intend to introduce a 'practice-oriented' rather than a 'practice-turn' approach and, in particular, a dynamic and systemic 'practice-oriented' approach to heritage. Although there is not a unified practice approach, most practice theorists agree that 'such phenomena as knowledge, meaning, human activity, science, power, language, social institutions and historical transformation' are objects of concern in practice theories (Schatzki 2005, 11). They also acknowledge the dependence of activity on shared skills or understandings, which are typically viewed as embodied (Schatzki 2005, 12). A review of contemporary practice theories indicated that 'the field of practice is the total nexus of interconnected human practices' (Schatzki et al. 2001, 11).

One of the matters that practice theories can explore more is that of 'change' (Shove et al. 2012, 9). Understanding how social practices change is critical to inform public policy (Shove et al. 2012, 9). For behavioural sciences, if 'the source of changed behaviour lies in the development of practices' (Warde 2005, 140), 'understanding their emergence, persistence and disappearance is of the essence' (Shove at al. 2012, 9). Shove et al. (2012) stress the significance of understanding change in social practices for informing policy initiatives that promote more sustainable ways of life. According to the authors, such initiatives should be informed by 'an understanding of the elements of which practices and systems of practice are formed, and of the connective tissue that holds them together' (Shove et al. 2012, 9). Agents and structures become two interdependent sets of phenomena through social practices (Shove et al. 2012, 10; see also Giddens 1984, 2).

Since my focal point is on dynamic and complex practices, I draw heavily on the work of Shove et al. (2012) which explores the ways in which social practices emerge, persist, shift and disappear. The authors argue that social practices consist of elements that are integrated when practices are enacted, and that practices emerge, persist and disappear as connections between defining elements are made and broken (Shove et al. 2012, 33). More specifically, they argue that social practices emerge, persist, shift and disappear when connections between materials, meanings and competencies are made, sustained or broken.

Shove et al. adopt an 'elemental' approach which de-centres the human actor. They do so because this focus aligns with their 'argument that in the moment of doing, practitioners (those who do) simultaneously reproduce the practices in which they are engaged and the elements of which these practices are made' (Shove et al. 2012, 21). As the authors further contend, by 'paying attention to the trajectories of elements, and to the making and breaking of links between them', it is possible 'to describe and analyse change and stability without prioritising either agency or structure' (Shove et al. 2012, 21). I would argue, however, that this can be potentially problematic. As will be demonstrated in the remaining chapters of this book – especially in Chapter 6, where heritage dissonance is examined as a dynamic social practice – the ways in which the interconnections of the same elements evolve over time varies depending on the lens of each 'agent' or 'stakeholder' group. There is a dimension of perception that should be considered while mapping the dynamic interconnections of elements.

The authors also argue that if practices are approached as ongoing integrations of elements, it is essential to explore what happens when requisite connections are no longer made. When and how are links broken and 'what is the fate of elements that are stranded as a result?' (Shove et al. 2012, 29). The authors examine everyday practices to conclude that when links are broken materials, meanings and forms of competence either vanish with little or no trace, remain dormant or take a new lease of life within and as part of other practices (Shove et al. 2012, 30).

Based on this work, I contend that heritage as a social and cultural practice consists of elements that are integrated when heritage practices are enacted. Heritage as a practice is therefore much more than a 'complex, interdependent, and open web of things, people, and relationships that reside within the larger social, cultural and natural environment that is continually in a state of flux' (Jung and Rowson Love 2017b, 3). It is a dynamic, socio-cultural practice in flux which emerges, evolves, 'dies' and revives continuously through the dynamic interconnectedness of key elements. In my approach, I will not exclude the 'human actor'. On the contrary: I will unfold the structure of a system from the lens of each actor as necessary.

A heritage practice does emerge, persist, disappear or even revive as connections between its defining elements are made and broken, viewed through the lenses of its agents. But what are these elements? A cross-cultural study carried out by Fouseki, Newton et al. (2020) on residents' decision-making on heritage conservation and energy efficiency in historic buildings identified 'materials', 'values' (meanings), 'competencies' (skills), 'senses and affect', 'space and place', 'time' and 'resources' as the core dynamic elements (see also Chapter 3 of this book). I argue that in the diverse contexts examined in this book heritage emerges, shifts, 'dies' and revives as a result of the interconnections of the elements above. The 'heritage life cycle' thus continues constantly, even if this implies that heritage acquires a new form, function, use or purpose.

Before proceeding with the analytical description of the 'heritage dynamics' approach, it is essential at this stage to define the core elements of 'heritage social practices'. Materiality, in this book, connotes the physical fabric of heritage degradation and material change of heritage objects, sites or places. 'Materials' can encompass objects, infrastructures, tools, hardware and the body itself (Shove et al. 2012, 21). Indeed, as Røpke (2009) suggests, there is now broad agreement that things should be treated as elements of practice. 'Values' and 'meanings' signify the intangible meanings that different individuals or groups of people attach to heritage objects, sites or places. 'Place' and 'space' denotes both small-scale (such as homes) and large-scale entities (such as neighbourhoods and cities). In some cases I will include 'environment' as part of this definition. 'Competencies', 'skills' and 'knowledge' connote the 'know-how', the background knowledge of how to perform a practice, the 'practical consciousness' (Giddens 1984) of someone. 'Time' is understood in multiple ways in each chapter. It may refer, for instance, to the ways in which 'time' is experienced by the 'agents' of a heritage practice or to the 'time span' that a heritage practice covers. 'Resources' can connote the financial, human or other resources needed to materialise a heritage action. Occasionally I will stress that fluidity of elements. For example, museum objects may be classified as 'materials' on some occasions or as 'resources' on others.

So far, I have conceptualised heritage as a dynamic, socio-cultural practice; it emerges, shifts, disappears and revives depending on how the interconnection of materials, values, senses and emotions, places and spaces, time and resources is sustained, evolving or broken. In order to explore the dynamic interconnections of the aforementioned elements better, it is important to draw on complexity, system and assemblage theories which will allow the deconstruction of the interconnected elements.

Heritage dynamics – complexity, system and assemblage theories

I mentioned above that I conceptualise heritage as a 'complex' and 'dynamic', 'systemic' practice, the emergence, continuation and transformation of which depends on the interconnectedness of several key elements. I also highlighted the need to incorporate the role of 'agency' in 'practice-based' approaches, a direction towards which actors-network theory can provide assistance. In this section I would like to delve a bit deeper into the notions of 'complexity' and 'dynamic systems'. If we accept that heritage is a social practice that is 'complex', 'dynamic' and 'systemic', then we need to unfold these characteristics in greater detail. To do so I will draw on theories which may seem related, but are not often in dialogue with each other in current literature. The theories I will utilise underpin the ways in which I approach heritage and 'heritage dynamics', as well as the methodology used for unpacking the dynamics of heritage in subsequent chapters.

Complexity theory and critical realism

The first theories I would like to present are fundamental in deconstructing the 'complex' nature of heritage as a dynamic social practice. These include complexity theories and critical realism. As with most definitions, there is not a universally agreed definition for 'complexity theory'. This is partly due to the fact that each discipline has approached complexity theories differently (Manson 2001).

Complexity theory could be traced back in the 1920s in studies on the 'philosophy or organism' (Manson 2001, 406), but has evolved since across a wide array of disciplines including physics, chemistry, biology and environmental science, among others (Ramage and Shipp, 2009). Complexity theory, also known as non-linear dynamical systems theory, was consolidated during the 1970s and 1980s in a range of sciences (Basile et al. 2018; Waldrop 1993). Since these 'hard sciences' 'assumed stability, equilibrium, linear change, cyclicality, robustness, and simple models generating simple behaviour', new approaches to complexity theory and systems in the 1980s emphasised 'instability, far from equilibrium, sudden change, sensitivity to initial conditions, and complex behaviour from simple models' (Mingers 2014, 35).

Despite the varied disciplinary approaches to complexity theory, there are certain epistemological attributes that characterise complexity theories. First, complexity theory rejects linearity between constantly changing entities (Manson 2001, 406). Second, complexity theory rejects reductionism as it is interested in exploring how complex behaviours emerge or evolve over time as a result of interactions among the various components of a system (Manson 2001, 406). Third, complexity research employs techniques to examine qualitative characteristics of a system (Manson 2001, 406). Byrne thus rightly contends (1997) that complexity theory shares ontological assumptions with critical realism in that what is observed is real, albeit marked with chaos and complexity, non-linear relationships, multiple causality, intersections of the micro and macro, interplay between structures and agency, and so on (Byrne, 1997; see also Dent, 1999). The emphasis on non-linearity is critical here. This notion implies that there are no obvious direct cause and effect connections in that changes in a system may result in no effects, unanticipated effects or multiple effects (Byrne and Callaghan 2013, 4). The same event may also lead to different outcomes each time.

Rather than predictability fostered in systems thinking approaches in the 1960s and 1970s, complexity theory aims for understanding and explanation, and is concerned with change over time (Byrne and Callaghan 2013, 292). One of the key underlying assumptions in complex theory is that 'systems' are subject to constant change. Therefore complexity theory can enable the unpacking of contextual and dynamic development and interplay of systems (Byrne and Callaghan 2013, 292).

Complexity theory is informed by 'critical realism'. Critical realism has been developing since the 1970s with the aim of re-establishing a realist view of being in the ontological domain while accepting the relativism of knowledge as socially and historically conditioned in the epistemological domain (Bhaskar 1997). It also aimed to highlight that the process of science is applicable in both natural and social worlds, with the social world putting inevitable limits on that process (Bhaskar 1997). Critical realism 're-asserts the primacy of ontology over epistemology – that is, it asserts the existence of an independent, external world about which we may acquire knowledge, while recognising the inevitably fallible and contextual nature of that knowledge' (Mingers 2014, 4).

Critical realism 'clearly embodies systemic and holistic themes at its very heart, with concepts such as totality, holistic causality, emergence, open systems, autopoiesis, and levels of stratification' (Mingers 2014, 28). Interestingly, although these concepts have been discussed in systems theory and systems thinking, there is almost no reference to this literature within the writings of Bhaskar (or those of other critical realists) (Mingers 2014, 28).

Critical realism is 'deeply and fundamentally systemic in character' in that it is 'couched almost exclusively in systemic terms' (Mingers 2014, 4). In critical realism the world is conceptualised as consisting of structures and mechanisms that generate the events (Bhaskar et al. 1998). These structures are distinct from the events they generate. Events occur at a particular point in time, but the structures are relatively enduring, exercising or not exercising their causal powers in interaction with each other. A distinction is also recognised between closed and open systems where open systems permit constant conjunctions of events but closed systems do not (Mingers 2014, 36).

The attributes stressed in complexity theory echo 'critical systems thinking' approaches, according to which the world is perceived as composed of complex systems. A complex system connotes 'a set of interrelated elements' where the whole – that is, all the elements and their interrelationships together – are greater than the sum of the parts (Byrne and Callaghan 2013, 4). To put it simply, 'systems thinking is a way of seeing and talking about reality that helps us better understand and work with systems to influence the quality of our lives' (Kim 1999, 2). A 'system' in the most basic sense is 'any group of interacting, interrelated, or interdependent parts that form a complex and unified whole that has a specific purpose' (Kim 1999, 2). Its origins, like those of complexity theory, lie in philosophy, and have since spread across a wide range of disciplines.

One of the first scholars to discuss systems thinking is the biologist von Bertalanffy. For von Bertalanffy general system theory is a general science of 'wholeness' (1972). As a response to the 'hard sciences' approaches to systems thinking, characterised by linearity, predictability and quantitative modelling back in the 1960s and 1970s, 'critical systems thinking', which emerged in the 1980s, specifically recognised our inability to understand the 'whole system'. It was concerned with how 'the theoretical partiality of existing systems methodologies limited their ability to guide interventions in the full range of problem situations' (Jackson 2020, 841). It therefore called for complementarism and pluralism in systems practice (Jackson 2019).

Critical systems thinking employs a multimethodology known as 'critical systems practice' (Jackson 2019). Critical systems practice (CSP) implies that traditional scientific methods, based upon reductionism and objectivity, are inappropriate in confronting complexity. CSP 'sees systems thinking as an appropriate complement to reductionism and objectivity because it promotes the importance of holism, interrelationships and emergence and values a pluralism of theoretical and methodological perspectives' (Jackson 2020, 842).

I have shown so far that complexity theory, critical realism and critical systems thinking are connected theoretically, conceptually and methodologically. In particular, the concept of 'aggregate complexity' that underpins systems thinking (Manson 2001, 409) is imbued with attributes that are fundamental in critical systems thinking. In order to deconstruct 'aggregate complexity' it is essential to examine relationships between entities, internal structure, surrounding environment, learning and emergent behaviour and the different means by which systems change.

Based on the above so far, I conceptualise heritage and its dynamic transformation as a 'systemic, social practice', the emergence and continuation of which depends on the interconnectedness of various elements (such as materials, values, place, time, etc.). As a dynamic and systemic process, the 'agents' are omnipresent even if they are not visualised on a system dynamics diagram/output. The relationships between the elements are non-linear, with multiple causalities leading to unanticipated outputs. Events can be sudden, of short duration or long-term; in most cases they are unpredictable.

Assemblage theories

An additional set of theories which share commonalities with 'complexity theory', 'critical realism' and 'critical systems thinking' is related to 'assemblage theories'. This set of theories originate from the work of Deleuze and Guatteri, but have deviated since and adapted in the discipline within which they were formulated. Given the diversity of assemblage theories owing to the diversity of disciplines on which they have drawn, I will first summarise the approaches developed by Deleuze and Guatteri and will then proceed with DeLanda. I will then refer to Buchanan's critique regarding contemporary approaches and re-interpretations of 'assemblage theories' before concluding with key points articulated by all 'assemblage theories' which, although they reflect different approaches, are important for the proposed heritage dynamics framework.

For Deleuze and Guattari an assemblage constitutes the productive intersection of a form of content (actions, bodies and things) and a form of expression (affects, words and ideas) (Buchanan 2015, 390). The form of content and the form of expression depend on each other. In other words, the relationship between the form of content and form of expression is one of reciprocal presupposition (one implies and demands the other, but does not cause or refer to it) (Buchanan 2015, 390).

Assemblages may be defined as the

> causally productive (machinic) result of the intersection of two open systems, and their properties are emergent in the sense in which that concept is deployed in logic, that is, not part of, and so not foreseeable in light of, either one or the other system considered in isolation, but instead only discernible as a result of the intersection of both such systems. (Marcus and Saka 2006, 103)

Deleuze and Guattari mediate the playful and critically aesthetic (of the 'art and architecture' tradition of modernism) and the formal and technical (of maths, set theory, topology). The 'playful' and 'critically aesthetic' 'indulges and even celebrates the intractably unpredictable and contingent in rapidly changing contemporary life' (Marcus and Saka 2006, 104). The formal and technical 'hopes for an understanding of the structural principles of order (and disorder) within the play of events and processes' (Marcus and Saka 2006, 104). An assemblage thus acts on 'semiotic' flows, 'social' flows and 'material' flows (Deleuze and Guattari 1988, 22).

As mentioned above, a growing number of disciplinary fields (including heritage studies) now draw upon the assemblage (*agencement*) theory of Deleuze and Guatteri (1988). In most cases, the theory of Deleuze and Guatteri is used as a point of departure; it then evolves into something different from the original theory. The ways in which assemblage theory has diverged over time from its original creators have triggered criticisms among a few scholars who insist that the theory of Deleuze and Guatteri should not be misinterpreted (see, in particular, Buchanan 2015).

In heritage studies, the work of DeLanda on assemblage theory has been particularly influential. DeLanda treats the assemblage as a complex aggregate that grows exponentially. That is, that assemblages are wholes whose properties emerge from the interactions of their parts (DeLanda 2006a; 2006b, 5). Quite similarly to this, Jane Bennett defines assemblages as 'ad hoc groupings of diverse elements of vibrant materials of all sorts' (2010, 23). For Buchanan (2020, 113), however, these definitions tend to approach an assemblage as an 'entity' instead of a 'dynamic arrangement between two (or more) semi-autonomous formations that encompasses the organization of bodies and the organization of discourses'. In understanding assemblage, in our case a heritage assemblage, as a dynamic arrangement between two or more formations, a series of questions raised by Buchanan can be of relevance here. Buchanan proposes a list of critical questions that scholars should consider when examining the applicability of assemblage theories which are of particular relevance to the objectives of this book. The first question is how did the assemblage come into being? The second is what elements were selected in the process and in what way? The third is what power of selection was in operation? The fourth is under what conditions were these elements brought together? The fifth is how did the various elements interact with each other over time? The sixth is what caused the elements to interact in the way that they did? The seventh question is how did these material things interconnect with one another, so bringing together 'material' and 'immaterial' dimensions of the system (Buchanan 2020, 113)? These are only some of the many questions to explore.

One of the possible reasons for the diversion of contemporary assemblage approaches from the original assemblage theory is the problematic translation of the term '*agencement*' into 'assemblage'. The term 'assemblage' is the English translation of the French word '*agencement*', which refers to the 'action of matching or fitting together a set of components (*agencer*), as well as to the result of such an action' (DeLanda 2016, 1). DeLanda points out that the English translation connotes the second meaning, formulating the impression that assemblage is the product of assembling, while the original meaning refers to both the process and the product. Buchanan (2015, 383) clarifies that it was Brian Massumi who translated the French word *agencement* which, as John Law has noted, encompasses a range of meanings that include 'to arrange, to dispose, to fit up, to combine, to order' (Law 2004, 41). Therefore, Buchanan suggests that *agencement* could be translated just as appropriately as arrangement, in the sense of a 'working arrangement', provided it was clear that it described an ongoing process rather than a static situation. For Buchanan the term ensemble or assembly implies a static situation, which is different from what Deleuze and Guatteri aimed to denote with the use of the term '*agencement*'. Interestingly Buchanan reminds us that Deleuze and Guatteri used the term '*agencement*' in translation of the German word *Komplex* (as in the 'Oedipus complex' or the 'castration complex'). And yet, for Buchanan, the connection between Freud's complex and the concept of the assemblage has been almost completely ignored (Buchanan 2015, 383).

One of the main criticisms that Buchanan addresses in regard to the new readings and approaches of Deleuze's and Guatteri's assemblage theory is the over-emphasis on the material objects. Buchanan argues that, although for Deleuze and Guatteri a material object can form part of an assemblage, such an assemblage is not defined by them. In other words, an assemblage can exist without objects (Buchanan 2015, 385). On the contrary, for Buchanan, more materialist permutations of assemblage theories such as the actors network theory celebrate the material (non-human) and their agential power, something that for Deleuze and Guattari is inessential (Buchanan 2015, 386).

Buchanan is rather critical of the over-emphasis of 'assemblage theorists' on the material (non-human) dimension. He argues that by focusing on non-human actors there is a risk of missing what is central to the assemblage. For Buchanan, what is central in the theory of Deleuze and Guattari is not the examination of an assemblage that consists of material and immaterial agencies, but rather the necessity of employing an assemblage process in order to disentangle the multiple and complex reality (Buchanan 2015, 386–7).

Buchanan is, in particular, critical of DeLanda's 'Deleuze 2.0' approach. DeLanda (2006a; 2006b) approaches the assemblage as a complex aggregate that grows exponentially in scale and complexity. For him, assemblages are 'wholes whose properties emerge from the interactions between parts' (DeLanda 2006b, 5). This enables DeLanda to offer an account of assemblages as ontologically 'unique, singular, historically contingent, individual' (DeLanda 2006b, 40). He frames the assemblage as a new way of thinking about part–whole relations, 'essentially pitching it as a new kind of causality, one that acts without conscious intention or purpose' (Buchanan 2015, 388).

To sum up, Buchanan's criticisms are that first the assemblage does not constitute a part–whole relation. Second, an assemblage is not the product of an accumulation of individual acts. Third, the assemblage does not change incrementally. For Buchanan, the central questions that assemblage theories should endeavour to address are 'what is that structure of authority?' and 'how it is constituted?' (Buchanan 2015, 338).

Assemblage theories and system dynamics

At this point, it is worth pointing out that DeLanda's assemblage theory does to some extent echo systems thinking. Systems thinking approaches the whole as a sum of parts. System dynamics can be used a method to understand how the 'components' interact over time, unveiling the conditions and factors that trigger an important change (Sterman 2002). In a similar way to DeLanda's definition of assemblage as consisting of heterogeneous components, a system in systems thinking consists of heterogeneous elements. The assemblage 'actively links these parts together by establishing relations between them' (DeLanda 2016, 2). For DeLanda assemblages are 'social wholes'; they emerge through 'interpersonal networks or institutional organisations that cannot be reduced to the persons that compose them, but that do not totalise them either, fusing them into a seamless whole in which their individuality is lost' (DeLanda 2016, 10).

Similarly, in systems theory and systems thinking, a system comprises heterogeneous elements that are interconnected with each other. As in systems theory, where each variable may form a separate system itself, 'the parts matched together to form an ensemble are themselves treated as assemblages, equipped with their own parameters, so that at all times we are dealing with assemblages of assemblages' (DeLanda 2016, 3).

However, for DeLanda there is also a distinct difference between 'assemblage theories' and 'system' or 'practice theories'. For him the assemblage theory has a 'material'-oriented approach in which an assemblage consists of sub-assemblages, each of which can retain its autonomy but which when in ensemble create a new whole (DeLanda 2006b, 9). In other words, in 'emergent wholes' (new 'wholes' emerging from the interactions of sub-wholes)

> the parts retain their autonomy, so that they can be detached from one whole and plugged into another one, entering into new interactions. (DeLanda 2006b, 9)

In practice theories the same principle can apply, but the focus here is on how a practice is sustained. The underpinning premise in practice theories is that if the links between the different components (or assemblies, if we want to use this terminology) are broken, the practice is not sustained. Although there is a variation between the two approaches (as interpreted by DeLanda), this premise is not substantially different from assemblage theory. In assemblage theory, if the

> properties of a social whole are viewed as produced by the interactions between components, and their existence and endurance explained by the continuity of those interactions, then the properties are contingent: if the interactions cease to take place the emergent properties cease to exist. (DeLanda 2006b, 12)

In system dynamics, the focus is upon how the interaction of the various parts (assemblies) evolves over time. In some ways, systems thinking brings practice and assemblage theories together.

To summarise, assemblages, for DeLanda, have a fully contingent historical identity. As such, each assemblage firstly constitutes an individual entity – an individual, a person, an individual organisation, an individual community, an individual city (DeLanda 2006b, 19). Secondly, assemblages always consist of heterogeneous components. For instance, a historic city as an assemblage consists of people, the architecture, the natural parks/green spaces, the symbolic and/or everyday practices of the community, etc. Thirdly, assemblages can become component parts of larger assemblages (DeLanda 2006b, 20). For instance, a historic building is an assemblage consisted of people working and/or visiting, as well as the building fabric and the movable artefacts. The historic building can also be a component part of the wider city or area in which it is located.

Assemblages result from interactions between their parts. Once an assemblage is in place it begins to act as a source of limitations and opportunities for its components (a phenomenon known as 'downward causality') (DeLanda 2006b, 21). This implies that assemblages would cease to exist if their parts stopped interacting with one another.

> The downward causality is needed to account for the fact that most assemblages are composed of parts that come into existence after the whole has emerged. (DeLanda 2006b, 21)

For example, a historic area can emerge as an assemblage as soon as its component parts are attributed a heritage value. Values and buildings are two components that create the assemblage of a historic area (downward quality). However, if a building is not being valued, then a historic area will cease to exist and may vanish through abandonment and obsolescence (upward causality).

Assemblage theories and actor network theories

Harrison (2012) has attempted to connect 'assemblage theories' and 'actor network theories' in heritage studies. Since in 'assemblage' theories, as interpreted by DeLanda, 'agency' is obscured by the emphasis on the materiality of an assemblage, linking actor network theories with assemblage theories can help to overcome this obstacle. The leading figure in actor network theory is Bruno Latour, a French philosopher, sociologist and anthropologist. Latour used the term 'actor' or 'actant' to connote anyone or anything modifying any particular state of affairs: the 'agent' or 'actor' is a conduit for change (Latour 1996; 2007). This approach

> shifts the emphasis from what objects 'symbolise' to the affective qualities of things, and the ways in which material objects are involved in particular forms of interactions that create social 'features', such as inequalities or shifts in power, through momentary or more persistent networks of social connection. (Harrison 2012, 32)

In heritage, the question of 'agency' is imminent – especially when considering heritage as a production of the past in the present, which immediately leads to a reassessment of who and what is involved in the process of 'making' heritage, and 'where' the production of heritage might be located within contemporary societies (Harrison 2012, 32). For Harrison (2012) agency is contingent and emergent within social collectives, involving human and non-human actors and taking many different forms that involve individuals or groups of people such as bureaucrats, local stakeholders, NGOs or tourists and heritage 'things'. This approach aligns with DeLanda's approach to assemblage as comprised heterogeneous, human and non-human elements. Thinking of assemblages as heterogeneous groupings of humans and non-humans

> focuses our attention on the ways in which things and people are involved in complex, interconnected webs of relationships across time and space, rather than seeing objects and ideas about them as somehow separate from one another. (Harrison 2012, 35)

This approach also enables us to focus on the formation and reformation of social processes across time and space (Harrison 2012, 35).

Assemblage theories and 'critical system dynamics'

Buchanan makes reference to the concept of 'boundaries', a concept fundamental in systems thinking and system dynamics as explained below. He uses the term to connote that both the 'internal' and 'external' limit of a 'text' (a term used broadly to encompass policy and the built environment) have boundaries that 'cannot be crossed without becoming something different from what it was' (Buchanan 2017, 467). The 'internal limit' is the sum of the total of possible variations it can accommodate; the 'external limit' is defined by the restrictions history itself places on the number of possible variations (Buchanan 2017, 468). The 'act' to which

Buchanan refers is a 'narratological concept' and as such is in a process subject to constant transformation (Buchanan 2017, 468). Conveniently for this analysis, he uses the example of a historic building to illustrate the concepts of 'external' and 'internal' limit. The 'internal limit' of a historic residential building is demarcated by the number of variations it can accommodate; as such it encompasses questions on what constitutes a historic building in a material-semiotic sense (Buchanan 2017, 470). The 'external limit', on the other hand, is determined by the external restrictions imposed by legal or other forces. In other words, what constitutes a heritage building in a cultural and political sense is a key question in this process. The building, in this example, is the 'actant' and the process of change or valuation is the 'act'.

What Buchanan describes above aligns with Deleuze's and Guattari's approach to assemblage. According to their approach, what needs to be determined is, firstly, the specific conditions under which 'matter' becomes material. For instance, how are building materials such as bricks, timber and steel perceived as the appropriate material for housing? Secondly, this approach attempts to identify the specific conditions under which semiotic matter becomes expressive. For instance, who makes the decision – and how – on how a specific arrangement of materials is 'fitting' for a person to live in while another arrangement is not (Deleuze and Guattari 1988, 67)? These 'formalisations are arbitrary and mobile as they vary considerably from country to country and more especially from one class perspective to another' (Buchanan 2017, 472; Buchanan 2020, 132). Formalisation implies a principle of both inclusion and exclusion. However, the principle of inclusion and exclusion for one dimension (content) may be in conflict with the principle of inclusion and exclusion for the dimension of expression. An 'assemblage's' work is to bring these two dimensions together. As a result

> we have to stop thinking of the concept of the assemblage as a way of describing a thing or situation and instead see it for what it was always intended to be: a way of analysing a thing or situation. (Buchanan 2017, 473)

Another important element of relevance to 'heritage dynamics' is that assemblage theory in the work of Deleuze and Guattari has always been concerned with questions of power (Webb 2009, 30). Unfortunately this aspect of 'assemblage theory is all too often forgotten', with the consequence of 'making the assemblage seem as though it is merely another way of saying something is complicated' (Buchanan 2015, 382). As he observes

> one of the great insights of assemblage theory ... is that it shows that material objects can and frequently do have agential power. (Buchanan 2015, 386)

'Assemblage' theories in heritage literature

> We should not be deceived into thinking that ... heritage is an acquisition, a possession that grows and solidifies; rather it is an unstable assemblage of faults, fissures and heterogeneous layers that threaten the fragile inheritor from within or underneath. (Foucault 1980, 146)

I have referred above to some heritage work that has engaged with mainly 'assemblage' and 'actor network theories' and less with 'systems thinking'. In this section I would like to expand on how these theories have been utilised by heritage scholars in order to identify gaps that the 'heritage dynamics framework' aims to address.

Sharon Macdonald has been one of the first heritage scholars to approach heritage as an 'assemblage' (2009). In her article looking at the assembling and postwar re-assembling of Nuremberg, she examines how heritage 'may act as a mediator even while it is being reassembled and, in particular, how it may mediate, or shape, a city and its citizens, present and future' (Macdonald 2009, 118). Macdonald argues that 'taking an assemblage perspective on heritage directs our attention less to finished "heritage products" than to processes and entanglements involved in their coming into being and continuation' (Macdonald 2009, 118). She further contends that an 'assemblage perspective' serves to focus 'on tracing the courses of action, associations, practical and definitional procedures and techniques that are involved in particular cases. In so doing, it takes into account not only the human and social but also the material or technical' (Macdonald 2009, 118). By doing so, it is possible to unfold 'multiple, heterogeneous and often highly specific actions and techniques that are involved in achieving and maintaining heritage' and to identify 'how certain pre-existing elements are taken up into a reshaping assemblage' (Macdonald 2009, 118). Although Macdonald has not engaged with the 'assemblage theories' of Deleuze and Guattari or DeLanda in this paper, she did in a way introduce a preliminary perspective on 'heritage dynamics' with her focus on heritage processes of 'coming into being' and 'continuation'.

Bille (2012) used 'assemblage theories' as a theoretical mechanism for unpacking the process of heritage definition in the case of the international valorisation of Bedouin heritage in Jordan on UNESCO's list of Masterpieces of the Oral and Intangible Heritage of Humanity. Bille (2012, 107) has approached heritage not as an assemblage, but rather as a process of assembling 'that emerges from the interactions of social entities operating on a smaller scale'. Like most heritage scholars, he draws upon the work of DeLanda (2006a; 2006b) and defines a heritage assemblage as 'an assemblage of discourses, documents and persons linked to pasts, practices, or materials'. However, according to DeLanda, assemblages are wholes characterised by 'relations of exteriority' – meaning that they may be detached from such exteriority and plugged into different assemblages in which their interactions also differ. In essence, an assemblage is made up of parts which are self-subsistent and articulated by relations of exteriority (DeLanda 2006b, 10–18).

Such a perspective is useful for heritage analysis, as Bille observes: 'taking this approach of assemblages into a heritage context enables us to take a critical look at the powers integral to the process of shaping a heritage application' (Bille 2012, 108). He goes on to demonstrate

> 'that the connections emerging between micro and macro levels of the social reality of a heritage assemblage are not only making use of intermediary positions, as DeLanda points out, but also reveal how individual levels may speak louder than even institutional or national levels. Further, it illustrates how shifting and fluctuating hierarchies of access to resources may potentially redistribute power, and step in and out of the process of assemblage. (Bille 2012, 108)

Through the case study analysis he showed 'how simultaneous discourses are contained within one sphere of the UNESCO application and draw on strained commitments to tangible heritage management' (Bille 2012, 119). This follows DeLanda's insight that in such assemblages 'the reason why the properties of a whole cannot be reduced to those of its parts is that they are the result not of an aggregation of the components' own properties but of the actual exercise of their capacities' (2006b, 11).

Despite these preliminary references to assemblage theories in the context of heritage, it is John Pendlebury who specifically advances the application of 'assemblage theory' in heritage conservation (2013). He argues that 'a distinct conservation-planning social entity has developed that may be described as an "assemblage" and that the values and validated practice of conservation-planning are constructed as an authorised heritage discourse (AHD)' (Pendlebury 2013, 709). As an entity, conservation planning has 'its own distinct history, stories, institutions and institutional context and relationship with actors and interests outside the heritage sphere' (Pendlebury 2013, 710). His definition of assemblage is also informed by the work of Manuel DeLanda (2006a; 2006b), as is most modern heritage work. Based on this, Pendlebury defines an assemblage as a 'social entity' which has been 'constructed through specific historical processes and from heterogeneous parts' (Pendlebury 2013, 710). He stresses that the ability of assemblage theory to 'co-join different actors (individuals or organisations) and their narratives and stories with other dimensions – for example, legal and policy frameworks – and conceive these together as a definable and extremely complex and nonstatic social entity' is very useful for understanding the dynamics of heritage (Pendlebury 2013, 711). He also emphasises the usefulness of assemblage theory in bringing attention to non-human dimensions, as it facilitates the 'coming together of the various other dimensions of the assemblage with the materiality of buildings and places that constitute the practice of conservation-planning' (2013, 711). For Rodney Harrison (2018, 1375) a 'heritage assemblage' encompasses the whole set of relations and processes in heritage, including definitions and discourses, in 'specifying both the forms of endangerment and the appropriate means of intervening in that condition'; the relations between heritage experts and the other (human and non-human) agents; the routes and mechanisms through which heritage experts and their assembled materials return to a field office, state government heritage agency or office of an international NGO; the mechanisms through which the materials and data they have collected are subjected to institutionally specific processes of ordering and classification; and the manner in which such materials and data are connected to the institutions and networks.

Harrison also calls for an exploration of material infrastructure associated with heritage management practices such as conservation and visitor management. He defines these practices as 'technologies', the various mechanisms and apparatuses by which the heritage experience is created, and observes that

> In thinking of heritage as an assemblage, we are forced to dissolve the boundaries between that which is 'old' and that which is 'new' to consider each as part of the physical infrastructure that constitutes a piece of 'heritage'. (Harrison 2020, 32)

The decentralisation of the 'human agent' serves to refocus attention on 'things' and 'processes' as individual objects or variegated assemblages (Stirling 2020). From this a 'post-human' approach to critical heritage studies, which have typically prioritised 'people-centred' approaches to conservation and interpretation, has emerged and been recently introduced (Stirling 2020).

Hill (2018) draws upon the work of Harrison (2012) in order to examine how the range of living human actors in a historic city of the Plza Vieja introduces distinct variables that operate differently from those in a museum environment or cultural landscape. He argues that the size, physicality and sociality of built heritage inheres limitations on how the heritage object can be reassembled (2018). Therefore, according to Hill (2018), the options for re-assemblage are constrained because the relocation is a complex process and because communities associated with the buildings often resist such relocations.

To sum up, the heritage scholars who utilise assemblage theories as a means of understanding the complexity of heritage have mostly been influenced by the work of DeLanda rather than by the original work of Deleuze and Guatteri. According to this, a 'heritage assemblage' is approached as a constantly changing entity, a 'product of stabilising and destabilising processes' (Roppola et al. 2019).

What is less discussed, if at all, is the process of 'disassembly'. There is an implicit hypothesis that a heritage assemblage is going through constant formation and re-formation. However, as Littlejohn notes, 'disassembly' can occur when an assemblage 'disbands', offering insight into what socio-material relations it had gathered (Littlejohn 2021, 955). The process of 'disassembly' may be temporary and last for only a short period of time. It often triggers people to act by putting things back together again or arranging their elements in new combinations (Littlejohn 2021, 955). 'The more an assemblage disbands, the more scope there might be for it to mediate other interests and values when its parts are reassembled' (Littlejohn 2021, 955).

Overall, assemblage theories have been applied in heritage with a particular focus on mapping the complexity rather than understanding it: on the entity rather than on its dynamic transformations. When analysing a 'thing' or 'situation' through assemblage theory, we need to tackle two fundamental questions. The first question is what the material elements are that constitute this 'thing' – how are the materials arranged, what relations do they entail, what new arrangements or relations can the materials facilitate (Buchanan 2017, 473)? A second question is how the arrangement of things is justified – in other words, what makes this arrangement look right and proper. The assemblage thus connects the above dimensions (material, discursive and performative).

Relational theories and relational models in heritage research

The significance of investigating the complexity of heritage through unpacking the multiple interrelationships between 'human' and 'non-human' agents has also been stressed in 'relational theories' and 'models'. For Munroe (2016) relational models can provide useful frameworks for understanding the embodied and felt manifestations of the heritage experience that emerge out of the connections between people, texts, objects and places. Waterton and Watson (2013, 552) suggest that relational models 'stir [heritage] back in with being human and living, so that it emerges from the feelings of being, becoming and belonging in the flows and complexities that characterise life'. Relational studies of heritage are therefore aligned with the concept of affective–discursive meaning-making as they 'situate meaning-making within the interactions and negotiations between both human and non-human elements: narratives, discourses, museum practices, the materiality of the museum itself, objects, curators and other actors, places and the wider socio-political landscape of the museum' (Munroe 2016, 119). Yet Waterton and Watson (2013) point out that one of the most striking things about relational theories is that 'theory' refers to 'what to study', rather than suggesting how we go about researching those networks.

Harrison (2012) puts forward a relational ontology – a way of thinking about heritage – but there is no explicit methodology for examining these dialogical connections between people, objects, spaces and practices. Perhaps this is due to the fact that this research is

> in its relative infancy in heritage studies, and as yet we have not developed the appropriate tools to deal with the swirling and dynamic movements, flows and connections which characterise this way of thinking. (Munroe 2016, 119)

Similarly, methodologies for studying the affective and emotive implications of heritage are 'thin on the ground' (ibid.). To address this gap, heritage dynamics draw on the method of 'system dynamics', a methodological tool that can capture the complex, dynamic relations of heritage assemblages.

'System dynamics' thinking in heritage literature

While there is emerging work on 'systems thinking' in museum work, heritage studies and, to a less but still significant extent, heritage management have not engaged with 'systems thinking' approaches, despite the acknowledgement that heritage does constitute a complex and dynamic 'assemblage'. In their edited volume *Systems Thinking in Museums: Theory and practice* (2017a) Jung and Love provide an overview of the theory enhanced with practical applications on how such an approach can be implemented in museum practice on the ground. Although they do not go into much theoretical depth, their book provides a solid foundation for opening up research into this field.

Discussions on the potential of systems thinking in the museum world have commenced much earlier, however. Sutter, for instance, calls for the adoption of systems thinking underpinning the work of human ecology to discuss sustainable development for museums (2006). Sutter proposes a model of adaptive renewal cycle developed by Holling (1992). An adaptive renewal cycle is triggered by some disturbance, which is then followed by a phase of reorganisation and a consequent phase of slow exploitation in which 'succession leads to complex relationships and the amount of stored capital increases accordingly' before the system enters a conservation phase (Sutter 2006, 209). However, it was Avrami (2012) who was one of the first heritage scholars, if not the first one, to use the method of system dynamics in order to map the transformation of heritage conservation and mechanisms of sustainability. Although she did not use system dynamics modelling, she drew on system dynamic tools in order to showcase that the historic built environment 'is not merely an agglomeration of buildings and places' but instead

> a complicated system of relationships that involves not only the products of design, planning and construction, but the complex processes associated with their creation and management. (Avrami 2012, 107)

Avrami highlights the usefulness of a systems approach for unpacking the 'ways in which those relationships influence the system as a whole as well as its components' (Avrami 2012, 107). Xu and Dai (2012), as well as other scholars in tourism research, have even applied system dynamics modelling in understanding the impact of heritage on sustainability.

Building upon the theoretical work reviewed in this chapter, I intend to propose a theoretical and methodological approach to the dynamics of heritage. I thus propose a 'heritage dynamics' framework which will hopefully enable future heritage scholars better to comprehend the dynamics of heritage and inform decisions for heritage management and sustainability in the future. Sporadic attempts to address 'heritage dynamics' have already occurred, albeit with a different focus. The *'Heritage dynamics: Politics, authentication and aesthetics'* project, for instance, looks at cultural dynamics in relation to the framing of heritage. It represents an anthropological perspective and pays special attention to the affective power of heritage and its interface between religion, arts and politics (e.g. Bakker 2013; Hudson and Balmer 2013; Meyer and De Witte 2013; Van de Port and Meyer 2018). The term 'heritage dynamics' also appears in some papers as part of a discussion of how declined heritage sites are being transformed and revived (e.g. Bouquet 2013). In this research, heritage dynamics are not theoretically conceptualised using relevant theories, such as systems thinking and complexity theories, or relevant methods, such as system dynamics. There is some limited heritage and museum-related literature using systems thinking as a conceptual framework (e.g. Barile et al. 2012; Avrami 2012; Jung and Love 2017a) in order to stress the significance of thinking heritage and museums as a system of interconnected and interdependent social, economic, environmental and other dimensions. However, these studies lack methodological systemic frameworks better to deconstruct the dynamic interconnected heritage dimensions. Moreover, the material change of heritage is not considered in the aforementioned studies.

My theoretical approach towards 'heritage dynamics' echoes similar approaches to 'cultural dynamics'. According to 'cultural dynamics', culture is composed of a number of distinct elements (or traits) which bear varying relationships to one another (Buskell et al. 2019, 2). Such traits may include beliefs, myths, stories and material artefacts, societal structures practices, norms and institutions such as kinship systems or subsistence strategies (Buskell et al. 2019). 'Many of these elements bear connections, or relational properties, to one another that impact the acquisition, maintenance, and transmission of other traits' (Buskell et al. 2019, 2). The authors advocate a systems approach in modelling cultural systems as a means to capture:

> an explicit representation of multiple traits (perhaps of multiple trait types); trait relationships of different valence and character;

and how traits and their relationships generate dynamic interactions over time. (Buskell et al. 2019, 3)

Why and for whom is a 'heritage dynamics approach' important?

In this chapter I introduced the 'heritage dynamics approach' that underpins this book. I argued that this approach enables heritage scholars and practitioners better to comprehend trajectories of change over time that can enable a better understanding of the present while developing future strategies for adapting to change. I conceptualised 'heritage' as a dynamic, complex, socio-cultural process, the continuation or discontinuation of which depends on the ways in which 'values', 'materials', 'skills', 'place/space', 'senses/emotions', 'time' and 'resources' interact with each other viewed from different perspectives.

As a framework, heritage dynamics re-orientate our perception of time. Instead of perceiving time 'as a linear elasticity that speeds up and slows down processes that find their spatial expression in uneven development' (Blunt et al. 2021, 150), a heritage dynamics approach motivates us to adopt a non-linear and 'pluralistic understanding of time' (Blunt et al. 2021, 150). A non-linear conceptualisation of time has the potential of correlating events which are distant from each other (DeSilvey 2020). As with space, time – from a heritage dynamics lens – is a relational, 'emergent property of objects' (DeSilvey 2020), as well as embodied. More importantly, heritage dynamics advances our conception of 'heritage assemblage'. Instead of approaching heritage as a complex 'entity' or 'arrangement' of objects, texts and practices, we can approach heritage through heritage dynamics as a dynamic and systemic socio-cultural practice which emerges, shifts, 'dies' and revives periodically. Consequently heritage can be approached as a 'renewable' resource that acquires new lives over time. A 'heritage dynamics' approach encourages us not only to develop and apply the appropriate methods for doing so, but also to raise critical heritage dynamic questions while informing policy and practice.

2
Urban heritage dynamics

Introduction

In March 2012 I visited the Royal Arsenal in Woolwich with my MSc Sustainable Heritage students for the first time. I recollect that it took us a while to orientate ourselves within the Royal Arsenal on our way towards the Berkeley Homes offices where we were hosted for the day. The area resembled a construction site with a few high-rise, newly constructed residential buildings with adaptively reused historic buildings located in between. During our visit we were struck by the sense of abandonment and remoteness of the Royal Arsenal and by the stark difference of the ongoing building developments with the culturally diverse and vibrant Woolwich town centre, located on the 'other side' of the road that disconnects the two areas. It was apparent that a new area was about to be born – one that would fuse the 'old' with the 'new' architecture while attracting a 'new', affluent community.

The division between the Royal Arsenal and Woolwich town centre was exacerbated by the presence of a brick wall, dating from the 1980s and built during the expansion of Plumstead Road, which separates the two areas. The wall constitutes a physical boundary as well as a symbolic and social demarcation between the 'old' and 'new' communities. Since my first visit in 2012, the area has been radically transformed. The Royal Arsenal is no longer characterised by remoteness and emptiness. Yet I am still not convinced that the social friction between the 'old' and 'new' communities has really faded away.

It is the aim of this chapter to examine how heritage emerges, changes, disappears and revives in the dynamic urban transformation context of the Royal Arsenal. By doing so, I intend to contribute an urban heritage dynamics theory that frames the dynamic change of heritage and its interactions with the social, economic and other surrounding conditions. My focal point of investigation is the heritage and socio-economic dynamics of the Royal Arsenal, a formerly industrial area of historic military significance, and its surrounding 'impact' area of Woolwich town centre. In order to establish the dynamic transformations in both areas, I intend to map the parallel evolution of the official (listed) and unofficial (non-listed) heritage alongside the wider socio-economic changes in the area. By doing so I aspire to identify at what point these parallel 'journeys' meet, interconnect and influence each other. Ultimately I endeavour to unfold the parameters that can lead to 'sustainable urban transformation' as revealed by these parallel journeys.

By the term 'sustainable urban transformation' – the focus of this chapter – I am referring to the sum of social, economic, cultural and environmental processes that direct urban development towards sustainable futures (see also McCormick et al. 2013, 1). In other words, this term connotes the

> comprehensive and integrated vision and action which seeks to resolve urban problems and bring about a lasting improvement in the economic, physical, social and environmental condition of an area that has been subject to change or offers opportunities for improvement. (Roberts 2000, 18)

Transformation implies that an area changes from a current, 'undesired' (for some individuals) state to a new, 'desired' (for some individuals) state. In the context of urban development, the term 'decline' is often used to connote a range of 'undesirable' conditions, such as unemployment, social exclusion and inequalities, physical decay, worsening living conditions and depopulation (see, for instance, Medhurst and Lewis 1969, 2). A related term to 'decline' is the term 'decay', which often insinuates 'physical decay of buildings, the declining attractiveness of the environment, the disappearance of activity, the growth of "undesirable" activity or even the quality of its administration' (Medhurst and Lewis 1969, 2; see also Lang 2005). Indubitably, however, transformation and change is not an 'a-human' process, as implied in the aforementioned definitions. An individual or a group of individuals are driving a process of transformation. Yet at this stage, it will be useful to deconstruct the attributes of the process before proceeding with a discussion on stakeholders involved in transformation projects.

The process of urban transformation is 'a fragile and dynamic process rather than a linear chronological continuum' (Degen 2018, 16). As a non-linear process, urban change is characterised by multiple temporalities exercised on multiple scales, from the home to the city level (Blunt et al. 2021). Living with urban change is mediated by memories of the past and experienced in the present through multi-layered and ambivalent ways (Blunt et al. 2021).

Each temporality and each form of change has its own pace. The pace of change refers to the different, often contradictory temporalities experienced at different scales (Blunt et al. 2021). In the regeneration of social housing at Hackney, for instance, Blunt et al. (2021) demonstrate how 'living of time' evolves for the

> urban dwellers, whose everyday rhythms in this period of waiting and uncertainty stand in stark contrast to the pace of change in the wider neighbourhood and city. (Blunt et al. 2021, 150)

The urban space and the urban dwelling become a sphere of 'dynamic simultaneity' (Anderson 2008). In view of this, the urban space is always being made, constantly waiting to be determined by the construction of new relations (Anderson 2008, 231). Because the urban space is constantly being made, it is always unfinished (Anderson 2008, 231).

The pace of change will dictate whether a place is moving towards decline or development. As Beauregard (1993) notes, decline in population and employment does not always imply an overall decline. It is the composition and pace of change that matters, as well as the resultant distribution of costs and benefits (Beauregard 1993). The pace of change is important because if change occurs at a steady pace, adequate time is provided to the urban system to adapt to unpredicted changing circumstances. If changes are embedded gradually, they can be integrated more organically into the system. On the other hand, a dramatic, invasive change can lead to unintended social and economic consequences such as physical or 'affective displacement', social and economic inequalities and change of physical environment (see also Blunt et al. 2021). It could be argued that the conservation and adaptive reuse of heritage buildings and sites permit this organic change to occur because the change that is introduced builds upon existing time layers and physical remains. And yet, the adaptive reuse of heritage buildings may not always ensure that the change introduced is socially sustainable. Both the *type* of adaptive reuse as well as the pace of change constitute two critical factors for social sustainability.

Adapting to expected or unexpected change is key to sustainability. First, adapting to change presupposes acceptance of change. A heritage-driven regeneration project is a major change in itself. From a sustainable urban transformation point of view, a heritage-driven regeneration project aims to reverse undesired change. However, the project itself can cause new undesired changes, especially if it lacks involvement and participation, as will be seen below.

Methodology

The meta-interpretation analysis of the Royal Arsenal and its surrounding area is based on thorough research conducted over the last five years by the author and MSc Sustainable Heritage students. The chapter thus draws on a diverse array of data, including annual photographs taken by my students and myself over the last ten years during our annual study visits to Woolwich; semi-structured interviews with local residents and online questionnaires distributed to local Facebook groups; Google Maps showing the changes of the townscape over the years; in situ observation notes; conversations with key stakeholders; masterplans of the area; data on listed buildings drawn from Historic England (including the Heritage at Risk list), the *Survey of London*, vol. 48, of Woolwich (Guillery 2012) and Alan Baxter's heritage study of Woolwich Centre.[1] I chose the Royal Arsenal as my focal study due to my in-depth, longitudinal, self-experiential insight into the transformation of this place. Although my self-experiential insight cannot be quantitatively measured, it offers an 'insider's' perspective, while also being an 'outsider'.

Urban dynamics

In order to achieve my aim of developing an 'urban heritage dynamics' theory, I will first summarise through a critical lens 'urban dynamics' theory on how cities grow, decline and revive. Before addressing some of the most influential work on urban dynamics, it is important to define what is meant by 'urban'. As with all terms, there is a multitude of approaches and definitions. For me, 'urban' refers to a place and space where a growing population lives – there is density, diversity, liveliness, a constant sense of motion and construction (see Roy 2016). The notion of change is inherent in the conceptualisation of urban. In view of this, urban dynamics, as a term, is slightly oxymoronic since an urban system is constantly dynamic and subject to change. However, in the context of this book urban dynamics can locate the focus of an urban study on the dynamic forces that drive change in cities.

Varied methods and approaches have been adopted in urban dynamic studies, an indicator of the 'interdisciplinary attractiveness' of the field. Insights into urban dynamics have been gained, for instance, through spatial and temporal patterns (Ramachandra et al. 2012) and GIS-based cellular automata (Batty et al. 1999). Special focus has been placed on modelling the urban dynamics with the aim of providing guidance and recommendations for future urban policies and strategies (e.g. Forrester 1969; Orishimo 1987; Bertuglia 2013; Batty 2005; Alfeld 2009; Pumain and Reuillon 2017). The disciplinary lens will inevitably determine the focus of exploration in each study. With this chapter, I contribute a new lens to studies of the 'urban'– the lens of heritage. By doing so, I strive to render heritage an integral component of urban studies and policies from now on. I thus argue that the ways in which cities evolve, grow and decline depend not only on the dynamic interconnections of available land, housing, industries and populations (as traditional urban dynamic theories contend), but also on the ways in which heritage emerges, evolves, disappears or revives in an urban setting. Before unravelling this argument further in the following section, I would like to consider a few of the most predominant urban dynamic theories which, despite their drawbacks, can provide a point of departure.

As noted above, urban dynamic theorists argue that three primary forces underlie urban growth and decline. These include

> migration guided by perceptions of relative attractiveness of an area, aging of housing and business structures, and the feedback connections among population, housing and jobs. (Alfeld 2009, 69)

System dynamics has been used to understand urban dynamic forces. The method of system dynamics provides a 'management tool for urban policy analysis', offering insights to urban analysis and policy-makers (Alfeld 2009, 69). System dynamics can be used to develop an urban dynamics model that allows computer simulation of alternative policies to revive a declining city; it can also reveal why certain policies in the past have failed while others have succeeded.

A diachronic, albeit controversial (Gray et al. 1972; Jaeckel et al. 2012, to name just a few) example of system dynamics applied in the context of urban policy is Forrester's *Urban Dynamics* theory (1969). The practical problem with which Forrester deals relates to the decline of cities over time. Forrester encapsulates the urban decline problem as follows:

> During the initial growth phase the area is attractive and can accept additional population. But if carried far enough, the influx of people overcrowds the area, reduces the attractiveness, reduces the population inflow, and increases the outflow until population growth stops. By this process population rises and falls to maintain the attractiveness of the area in balance with that of the surrounding environment. The change in economic circumstances that occurs while growth is giving way to stagnation is caused by the changing proportions of people, housing, and industry. During the growth stage new construction outruns the aging process so that the decaying part of a city is little noticed in relation to the ever rising new construction. But as the land area becomes filled, new construction can take place only as the old is demolished. An equilibrium is established in which the demolition rates and construction rates must be the same. (Forrester 1969, 59)

In his urban dynamics model, Forrester deconstructs the parameters that drive urban decline and aspires to offer a tool for policy-makers that can be used to test the best scenarios or strategies for urban renewal. In more detail, Forrester's urban dynamics model looks at the dynamic interactions between housing structures, business structures and population in an American city over a 250-year period. He classifies the business structures into new, mature and declining business structures (industries); the housing into premium, worker and underemployed; and the population into managerial/professional, labour and underemployed groups.

According to Forrester's model, an empty land is transformed into a thriving area before it starts declining again, if certain conditions are met, leading to either abandonment or overcrowded housing buildings and/or obsolete industries (Diemer and Nedeleciu 2020, 4). Forrester argues that new housing attracts a managerial, professional population, but that once this deteriorates it is occupied by worker-housing, usually overcrowded. The third subsystem of population consists, according to Forrester, of managerial/professional, labour and the underemployed (unemployed and unemployable people, people in unskilled jobs, those in marginal economic activity and those not seeking employment but who might work in a period of intensive economic activity). A simplified version of this model was adapted by Alfeld and Graham (1976) (see also Ghaffarzadegan et al. 2011).

Their model comprises the same three 'stock variables' as with Forrester's model, i.e. business structures, housing structures and population. The behaviour generated by the model is also similar to Forrester's initial model. According to this representation, during the early years of an urban system's development when land is plentiful, exponential growth in housing, business structures and population is observed. The increasing number of business structures attract developers to invest in housing. This mobilises new job opportunities, leading to population growth via migration. As the growth continues, the available land becomes scarce and the space available for business or housing therefore becomes limited. Such space limitations slow down the rate of housing and business construction until the available land is completely full (Ghaffarzadegan et al. 2011).

The slowing growth of business structures leads to the reduction of employment opportunities and a gradual slowing of population growth through migration. However, housing construction, although also affected by space limitations, 'does not slow as quickly, due to a bias for housing over business (job-generating) structures' (Ghaffarzadegan et al. 2011). If the housing structures keep attracting a population that cannot be employed in the existing business structures, then signs of poverty and material decay will begin to appear. If unemployment levels are increasing, then the chances for housing abandonment also rise, since the living population will be either unable to maintain the housing or will endeavour to move to another area for employment.

The usefulness of the URBAN1 model (as with any urban dynamics model) lies in the fact that it does not only generate useful insights into the causes of urban decay, but 'can also help policymakers design policies to improve decaying cities or prevent stagnation and decay in urban areas that are still growing' (Ghaffarzadegan et al. 2011).

An additional insight that the urban dynamics model affords is that the total attractiveness of an urban region must be considered relative to the attractiveness of surrounding regions (Forrester 1971). For instance, if the attractiveness of a region increases temporarily relative to others due to the increasing number of job opportunities, then attractiveness must fall until equilibrium is again reached. Forrester suggests that increasing business structures and reducing the quantity of available housing will balance any change to overall attractiveness (1971).

Despite the usefulness of Forrester's urban model (and its future amendments), the model has been criticised for its inability to deal with the suburbs, failing to answer the question of where do people go when they live in a city (Gray et al. 1972, 143). An additional criticism is that Forrester's model precisely defines a stagnant and declining city, but not a healthy one; it is also perceived to lack a robust theoretical foundation

(Gray et al. 1972, 143–4). Moreover, according to critics, Forrester's model is based neither on empirical data collected for a specific city (Averch and Levine 1971, 152) nor on existing studies and literature (Dunn 1970, 217), but it rather provides a generic model intended to apply to various cities (Berlinski 1970).

Since Forrester's theory was not backed up by empirical data over time, researchers in recent years have attempted to improve the theory through the acquisition of empirical evidence. For instance, Sanders and Sanders have demonstrated that the fraction of residents migrating into or out of the city (zone) is modulated by the attractiveness of the city compared to its environment or other zones (2004). The key variables mobilised in the dynamics of the city are population growth, economic activity, pressure for new housing, pressure for industrial areas, land-use zoning, available land, built-up area, level of services and building height restrictions. Meerow et al. (2016), for instance, provide a more holistic system as they identify four subsystems: governance networks, socio-economic dynamics, urban infrastructure and form, and networked material and energy flows.

Despite the criticisms raised, especially in the early years of the publication, Forrester's model remains one of the most influential and commonly cited models (Lane and Sterman 2011; Lane 2007). Although up to 1995 (Alfeld 1995), the model had not been widely accepted in the United States, it has become more influential elsewhere. This, I argue, is because despite its flaws the model provides a basic, simple and validated structure of urban growth and decline. As Richardson observes:

> Urban Dynamics was a breakthrough, or more appropriately a breakaway, which led in spirit, if not in strict content, to the breadth of papers in this issue, which in turn hint at the breadth of applications in current practice around the world. (1999, 440)

Similarly, Saeed's comments in his work on applying the model in the context of a developing country also reveal Forrester's influence:

> Many years ago, I asked Professor Forrester in a casual conversation about his take on the developing countries. I was a bit surprised to learn that his perspective on where the developing countries stood (at a mature economy level) and where they were heading (stagnation/downward) was very different from what the contemporary literature on economic development assumed (at early stages of growth and heading upward). He also referred me to his Urban Dynamics model (Forrester 1969) as an appropriate policy

framework for economic development, even though this model originally addressed urban issues in the United States rather than in any developing country. I have to admit I did not immediately understand Forrester's perspective and in my mind even called his familiarity with the issues faced by the under-developed world to question. However, although it has been over a decade since we had this conversation, I have not been able to put it to rest. In fact, the more I have thought about it, the more I have come to appreciate Forrester's unusual view of economic development and the appropriateness of his Urban Dynamics model as a policy framework for it. (Saeed 2010, 3)

Saeed compares Forrester's model with the creative destruction theory by which the 'creative' demolition of aging infrastructure can be a catalyst for urban renewal. Although I strongly disagree with the contention that urban renewal can be achieved through 'creative demolition', I contend that urban dynamics can capacitate the understanding of the complexity of urban heritage systems as long as they are complemented with additional trans-disciplinary and cross-disciplinary analytical tools which can enable a better understanding of the social dynamics (Fouseki and Bobrova 2020). It is my aspiration in this chapter to add a socio-cultural lens to urban dynamic studies – the lens of heritage – and thus to propose an 'urban heritage dynamics' approach that will hopefully be useful for urban planning in heritage areas.

Urban heritage dynamics

How is urban dynamics relevant or useful (or how can it be) for studying the dynamics of urban heritage areas? In this section I utilise the urban dynamics theory of Forrester and his followers as a point of departure in order to shape an 'urban heritage dynamics' theory. I do this by juxtaposing the urban dynamics theory with the ways in which the Royal Arsenal and its surrounding area in Woolwich have changed. I also draw on the findings of a longitudinal study evaluating the impacts of the Townscape Heritage Initiative – an initiative funded by the Heritage Lottery Fund that aimed to support the 'regeneration' of declining areas through heritage conservation – in order to reinforce my analysis (Reeve and Shipley 2014).

As I have demonstrated above, urban areas are complex and dynamic systems affected by external social, political, economic, environmental or other influences (e.g. Fouseki and Nicolau 2018). Not only are cities complex and dynamic, but they are also adaptive systems, in that they constantly adapt to inevitable change (Batty 2009). Similarly, historic cities exemplify 'complex systems composed of multiple dimensions (such as social, cultural, political, economic and environmental) that are in dynamic interaction with each other' (Fouseki and Nicolau 2018, 230). However, most theories of urban change provide only a partial insight into what is a complex process (Roberts 2000, 21; Diemer and Nedelciu 2020, 1).

In order to address this gap, I endeavoured elsewhere to visualise the dynamic interaction of social, economic, environmental, heritage and political parameters that are mobilised during a heritage-led regeneration project (Fouseki and Nicolau 2018). At this point, I will encapsulate and contrast this visualisation with the urban dynamics model before proceeding with the application of the 'urban heritage dynamics' theory in the case of the Royal Arsenal.

In 2018 I developed on Vensim a causal loop diagram depicting the dynamics of 'heritage-led urban transformation programmes' funded through the Heritage Lottery Fund Townscape Heritage Initiative (THI) (Fouseki and Nicolau 2018). The construction of the diagram was based on a longitudinal study carried out by the Oxford Brookes University (Reeve and Shipley 2014). It is worth mentioning here that environmental changes were beyond the scope of this longitudinal study. Moreover, only limited data related to residents' sense of wellbeing and belonging were collected. Despite the flaws of the longitudinal survey, this study serves as a solid (and sole) foundation for urban heritage dynamics due to the predominant lack of longitudinal research.

The causal loop diagram published by Fouseki and Nicolau (2018) depicts nine loops. A 'heritage loop' signifies a reinforcing relationship between regular maintenance of built heritage, physical condition of built heritage and 'environmental', 'townscape' aesthetics. The 'heritage loop' reinforces the willingness of private investors (e.g. developers) to invest in the area due to their anticipation that the regeneration will result in higher property values. At this point an 'economic reinforcing loop' is inaugurated. The willingness to invest generates new housing, but also restoration and adaptive reuse of old buildings as businesses or residences. The 'new' housing tends to be inhabited by affluent 'newcomers' who hold the 'confidence' to spend. The arrival of 'newcomers' contributes to population growth. However, there is a risk of decline in social cohesion as the 'older' community will either be dislocated or feel disconnected. This observation was not remarked by the Townscape Heritage

Initiative study, but it has been adequately noted in the literature and will further be evidenced by the case study analysis.

It is at this point that the 'economic and social reinforcing loop' may start evolving into 'balancing loops'. The THI study illustrated that a 'social reinforcing loop' presupposes strong local self-esteem, which can be achieved if local community members participate actively in the regeneration plans and if their needs are fulfilled by the plans. More importantly, the Townscape Heritage Initiative pinpoints that if local needs are addressed, economic resilience is more likely to be achieved, guaranteeing employability and better quality of life. In the case of the adaptive reuse of buildings for social-cultural or other forms of enterprises, improvement on the economy of the surrounding region was observed. This led to the opening of new businesses and the increased demand for adaptive reuse of heritage encouraging more newcomers to the area.

How does the 'urban heritage dynamics' theory differ so far from the 'urban dynamics theory'? In the 'urban heritage dynamics' approach, urban 'renewal' occurs – not on empty land, as per Forrester's model, but on a land occupied by 'obsolete structures' of heritage significance. The principle is that 'obsolete structures' are revived through adaptive reuse triggering wider renewal on a greater scale. The 'balancing factor' – the factor that may change this reinforcing relationship – is the degree of concerted strategy and planning across the entire area. If absent, this can have a negative impact on the implementation of the project.

Contrarily, the urban dynamics model looks at the growth and decline of an empty land which is gradually filled up with housing and business structures. This results in population growth before a decline begins – marked by deterioration of the material fabric, closure of business, overcrowding of houses, unemployment and eventually depopulation. The causal loop diagram represents a point in time of neglect and abandonment during which existing heritage structures deteriorate. The solution employed is that of conservation and adaptive reuse rather than demolition, which would offer new land. The dynamics diagram shows that an economic and social revival can be mobilised through this tactic as the townscape improves, new businesses operate, employment opportunities emerge, the attractiveness of the area is raised and newcomers move into the area. However, this model does not withstand external shocks (such as the 2008 global economic crisis, by which the Townscape Heritage Initiative cases were affected) well if the adaptive reuse has not responded to the community's needs and heritage values.

The system depicted in the analysis is an 'open system' in that it takes into account the 'economy of the surrounding area', as well as the willingness of external investors and developers to finance the project. In addition, a series of variables related to the social wellbeing, beyond the attractiveness, of the area have been identified. These include the alignment of resources to local needs, local self-esteem and active local involvement, essential elements for resilient regeneration. To this end, the growth and decline of an urban area depends on multiple variables extending far beyond the connection between industries, businesses and population. In the next section I will elaborate even further on the 'urban heritage dynamics' theory through an in-depth analysis of the Royal Arsenal, Woolwich (London).

Urban dynamics in the Royal Arsenal and its surroundings

In this section I intend to unravel how heritage emerged and evolved in the Royal Arsenal over time, as well as the socio-economic consequences of 'heritage revival' in the area. Such exploration is significant for understanding the conditions under which heritage can be a catalyst for sustainable development. As I have explained, heritage is a dynamic and systemic socio-cultural practice, the continuity of which depends on the dynamic interactions between 'meanings', 'senses', 'space', 'skills', 'materials', 'time' and 'resources'. 'Urban heritage dynamics' are likewise driven and shaped by analogous interconnections.

The Royal Arsenal case study demonstrates that, until the 1980s, the evolution of the area aligned with Forrester's 'urban dynamics' hypothesis. As illustrated later in the chapter, the originally empty riverside land was progressively occupied by 'housing' and 'industry' structures (to use Forrester's terms); they were associated with the military function of the area as a place where weaponry or other military-related material was produced (Hogg, 1963). The construction of 'housing' and 'industries' mobilised population growth and employability. With the end of the Second World War, however, the closure of most factories forced the majority of workers either to share houses or move outside the area (Stevenson 2007, 13). The gradual abandonment of the area led, inevitably, to the material degradation of the building infrastructure. Within the context of growing obsolescence, discussions for reviving the declining Royal Arsenal began to surface during the 1960s, but were only materialised at the beginning of the twenty-first century. It is at this point that Forrester's model does not suffice to interpret the transformation of the area. The Royal Arsenal may have looked like an 'empty', abandoned land, but the process of revival was to be based on the existing 'housing' and 'industrial' building-stock which, in the meantime, was acquiring a new dimension – that of heritage.

The majority of the military and industrial buildings in the Royal Arsenal were listed in 1973 and the Royal Arsenal was designated as a conservation area in 1981 (Guillery 2012, 190). Thus a new urban dynamics model – an urban *heritage* dynamics model – is fundamental in order to comprehend the new dynamics actuated by the emergence of certain forms of heritage and the exclusion or erasure of 'other' heritage practices. I will manifest in my analysis of urban heritage dynamics below that the adaptive reuse of the built heritage for residential or commercial purposes attracted affluent 'newcomers' who invigorated the area. Concurrently, however, the display of a 'sanitised' version of the past through interpretation panels (Willems 2020) alongside the wider 'gentrification' cultivated a divisive feeling between 'old' and 'new' communities. In a context of 'social division', heritage and culture have been 'used' as a medium for social cohesion. The first such endeavour was the establishment of the Fire Power Museum in the early 2000s. It was located within the Royal Arsenal, but failed to attract enough visitors, leading ultimately to its closure (Stevens 2016). A new cultural hub, known as 'Woolwich Works' was recently inaugaurated on the same site. It remains to be seen whether or how this project will reunite the communities fostering social resilience.

Urban dynamics in the Royal Arsenal

The official closure of the Royal Arsenal in 1967 marked a new 'heritage' and 'transformation' life cycle. In fact, a series of new, non-linear, often parallel 'heritage' and 'urban' life cycles emerged. Figure 2.7 (p. 63) depicts a complex causal loop diagram, the design of which is based on the synthesis of a diverse data set comprised of online questionnaires, interviews and secondary socio-economic data (methodology above). For the purpose of a clear narrative, I will attempt to provide a 'linear storytelling' divided into distinct phases of major change over time, outlined through the interconnected, non-linear, parallel 'loops'. By doing so I will argue that obsolescence ignites parallel, new, non-linear dynamic cycles, often in juxtaposition with each other.

Royal Arsenal in decline

The Royal Arsenal has a lengthy military history. That of the area dates back to the early sixteenth century, when Henry VIII built a dockyard for the creation of his flagship *Henri Grace a Dieu*. Further east, the land known as 'The Warren' was used for testing guns; a gun wharf was constructed there in 1546 (MacDougall 2019).[2] Over the years the land was passed to different owners and was gradually occupied with cottages, stores and manufactories for guns and ropes (Guillery 2012, 130). The Royal Arsenal grew into a thriving area, providing employment to 80,000 people in the manufacturing of weapons and armaments during the First World War (Raynsford 2006). However, after the Second World War most factories closed down; by 1922 only 6000 people were still employed there (Guillery 2012, chapter 3, note 183).

Despite attempts to generate alternative forms of work after the Second World War, further decline ensued. In the 1950s the separate factories were merged to form the Royal Ordnance Factory (White 2014), while the eastern lands were sold to the London County Council (later the Greater London Authority). The road-building around the Beresford Gate contributed to the area's decline and abandonment, with numbers of employed people being reduced to 9000 from 80,000 back in the 1940s and buildings being deserted (Guillery 2012, note 183). In 1967, despite sporadic efforts to reuse a few of the surviving structures adaptively (such as the use of Buildings 47 and 48 for remote book storage for the National Central Library in 1962), the Royal Arsenal formally closed (Guillery 2012, 372). Many buildings were demolished as a result, while the area was characterised as 'disadvantaged'; it suffered from high unemployment and was in need of regeneration (Clark 2005). The closure of the Royal Arsenal denotes the phase of 'decline' and 'obsolescence' in the area (Fig. 2.1).

Obsolescence insinuates for planners the end of a building's life span. Such a stage is remarked by the 'declining performance of a building' and the rising expectations of users (Thomsen and Van der Flier 2011) or the '(possible) decline of usefulness over time' (Egghe and Rousseau 2000, 1005). It is thus an opportunity for a new 'life' often acquired through the demolition of obsolete buildings. However, obsolescence is much more complex than its direct linkage with building (material) deterioration implies.

In my attempt to classify 'obsolescence' under one of the main attributes I have identified as integral for the continuation of a dynamic practice, I endeavoured to allocate obsolescence under a specific attribute.

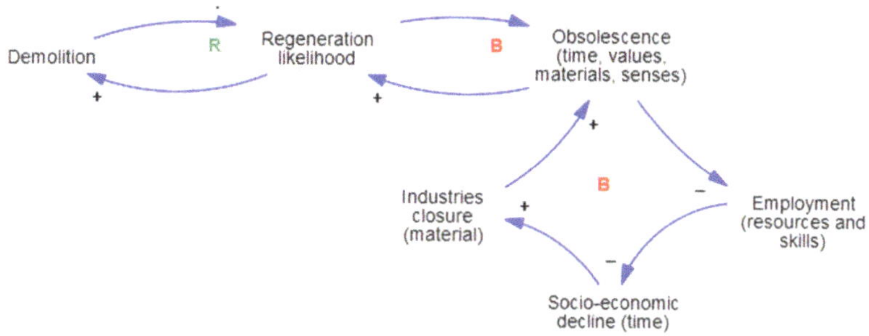

Fig. 2.1 Snapshot of causal loop diagram visualising 'urban heritage dynamics' at the Royal Arsenal. The diagram illustrates the driving factors contributing to decline.

Obsolescence evidently signifies material, time, sense and values, at the very least. It also bespeaks a moment in time, even as it leaves a time mark in the landscape/cityscape while alluding to a sense of 'permanent neglect' portended by deteriorated material buildings. More importantly, at the heart of revitalisation lie the 'people', while at the heart of obsolescence lies the absence of people, more so than the materials.

Post-decline valorisation and conservation

Abandonment and decline through obsolescence can result either in demolition or, as in the case of the Royal Arsenal, 'valorisation' (that is, attribution of a new value) of buildings as heritage (Fig. 2.2). The valorisation process is driven by feelings of fear of loss (sense/effect) (Robinson 2018, 199) – a fear that results in more 'material heritage' through the listing process.

Early discussions took place in the 1960s and early 1970s between government departments and Greenwich Council regarding the preservation of some of the Arsenal's more historic buildings; disputes also occurred over the removal of the Shot and Shell Foundry gates (Guillery 2012, 390). Such discussions, combined with ongoing developmental plans, most likely resulted in the purchase of the land by the GLC (Greater London Council) in 1967 and in the listing of several buildings in 1973.

The listing epitomises the 'official' recognition of heritage by national and local authorities and the shift of the development 'rhetoric' from one of demolition to one of preservation and adaptive reuse. The 'official' heritage may have overshadowed 'unofficial' heritage, however, as remembered and experienced by locals (especially those working on site). In any case, the idea of a museum as a 'commemorative medium' of

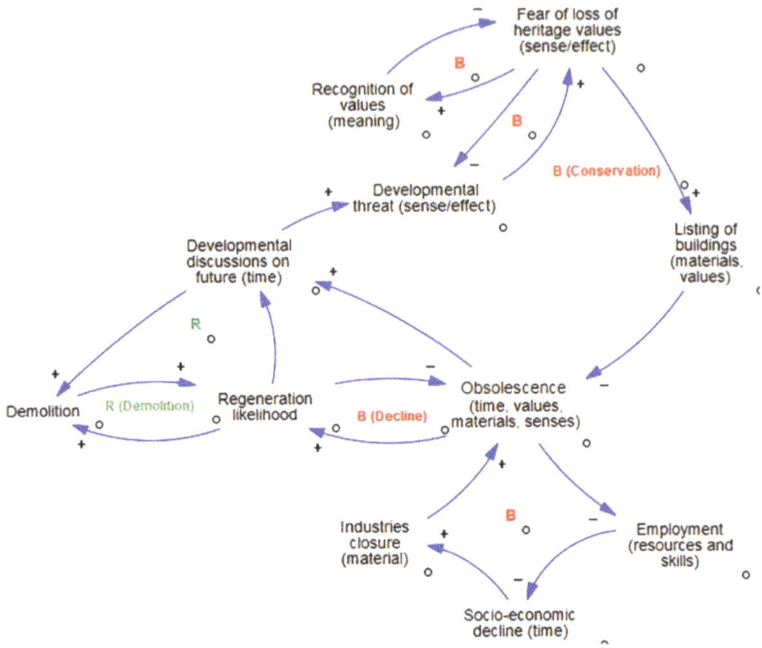

Fig. 2.2 Snapshot of causal loop diagram visualising 'urban heritage dynamics' at the Royal Arsenal. This snapshot illustrates the impact of 'listing' as a driving force for regeneration.

the history of the area – possibly serving as a 'bridge' between 'official' and 'unofficial' forms of heritage – emerged in 1978, in the proximity to the Royal Brass Foundry and Dial Square area (Guillery 2012). Ultimately the Royal Arsenal Conservation Area was declared in 1981 at the west end of 'a vast deserted area scattered with the half-used remnants of later structures, an eerie and desolate scene' (Guillery 2012, 190).

What we observe so far is a process of 'heritage up-scaling'. Conversations on the future of the area considered aspects of the heritage significance of the place ('values'); these culminated in the listing of buildings located in the Royal Arsenal in 1973 ('materials and values'), the emergence of ideas to construct a local museum ('place/space') and, eventually, the designation of the Royal Arsenal as a conservation area in 1981 ('place'). 'Official heritage' rose at a moment of decline and abandonment ('time') due to 'fear of loss' ('effect, senses') of heritage. The official recognition of certain 'values' was established through listing processes ('materials') and museum plans ('spaces'), but the completion of the latter was subject to 'resources'. In other words, the formulation of a new heritage life cycle introduced a new framework for the urban

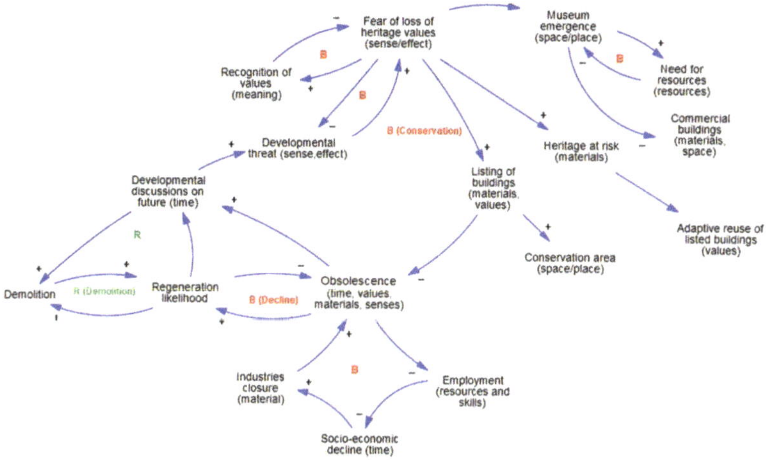

Fig. 2.3 Snapshot of causal loop diagram visualising 'urban heritage dynamics' at the Royal Arsenal. This snapshot illustrates the cultural revival achieved through listing and museum construction as a result of the fear of losing heritage values.

transformation of the place. It is at this point in time, therefore, that the two life cycles (heritage and urban transformation) cross over (Fig. 2.3).

Culture and heritage-led revival and regeneration

The 1990s were characterised by 'regeneration' plans. The land was transferred by the Ministry of Defence to English Partnerships, a government agency, and then to the London Development Agency with the aim of redeveloping the area (Clark 2005; Guillery 2012, 184). The area was zoned into residential (to the north-east), retail (to the south-east), employment (to the centre) and heritage and leisure (to the west). Developmental plans and discourses prompted further heritage actions on behalf of official heritage authorities. The Royal Commission on the Historical Monuments of England (RCHME) supplemented a suite of surveys in 1994–5 to unfold the historic significance of the site (Cocroft 2006). Future use was addressed by Inner City Enterprises, the condition of the buildings by Alan Baxter and Associates, archaeology by the Mills Whipp Partnership and site contamination by the Royal Ordnance (Guillery 2012). In this context of 'heritage' and 'urban' revival, a 'museum revival' also ensues. To this end, the Royal Artillery Museum at the Rotunda launched a fund-raising appeal in order to move to the former Academy, New Laboratory Square and Paper Cartridge Factory

(Buildings 17, 18, 40 and 41) (Guillery 2012; see also Cole et al. 2020). Simultaneously, Greenwich Council decided to relocate its borough museum and local history library at the Arsenal.

The 'heritage' revival was not always in harmony with the 'transformation' change. The widening of Plumstead Road in the 1980s, for example, was deplored as a 'disaster' for regeneration (Guillery 2012) as it separated the Royal Arsenal from the rest of Woolwich.

Merging the 'old' with the 'new'

One of the key regeneration moments was the purchase of the site by English Partnerships in 1997. A new masterplan, designed by Llewelyn-Davies, divided the area into four broad and flexibly projected uses, along with 22 subzones incorporating listed buildings. The zones were identified as residential (to the north-east), heritage (to the north-west), mixed heritage-leisure (to the south-west) and employment (to the south-east), where road links were best (Guillery 2012, 186; see also Llewelyn-Davies website[3]).

How does this zoning scheme compare with the previous scheme? The residential area remained in the north-east, as with the former masterplan. The use of the south-east side was transformed from one dedicated to retail to one focused on employment, while the western side was now intended to accommodate heritage and leisure activities. The new masterplan thus significantly reduced emphasis on retail. The project was completed in 2004.

Their project website reads:

> The site is an important historic area comprising **one of the largest concentrations of Grade I and Grade II listed buildings.** Llewelyn Davies **led a consultant team of over 20 disciplines** for the regeneration of the site, establishing the masterplanning framework and the delivery of the initial infrastructure of the site. The strategy was developed to **respond to the existing town centre and community, transport initiatives, employment uses and development potential of the area.**
>
> The site has now been successfully transformed into a vibrant, **mixed-use development by private residential developers.** The masterplan has been a developing benchmark as market demands have reshaped the disposition of uses on site. (author's emphasis) (https://www.ldavies.com/home-slider/royal-arsenal/)

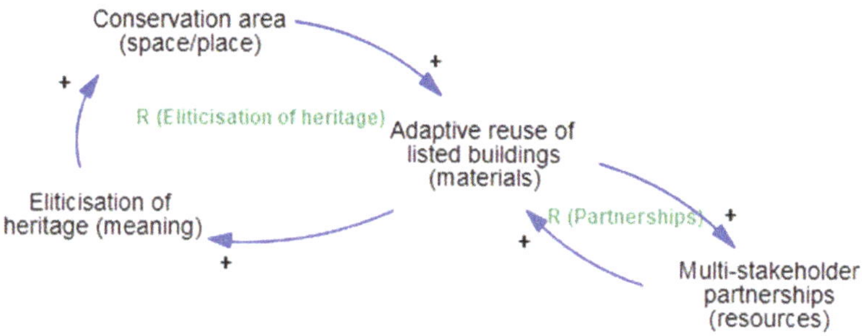

Fig. 2.4 Snapshot of causal loop diagram visualising 'urban heritage dynamics' at the Royal Arsenal. This snapshot illustrates 'growth' attributed to regeneration and partnership.

The description of the project begins with a statement on the heritage significance of the Royal Arsenal. The opening statement thus indicates that heritage provided the overarching framework within which the master plan emerged. The listed buildings ('materials') delineated the 'space' and 'place' boundaries of what 'could' and/or 'should' change or remain as is. The imposition of a boundary framework demanded multi-coordination and multiple 'skills' ('competencies'). The emphasis on 'responding to the existing town centre and community' is of particular interest due to the 'physical' and 'symbolic' disconnection of the Royal Arsenal via the Plumstead Road wall. The absence of a distinct retail zone (although some shops, such as a bakery and a flower shop, can be seen in the area) may be interpreted by a desire to interconnect the Royal Arsenal with Woolwich town centre. A partnership between developers, heritage professionals and planners is highlighted, but less so with the wider communities (Fig. 2.4).

Cultural revival

This new phase of construction and reconstruction is characterised by building works associated with the museum in 1999 and the instigation of archaeological excavations by Oxford Archaeology under the supervision of English Heritage (Guillery 2012, 186; see also Whalley 2004; Teague 2020). The development of the residential zone was assigned by LDA to Berkeley Homes Ltd in 2000 (Woodcraft 2015, 139). The core of the conservation area was leased to them and a planning consent was granted for a mix of private, social rented and shared ownership apartments and houses in new blocks and converted listed buildings in a poor state of repair, with severe contamination and important archaeology in the ground, which was excavated by Mills Whipp Partnership in 1994–5. Gradually the total number of homes increased in order to maximise profitability (Clark 2005). The prospect of a Crossrail station within the Royal Arsenal, partially funded by Berkeley Homes, boosted the attractiveness of the area for newcomers. The general trend so far has been increased height and density of buildings, as well as increased cultural and heritage activities.

Hitherto the aspiration of the regeneration aligns with Forrester's model in that the focus is the creation of new housing and new industries (including cultural and heritage industries) that will attract 'newcomers'. Yet how can heritage – and culture more generally – evolve in a rapidly changing urban environment? What are the social consequences of such a rapid transformation?

One of the first cultural endeavours during the regeneration phase was the establishment of the Firepower Royal Artillery Museum. The museum, funded through the National Lottery Heritage Fund (HLF), was initially housed in Building 17 between 1999 and 2001 before expanding to Building 41. Its construction thus coincided with the wider redevelopment works. However, despite the ongoing regeneration, the Firepower Museum closed on 8 July 2016 (Museums Association, 2016)[4], the result of its failure to meet its target of 200,000 visitors a year (Fig. 2.5).

Indeed, the absence of visitors, especially from the surrounding local area, was remarkable during our annual study visits. The physical

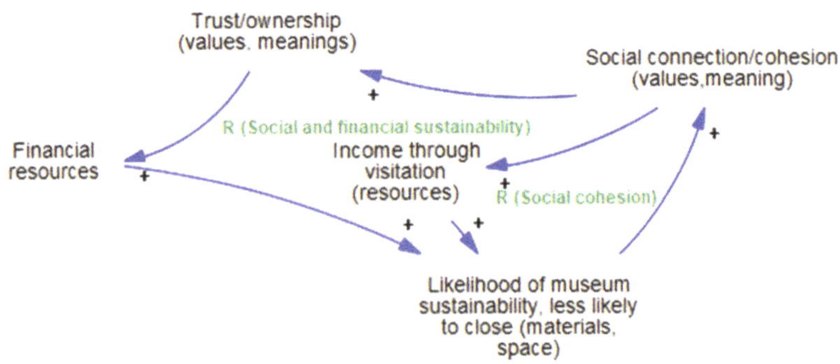

Fig. 2.5 This causal loop snapshot illustrates the key factors that contributed to the closure of the Firepower Royal Artillery Museum in 2016.

and social separation of the Royal Arsenal from the rest of Woolwich seems to have contributed (at least in part) to this trend. The challenge that the museum faced from its early stages was that of providing a vibrant central hub in an otherwise 'empty-feeling' land. This project pinpoints that a museum's social (and consequently financial) ('place, space') resilience is interdependent on the social resilience of the wider area ('space, place'). In other words, we cannot expect a museum to drive community cohesion if this is not already embedded into the society, and vice versa: we cannot expect a socially cohesive place, if a museum or a heritage site excludes segments of the society.

Despite the closure of the museum, the cultural legacy was retained. Buildings 17, 18 and 41, formerly housing the Firepower Museum, were transformed into a cultural centre known as the 'Woolwich Works' which opened in autumn 2021[5] (Fig. 2.6). The socio-economic and cultural impact of this venue remains to be seen.

In addition to the Firepower Museum, the Greenwich Heritage Centre was located opposite to the Firepower Museum. It is currently closed, but is about to move into Charlton House, outside the Royal

Fig. 2.6 'Woolwich Works' under construction, Royal Arsenal. (Photo taken by the author, 10 September 2021.)

Arsenal. The brief timeline of the Firepower Museum demonstrates that cultural sustainability cannot be guaranteed without commitment from local authorities and sufficient visitor footfall. A cultural approach was adopted including arts, indicating the role of arts in sustainability and moving beyond just heritage.

Social division

The socio-economic picture of the Royal Arsenal has changed dramatically since 2002, with the Arsenal site forming a 'pocket' of comparative affluence in Woolwich. In addition, the Royal Arsenal has some of the highest property values across Woolwich, as stated on the website of Berkeley Homes. This describes the 'Officers' House' as a 'unique architectural gem' with 'the original part of the building built over 250 years ago'.

> Artfully combining old and new, The Officers' House is a combination of Grade II listed apartments and contemporary new build. The original construction dates back to 1740 when The Officers' House was part of the Royal Military Academy. Now with a completely modern addition, this is your chance to enjoy such a historic setting in a building designed for 21st-century living.[6]

The combination of 'old' and 'new', 'Grade II listed' and 'modern' or 'contemporary', 'historic setting', combined with a twenty-first-century lifestyle is characterised as 'art-full', connoting Bourdieu's analysis of how art can only be perceived by those who have the necessary knowledge to appreciate. The social division is further re-affirmed by the online respondents to a structured questionnaire distributed to local Facebook groups in 2020 and in-depth interviews carried out since 2016. 'Speak out Woolwich', a group of local residents campaigning for a better Woolwich, has often commented on the implications of the physical and social divide between the Royal Arsenal and the town centre – a divide that is now hoped to be reduced, as illustrated in 'The new vision for Woolwich' masterplan.[7] Despite the positive intentions of the new vision, 'Speak Out Woolwich' has pointed out the lack of community involvement in conceptualising the vision, as well as the lack of integrating alternative forms of heritage into the masterplan.

Urban heritage dynamics beyond the Royal Arsenal

Up to now I have evaluated the dynamics of the Royal Arsenal as if it is a 'closed dynamic system' – either unaffected by external and peripheral forces or having no effect on the neighbouring areas. A 'closed system', in system dynamics, reflects Forrester's concept of endogenous systems (Richardson 2011, 211). According to the endogenous viewpoint, the dynamic behaviour of a system arises within its internal structure (Forrester 1968, 4). How are the boundaries of the internal structure of an urban system defined? An urban system contains a multiplicity of potential boundaries that can be selected for identifying the study area. For instance, urban system boundaries can be determined on the basis of the infrastructure, administrative units or the ways in which a community self-identifies with specific areas (social boundaries) (Tobey et al. 2019, 457).

In the case of the Royal Arsenal, I first construed the 'physical', geographical boundary of the area which bolstered the delineation of the focal area. However, I acknowledge that as much as an endogenous, 'closed system' approach may buttress an investigation of urban dynamics at the early analytical stages, we cannot deviate from the fact that this 'closed system' depends on external and peripheral systems. Such interdependence eventually modifies an urban system into an 'open system' – one that is 'causally related to exogenous activities' (Elliot et al. 2018, 81). It is thus the aim of this section to outline a few of the 'cross-boundary dynamics' that occur between the Royal Arsenal and its neighbouring areas.

I have hinted above that the 'physical' boundary imposed by the wall erected during the widening of Plumstead Road in the 1980s not only defined the geographical boundaries of the Royal Arsenal, but also introduced a 'social boundary' that disconnected the 'newcomers' of the Royal Arsenal from the 'old' community outside these boundaries. Here I would like to explore the 'symbolic' and 'cultural boundaries' as manifested through the presence of the built heritage. I will argue that the symbolic boundaries transcend the physical ones, evidencing the 'openness' of urban systems. I will also contend that these boundaries, whether they are social, symbolic or even physical, are not static and fixed, but rather fluid and subject to change. A physical boundary may provide the catalyst for the formation of symbolic and social boundaries that will ultimately overstep the physical boundaries; a symbolic boundary can be transformed into a social boundary as soon as a social group formulates an abstract idea into a specific form of social practice.

'Heritage values' constitute an indicative example of the interdialogical relationship between physical, social and symbolic boundaries. The ways in which certain forms of heritage (symbolic boundary) are valued by a social group (social boundary) within a physical space (physical boundary) may very well influence how heritage beyond the physical boundaries is valued and recognised. Therefore, although boundaries connote 'locations of difference' where any two adjacent points at least differ in some respect (Abbott 1995), they can also intermix at any point in time, overshadowing the initial difference that created them in the first place.

In Woolwich a series of examples serves to indicate the interconnection of symbolic and social boundaries beyond the narrow physical boundaries of the Royal Arsenal. For example, the swing bridge at Broadwater Estate of the Royal Arsenal Canal, built in 1812–14, was associated directly with the operations of the Royal Arsenal, although located beyond its physical boundaries. As soon as the Royal Arsenal declined, the bridge began to deteriorate following its abandonment in the 1980s. The urgent need to repair led to its listing in 1990 while recent redevelopment efforts of the Broadwater Estate, of which the canal is part, led to the inclusion of the bridge into the Heritage at Risk List.[8] Another example is the listing of the historic school (Gordon School) alongside a complex of four huts in 2008.[9] The huts were moved to the school's area in 1916 in order to provide places for children from the Well Hall Estate, built by the government for munition workers working at the Royal Arsenal. The hutments, intended to be temporary structures occupying areas of Well Hall and underdeveloped parts of Eltham Park Estate, were meant to house the increasing population of workers who had to commute daily to the area. The hutments were removed in the 1930s (1937) (Kennet 1985).[10] The huts were listed as they were viewed as the 'best surviving examples on the site of a paired arrangement of relatively rare temporary classrooms built in the early C20', with the site illustrating 'the contrast between the architectural exuberance of Edwardian board school design and the early use of functional, flexible structures to accommodate pupils'.[11] The huts have remained vacant and continued gradually to deteriorate, resulting in their inclusion in the Heritage at Risk list.[12]

Another place symbolically and socially associated with the Royal Arsenal but not located in its vicinity is the Progress Estate in Eltham. The estate accommodated individuals employed by the Royal Arsenal, despite the fact that the majority lived alongside Plumstead Road which crosses the Royal Arsenal site.[13] The blog administered by historian Ian Bull reads:

> The wartime expansion of the Arsenal soon strained local housing capacity around Woolwich to the seams. In addition to several thousand single women to be housed, the Arsenal also employed up to 7,700 boys. Many lived with their parents, but 1,000 or more had been sent from homes far away. Whole families also waited to move to Woolwich; many spread roots in the area at this time and their descendants remain today. The Ministry of Munitions not only built huts and hostels by the thousand to house the workers, but also built a model estate that stands today, now a green and leafy suburban area; the Progress Estate, nearly 1,300 homes on a 100-acre site, would have taken about 3 years to build in peacetime. The Ministry managed it in just 9 months. Of the hostels, perhaps the most poignant was the boys' hostel on the Churchfield Estate. Five blocks held 750 boys. These lads worked 62 hours a week in the Arsenal, mostly in making and filling small-arms cartridges. They typically earned slightly more than an adult 'civilian' labourer, and to avoid temptation the hostels looked after their money, making regular reports to the boys' parents or guardians. Conditions in winter in the flimsy timber huts must have been appalling.

The 'Progress Estate', built in 1915 by the Government as homes for the workers at the Royal Arsenal in Woolwich, was designated a conservation area in 1971; most buildings within the Royal Arsenal were listed during the same year. Listing is a social practice enacted by a specific social group (that of heritage professionals). As a social practice, listing transforms what was an initially symbolic boundary, bounded by the values and meanings, into a social boundary. It also has a physical dimension as it delineates what can or cannot occur physically on the building and its vicinity. The conservation appraisal describes the estate as

> the first and most spectacular of the Garden suburbs built by the government during the First World War to house munitions workers … a tour de force of picturesque design. (Sir Nikolaus Pevsner Buildings of England – London: 2, p. 307, cited in Greenwich Council 2007, 3)

Undoubtedly, the most characteristic area linked symbolically, socially and physically to the Royal Arsenal is Woolwich town centre. The story of growth in the western part of Powis Street affirms Forrester's model and similar stories in other urban areas. Initially the land behind Woolwich High Street was empty. However, the growing military presence since the 1780s alongside the expansion on the Warren, barracks on the common and an improved road link (Woolwich New Road) were a growth catalyst for the eastern part of the town centre marking the initiation of building construction (Guillery 2012, 190). Ironically, while the outbreak of war in 1793 contributed to reduced housing demand and construction in London, in Woolwich it led to increased work, population and housing demand. By 1815 Powis Street was fully built up with 158 properties and Hare Street was also complete (Guillery 2012, 192). Through the second half of the nineteenth century Powis Estate was, despite its divided ownership, managed as one by Henry Hudson Church (1827–1914); he was instrumental in the development of public works and new roads during the 1850s and 1860s.

The commercialisation of Powis Street had started before the expansion of the Arsenal, but certainly the Arsenal was an additional factor for more shops to open. Woolwich's street market was relocated and established in Beresford Square in 1888, attracting more shoppers and redevelopment (Guillery 2012, 198). The area continued to grow into a central commercial/shopping area (from housing to commercial). However, not unsurprisingly, the closure of the Arsenal in 1967 and of the Siemens factory in 1968 resulted in unemployment and loss of local custom while business rates kept increasing (Guillery 2012). Several shops started closing down in the 1970s and 1980s and big office blocks emptied, despite attempts to pedestrianise the eastern part of Powis Street and Beresford Square in the early 1980s and to 'clear' General Gordon Place in 1984. An interesting shifting pattern occurred at the time – a return to the residential character of the area by converting high office blocks into flats. This residential revitalisation encouraged brands such as Costa Coffee (2005) and Starbucks (2008) to open in the area (the revitalisation link to improvement of transportation links as in 2009 was the year in which the DLR extension to Woolwich was realised). However, many brands shut down, partly as a result of increasing rents but also possibly because of the forthcoming 'gentrification' of the area.

Beresford Square evolved into a square, a market and a meeting point, as well as a focal point for protests due to its proximity to the Arsenal. Unfortunately the closure of the Arsenal affected the planning perspectives around the square when the Greater London Council approved plans for widening Plumstead Road that assumed the demolition of Beresford Gate (Guillery 2012, 163). When the road passed through the Royal Arsenal in 1984–6, Beresford Square was pedestrianised, maintaining the Beresford Gate in place. This change contributed to the gradual decline of the market with several stall-keepers whose families had been trading in the area since 1888 leaving the area (Guillery 2012).

Woolwich town centre was designated as a conservation area in 2020 although discussions about the designation of a conservation area emerged much earlier. More recently the area became part of the Heritage Action Zones scheme (a scheme administered by Historic England and the respective local authorities), which aims to convert empty and underused buildings into creative spaces, offices, retail outlets and housing to support wider regeneration by attracting future commercial investment. This example demonstrates the loop of 'heritage diffusion' or 'upscaling' as some alternative forms of heritage are recognised while others remain excluded.

A similar example is the Covered Market on 14 Plumstead Road, which opened in 1936 and was listed in 2018 as a Grade II listed building, possibly due to the risks imposed by the development proposals. We read at the Woolwich Exchange, for instance, the revised redevelopment proposal in the area (https://www.woolwichexchange.co.uk/). The market was designated due to its 'architectural' and 'historic' interest. According to Historic England, the architectural significance lies in the fact that the roof is 'unaltered', constituting the earliest surviving example of the Lamella system. The historic interest derives from the fact that the market is a 'rare survival' of the dwindling number of Lamella structures in England; over 100 were built during the interwar period but only 16 are now thought to remain.[14] Although this is what is described as a justification, it is most likely that what drove the listing were community pressures and the fear of loss due to the rapid development in the area. As stated by 'Speak Out Woolwich', while developers applied in 2018 to demolish the market, local community action resulted in its listing and future reuse as a cinema.

Before examining the interactions with the other subsystems, it is worth mapping the life cycle of the market. How did the market emerge, how did it evolve, at what point in time did it become heritage (unofficially and officially) and what has been its evolution since then? According to Historic England, the market opened in 1932 due to the overcrowding of the earlier marketplace on Beresford Square. In 1936 the market was enclosed by a lightweight steel structure with a Lamella roof. It closed in 2017 and was converted into a multi-venue food hall, operated by Street

Feast on a rent-free deal. Unfortunately the market was abandoned once again in February 2019 due to a 'row with the council over a £20,000 bill to fix botched electrical works'.[15]

As mentioned above, the market received its designation as heritage as a result of controversial plans requesting its demolition prior to redevelopment. The move for the designation was instigated by the Twentieth Century Society which described the building as a big, uninterrupted space for people to gather. It was highlighted that several businesses, run by mostly Black, Asian and Minority Ethnic (BAME) communities, were facing dislocation. Mr Patel, a shopkeeper who worked as a newsagent on Woolwich New Road, said:

> I've been trading on the same spot for 35 years. It's always been at the heart of the community, we had a thriving Woolwich market which the council has let it run down over the years.
>
> We're all in favour of change … but we're part of the community and we make it tick. I had a laughable offer from someone from Tree Shepherd – 'if we relocate you to Abbey Wood, would you be happy with that?'

Another shop owner stated:

> I mean, we want to be part of this, we've worked our lives here. We should be allowed to be where we are and be given a place to trade from, instead of just being bought out and moved on. We want to be part of this community.

The community reactions forced the developers to amend their initial proposal by building the 'cinema within the former covered market building, with cafes, bars and restaurants above, as well as a public space for anyone to use' (Woolwich Exchange 2020). The developers stated on the revised plans:

> As well as delivering high-quality homes to meet the needs of the whole community, we will respect and enhance Woolwich's rich heritage and look **to breathe new life into** the former covered market. The site's unique position nestled between Royal Arsenal Riverside and the wider town centre creates an opportunity to forge stronger connections and provide new facilities for the growing community.

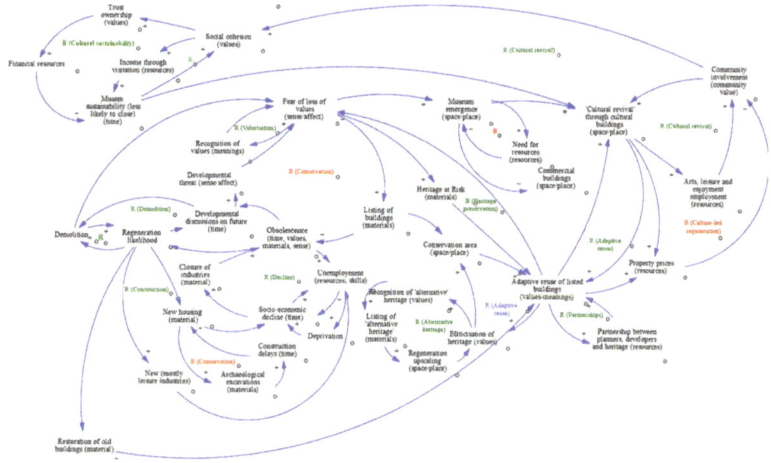

Fig. 2.7 Causal loop diagram summarising the interconnected variables mobilised during the regeneration of the Royal Arsenal.

To sum up (Fig. 2.7), the case of the Royal Arsenal illustrates how Forrester's traditional urban dynamics theory was validated after the closure of the Royal Arsenal site. However, the conservation (instead of demolition) and adaptive reuse of the historic buildings which were listed as a means of protection introduced a new 'lease of life'. It generated financial resources for the actual conservation of the buildings while opening up new leisure centres and places. Despite these successes, a social gap between 'old' and 'new' communities seems to exist and to be only widening. This poses the critical and still open question: Whose role is it to cultivate 'social cohesion' during a regeneration process? Is this the role of a 'heritage officer' (defined in the broadest sense), a 'planner' or a 'developer'? Or should we say that everyone is involved in a 'regeneration' programme? If so, how can such a role be fulfilled?

'Modelling' urban heritage dynamics

I would like to conclude this chapter by proposing a new 'urban dynamics model' which incorporates the heritage dimension of an 'urban system'. Before doing so, it is worth elucidating how I employ the ambiguous term 'modelling', as it can often be interpreted as a tool of prediction. As Bala, Arshad and Noh argue, a model can alternatively be defined as a substitute of an object or system (2017). A mental image in thinking, for instance, is a model representing a real phenomenon or behaviour

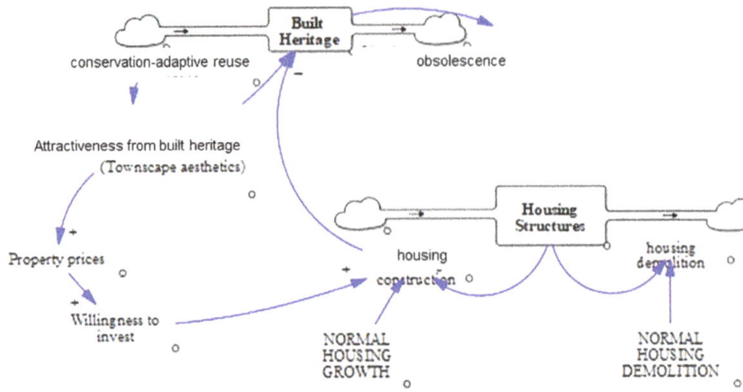

Fig. 2.8 Urban heritage dynamics model under construction.

(Bala et al. 2017). Accordingly, a simulation is not used for future prediction, but rather for describing the behaviour of a complex system (Sterman 2002). Subsequently, the 'urban heritage model' I present here is a visual representation of a mental model – a depiction of how an urban heritage system 'behaves' over time. I should also note that the 'urban heritage model' I portray here is not a simulation model. The latter is the subject of the ongoing 'CURBATHERI' (Curating Urban Transformations through Heritage) European project funded by the JPI-JPHE Global change and cultural heritage initiative (www.deepcities.eu). In the depiction of the model I will use the terms 'stocks' and 'flows'. 'Stocks' refers to anything (tangible or intangible) accumulated over time, while what drives the accumulation of stock over time is known as the 'flow' (Forrester 1987, 191).

My proposed 'urban heritage dynamics' model builds upon the Urban Model 1 by initially including the 'stock' of built heritage (Fig. 2.8). The rate of growth or decline of 'built heritage' depends on the rate of conservation through adaptive reuse or demolition respectively.

Evidence from the Royal Arsenal case and the Townscape Heritage Initiative indicates that the 'attractiveness of the area through aesthetics' is enhanced, triggering increase in property prices and thus motivating developers to place further investments. The developers' willingness to invest contributes to new housing construction which, ultimately, renders existing heritage at risk.

Earlier in this chapter I stressed the vital importance of concerted planning and community participation for achieving social and economic resilience. To this end I embedded the 'stock' of communities, which I connected with 'population' and the new 'stock' of 'cultural industries' (Fig. 2.9).

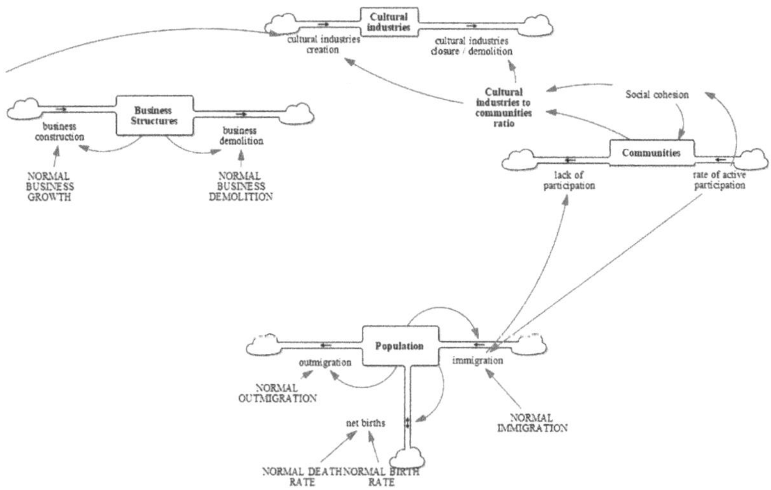

Fig. 2.9 Urban heritage dynamics model under construction.

By doing so, the assumption represented in the model is that if the community is not actively involved in the regeneration phase – or is 'priced out' due to increased property prices – outmigration will be exacerbated. Although the rate of outmigration may be balanced by the rate of immigration (that is, of newcomers moving into the area), the rapid change of 'outmigration' and 'immigration' will create division and affect social cohesion. Indeed, the social tensions created by the construction and population changes are missing from Forrester's model. Ultimately, it is not just about the number of people living in an area, but also about how connected these people feel as one community. Participation or lack of participation are depicted as the 'flows' to the 'communities stock'. In other words, the level of participation will determine how cohesive the community is, as well as how resilient the emerging cultural industries (such as museums) are. I purposefully created a distinct 'stock' for cultural industries, the vitality of which – unlike other industries – depends strongly on community participation. 'Cultural industries' are interconnected with 'business structures', however, in that they also occupy a fraction of the available land (Fig. 2.10).

Conclusion

In this chapter I have proposed an 'urban heritage dynamics' theory which can enable researchers and practitioners in charge of planning and

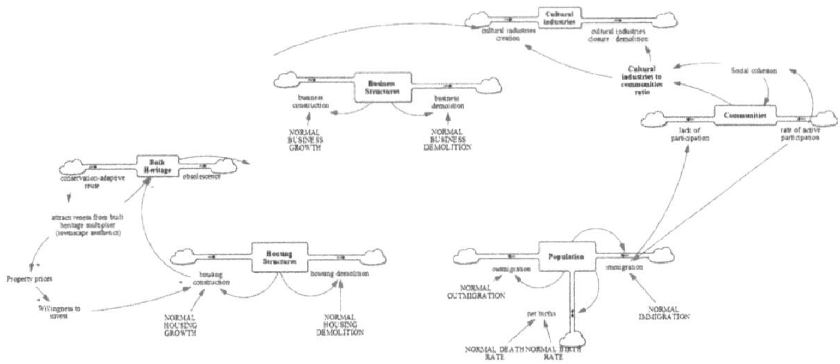

Fig. 2.10 Complete illustration of an urban heritage dynamics model.

managing 'historic urban areas' to unpack the underpinning forces that drive 'sustainable' or 'unsustainable' social and cultural change. By using the 'urban heritage dynamics' model, it is also feasible to test and visualise how certain actions and decisions in the present can trigger knock-on socio-economic and cultural effects in the future. I used 'urban dynamics' studies and models as a departing point. Most models in this field explore the dynamic interconnections between availability of land, number of housing and business structures and population. I argued that much as such models offer potentially useful tools for visualising and communicating the unintended consequences of decisions on urban growth and revitalisation, they fail to apply in urban heritage areas.

A historic urban area in decline may feel abandoned, an 'empty' land. However, the existing structures can provide the basis for revitalisation and rebirth. Through the case of the Royal Arsenal in Woolwich (and its surrounding areas) I showed that the site's obsolescence following the closure of factories in 1967 triggered a new life cycle – an urban heritage life cycle. Most existing structures were listed, provoking new ways of transformation that had to rely on a mixture of 'old' and 'new' structures. However, this transformation culminated in a social division between the 'old' and 'new', more affluent communities – a division exacerbated by the physical boundary that disconnects the Royal Arsenal from the nearby town centre. I demonstrated that such 'physical boundaries' can generate symbolic and social boundaries beyond the initial physical demarcation.

I concluded this chapter by presenting an 'urban heritage dynamics' model which has added three new 'stocks', including 'heritage', 'cultural industries' and 'communities'. I showed that, in the context of an urban heritage area, it is not adequate simply to observe the dynamic interconnections of the number of businesses, houses and population; one needs also to integrate more qualitative elements, such as 'heritage values', 'community participation' or 'community wellbeing' data. What remains to be completed in the future is the elaboration and further enhancement of the 'urban heritage dynamics' model, with equations that will allow the performance of simulations and so facilitate future practitioners to use this model as a practical tool for decision-making. This work currently forms part of the ongoing JPI-JPHE CURBATHERI (Curating Urban Transformations through Heritage – Deep Cities) project, of which Woolwich is one of the four main case studies (www.deepcities.eu).

Notes

1. https://853blog.files.wordpress.com/2019/01/woolwich-heritage-study-december-2018.pdf.
2. https://www.royal-arsenal-history.com/royal-arsenal-timeline.html.
3. https://www.ldavies.com/home-slider/royal-arsenal/.
4. https://www.museumsassociation.org/museums-journal/news/2016/03/01032016-fire power-museum-to-leave-london-home/# .
5. Woolwich as a major cultural destination | Woolwich Works | Royal Borough of Greenwich (royalgreenwich.gov.uk); UPDATE: Woolwich Firepower Royal Artillery Museum 'to leave by 2017' - former board member hits out | News Shopper; Contact us - Royal Greenwich Heritage Trust (RGHT).
6. The_Officers'_House_web_opt.pdf (lasoffittaimmobiliare.com).
7. https://853.london/wp-content/uploads/2019/02/speak-out-woolwich-submission-on-concept-masterplan.pdf.
8. https://historicengland.org.uk/listing/the-list/list-entry/1213695.
9. https://historicengland.org.uk/listing/the-list/list-entry/1392379.
10. http://www.ideal-homes.org.uk/greenwich/assets/galleries/progress-estate/hutments.
11. https://historicengland.org.uk/listing/the-list/list-entry/1392379.
12. https://historicengland.org.uk/images-books/publications/har-2018-registers/lon-har-register2018/.
13. https://www.royal-arsenal-history.com/royal_arsenal_family_members_posts/research-on-people-who-worked-in-the-royal-arsenal-woolwich-all-related-posts-here-on-comments.
14. https://historicengland.org.uk/listing/the-list/list-entry/1456184.
15. Woolwich Street Feast shuts after botched electrical work and Crossrail delay – https://853.london/2019/10/11/woolwich-covered-market-to-stay-as-spray-street-developers-review-plans/.

3
'Everyday heritage'

Introduction

Seven years ago I undertook a 'public engagement project' funded via UCL's Public Engagement Unit. Its aim was to organise events for local communities in Walthamstow (East London) on energy efficiency in 'old' buildings. The first step was to conduct in-depth discussions with residents on what they valued about living in an 'old' building and how they balanced these 'values' with the need to improve thermal comfort and energy performance. The second step was to hold workshops in which residents could design 3D models of their ideal, energy-efficient, future houses. They were given a notional budget of £10,000 and a list of options to choose from, accompanied by information on estimated costs and savings in carbon dioxide emissions. The third step was to display the models produced by the workshop participants at the William Morris Gallery. This provided an opportunity to discuss with visitors ways of rendering their properties energy efficient while preserving the heritage elements.

The residents, especially those with children, enjoyed the workshop, stating that it was the most engaging one they had attended. Several visitors also commented on how they wished this information had been available to them before they undertook damaging insulation works in their houses. This project instigated a new, under-explored area of research related to inhabitants' efforts to balance the needs of thermal comfort, energy performance improvements and 'heritage conservation' in 'old' residential properties (both listed and non-listed).

In this chapter I aim to unravel how elements of 'old' residential buildings (such as 'original architectural features') acquire or expend 'heritage value' over time. I do so by looking at the ways in which inhabitants of such buildings negotiate their decisions on heritage conservation, thermal comfort and energy performance improvements. I then turn to what I call 'everyday heritage' – that is, heritage experienced in everyday life through everyday routines and practices. In the context of urban landscapes where this term has recently occurred, 'everyday heritage' is understood as a '"catalyst of everydayness" for people … that comes to be evaluated by residents through its functionality and uses more than through its historic or official value' (Giombini 2020, 54). As such, everyday heritage

> conserved or organically evolved, can contribute to producing and organizing everyday social spaces in the urban landscape by changing its original function, form or meaning. (Mosler 2019, 781)

In the context of domestic, private places, 'everyday heritage' is associated with a complex and interconnected set of 'values' and 'meanings'. These may be attributed to specific architectural features or linked with the general experience of living in an 'old' home.

The concept of 'everyday heritage' is inherently dissonant. As I will show later in the chapter, the wide array of cultural and social 'values' assigned to an 'old' house may decline over time, due in part to material degradation and reduced functionality which may influence the 'everyday need' for thermal comfort and energy efficiency. I will demonstrate that values assigned to 'original' (heritage) features (such as aesthetics, historic, symbols of the past) are highly attributed at the time of moving to a residence. Over time such values decline, however, as the need to improve thermal comfort becomes more imperative. This trend leads often to the replacement of 'original features' (mostly windows) by new ones made from modern materials. Yet in recent years a new trend may be observed – especially in conservation and/or affluent areas (or areas undergoing 'gentrification'). This is the process of restoration (even at times replication) of 'original' (heritage) features, especially fireplaces, cornices and windows (see Fouseki and Bobrova 2018; Fouseki, Newton et al. 2020).

The chapter is a meta-interpretation of an in-depth, cross-geographic and cross-cultural study (the first of its kind). It involved conducting 59 in-depth, semi-structured interviews (totalling 206,771 words) with residents of neoclassical stone buildings in Athens (Greece), Victorian and Edwardian brick buildings in London (UK), 1940s Swedish-type timber structures in rural England, mostly brick Victorian buildings in conservation areas of Cambridge (UK) and stone buildings in the World Heritage City of Mexico (Fouseki, Newton et al. 2020). Each interviewee was given a code consisting of the initial letter of the area (i.e. W for Walthamstow, C for Cambridge, A for Athens) and the number of respondent (i.e. W1, W2, etc.). For those inhabiting the timber houses in rural England, the coding comprises the capital letter T and the consequent number. The rich interview dataset was double-coded through NVivo, a type of qualitative analysis software. The open coding resulted in 682 codes which were then clustered through 'axial coding' into broader themes. In parallel with the coding, I mapped 214 cause and effect relationships on NVivo; these were then later collapsed into a smaller number of causal relationships and visualised on Vensim, a software used for mapping and modelling the dynamic interconnections of a 'system' (Fouseki, Newton et al. 2020, figure 3).

'Qualitative cross-tabulations' were then performed on NVivo. These compared responses based on a series of attributes such as location, building age (nineteenth century, early twentieth century and the 1940s), construction materials (brick, stone, concrete mixed with brick, concrete mixed with stone, timber), desired thermal comfort (between 20 and 25 degrees, less than 20 degrees, more than 25 degrees), length of time living in the property (1–5 years, 6–10 years, 11–30 years, more than 30 years), length of time planning to live in the property (indefinite, planning to move soon, 1–5 years), listed status (listed, non-listed, partially listed (only facade), non-listed but in a conservation/protection area), ownership status (owner, landlord, private tenant, council tenant), type of area (conservation urban area, non-conservation rural area, non-conservation urban area, World Heritage area) and type of building (detached house, semi-detached house, terraced house, flat in block of apartments) (Fouseki, Newton et al. 2020). The meta-interpretation operated in this chapter allowed heritage researchers and professionals to ponder the systemic and dynamic nature of 'heritage values' which, up until now, have not been captured.

The term 'original features' connotes the values of 'originality' and 'authenticity', although the latter term was not specifically employed by any of the interviewees. It is also worth mentioning at this point, as explained below, that the terms are perceived in a different way to when they are used by heritage professionals. In that context 'originality' and 'authenticity' imply preservation of the 'original' state of condition, as defined by heritage professional and international charters on heritage conservation (see pp. 71–5 below). For the participants of this study, however, the 'original features' can (and should) be restored and refurbished so that they are fully functional.

We should also keep in mind that what are now called 'original features' fulfilled, at the time of construction, a functional role. Thus, from a 'heritage dynamics' (heritage life cycle) perspective, the 'original features' denote a shift from functionality to aesthetics, coined here as 'functional aesthetics'. 'Functional aesthetics' encompass both the 'aesthetic' and 'functional' values with which 'original features' are attributed (see Saito 2007 on 'functional beauty'). Sustaining 'functional aesthetics' is critical for the future sustainability of 'original features'. As I will illustrate, the material degradation of 'original features' culminates in a loss of functionality; this may in turn lead to restoration or replacement of 'original features' by modern products and materials. In this study, functionality was related to the provision of a thermally comfortable environment. The interview extract below succinctly summarises the dynamic interrelationship of 'original features', and the values associated with them, with the need to improve the thermal comfort (see also Fouseki, Newton et al. 2020).

> Yes, I really like the **original sash windows** ... but they were in very **bad condition** ... so they then needed to be either completely restored or taken out and **restoring sash windows is a very pricey job** and even if you do it properly ... you don't get the same insulation you would get with PVC ... So we went for double-glazing PVC ... We only did it last year, we couldn't afford it. We probably would have done it sooner although **we weren't necessarily agreeing**, because we liked the fact that it was sash windows and Jason was thinking it would be nicer to restore them, but when we saw how much it was going to cost and also **finding a specialist**, whereas with the PVC you could get almost anyone to quote, so it was less than half price in the end. And the decision you know, it was also because those houses, especially at the time, they weren't expensive houses, they weren't £200,000 and we just felt that spending money and restoring windows if you're in a conservation area in a nice neighbourhood, or ...somewhere where the Real Estates move premium it makes sense, but **spending money on restoring sash windows in this area, it didn't really add with the price of the house** ... to be honest it would probably hurt it, because people looking for housing in this area tend to be families who want to have a warm house, not necessarily a conservation type of house. (Participant: W5) (author's emphasis)

'Official' heritage discourses on 'originality' and 'authenticity'

Before making a detailed examination of inhabitants' attitudes towards the preservation or replacement of 'original features' by modern ones, it will be useful to review at this point how 'originality' and 'authenticity' are defined in international and national heritage policy documents. By doing so, I will unfold the emergence of 'originality' as a distinct 'heritage value', as well as map the wider context of legislation and administration within which most of the heritage, residential buildings are located.

The first official reference to the value of 'originality' can be traced in the 'Athens Charter for the Restoration of Historic Monuments' adopted at the First International Congress of Architects and Technicians of Historic Monuments in 1931. The Charter recommends that:

> In the case of ruins, scrupulous conservation is necessary, **and steps should be taken to reinstate any original fragments that may be recovered (anastylosis)** whenever this is possible; the new materials used for this purpose should in all cases be recognisable. (author's emphasis)

The Charter went through revisions in the following years, partly as a response to the changes imposed by the First World War (Gold 1998). Despite the changes, the emphasis is placed on the 'reinstatement' of 'original materials'. It also stresses the need to make modern materials distinguishable. Therefore the Charter accentuates the importance of 'materiality' in conveying the 'sense' of originality. Almost 30 years later, the still influential International Charter for the Restoration and Conservation of Monuments and Sites (Venice Charter) (ICOMOS, 1964) was adopted at the Second International Congress of Architects and Technicians of Historic Monuments. The Charter begins with the following statement:

> Imbued with a message from the past, the historic monuments of generations of people remain to the present day as **living witnesses of their age-old traditions**. People are becoming more and more conscious of the unity of human values and regard ancient monuments as a **common heritage**. The **common responsibility** to **safeguard them for future generations** is recognized. It **is our duty to hand them on in the full richness of their authenticity**. (author's emphasis)

'Authenticity' is associated with the 'evidential value' ('living witnesses of their age-old traditions') of the remains of the past, as well as with the 'truthful' information provided on those remains from 'authentic documents', as stated in Article 9:

> The process of restoration is a highly specialized operation. Its aim is to preserve and reveal the **aesthetic and historic value** of the monument and is based on **respect for original material and authentic documents**. It must stop at the point where conjecture begins, and in this case moreover any extra work which is indispensable must **be distinct from the architectural composition** and must bear a contemporary stamp. (author's emphasis)

The Venice Charter builds upon the principles of the Athens Charter, which are expanded to stress the 'moral' and 'shared' responsibility of present generations to 'respect' and 'sustain' monuments in their 'full authenticity' for future generations. Although the Venice Charter did not define 'authenticity' explicitly, it implicitly connotes that 'documenting the presence of original material was the determine authenticity' (Goetcheus and Mitchell 2014, 344). 'Authenticity' is also conjoined in the Charter with 'historic' and 'aesthetic' value. As a matter of fact, authenticity is portrayed as a prerequisite of the aesthetic and historic value of a monument. Consequently, with the ratification of the Venice Charter in 1964, a respect for authenticity in the sense of the 'genuine' and the 'original', uncontaminated by intrusions of another age, was dictated (Jones 2010, 185).

Despite the fact that both Charters reflected the conservation principles of the time in which they were developed, they have influenced – and continue to influence – official heritage management practices in many countries (Goetcheus and Mitchell 2014). The discourse on 'authenticity' and 'originality' is so dominant that it can be detected in 'everyday heritage' responses. For example, respondents living at the World Heritage Historic Centre of Mexico demonstrated a sense of appreciation of 'facadism' – possibly a projection of the values underpinning the listing in the first place (Fouseki, Newton et al. 2020). This phenomenon may be further explained by the inclusion of Mexico's Historic Centre into the World Heritage List, a process that stresses 'authenticity' as one of the key prerequisites for World Heritage listing.

Indeed, in the 1990s UNESCO's Operational Guidelines it is specified that each World Heritage Site should 'meet the test of authenticity in design, material, workmanship or setting and in the case of cultural landscapes their distinctive character and components' (McBryde 1997, 94). This approach clearly highlights the importance of 'tangible' qualities of heritage. The materiality of heritage is used as the undebated evidence of 'genuineness'.

Certainly the 1994 Nara Conference on Authenticity introduced a shift towards the importance of intangible qualities relevant to authenticity, as can be observed in the 2019 Operational Guidelines (Jones 2010, 185). Indeed, revised Operational Guidelines associate 'authenticity' with the credibility and truthfulness of the 'information sources' on which the attribution of value to heritage is based.

> The ability to understand the value attributed to the heritage depends on the degree to which **information sources** about this value may be understood as **credible or truthful**. Knowledge and understanding of these sources of information, in relation to original and subsequent characteristics of the cultural heritage, and their meaning as accumulated over time, are the requisite bases for assessing all aspects of authenticity. (author's emphasis)

The Operational Guidelines make explicit reference to the Nara document on Authenticity (1994), which called for broadening the scope of the concept of authenticity using similar terminology. The Nara meeting on which the Nara document was based originated from the need of Japanese conservation practitioners

> to extend the range of attributes through which authenticity might be recognized in order to accommodate within it mainstream Japanese conservation practices, namely the periodic dismantling, repair and reassembly of wooden temples, so that Japan would feel more comfortable about submitting World Heritage nominations for international review. (Stovel 2008, 9)

Despite its initial local focus, the Nara document introduced universally applicable principles that re-orientated the way in which 'authenticity' could be explored in World Heritage nominations. For instance, Article 11 of the Nara document states that:

> **All judgements about values** attributed to cultural properties as well as the credibility of related information sources **may differ from culture to culture**, and even within the same culture. It is thus not possible to base judgements of values and authenticity within **fixed criteria.** On the contrary, the respect due to all cultures requires that heritage properties must be considered and judged within the cultural contexts to which they belong. (Article 11)

However, although Article 11 stresses the need to contextualise how authenticity is approached in each cultural group, an attempt to 'measure' authenticity systematically and credibly is also mentioned. In Article 12, for example, the Nara document advocates that 'within each culture, recognition be accorded to the specific nature of its heritage values and the **credibility** and **truthfulness** of related information sources'. It continues

> Aspects of the sources may include form and design, materials and substance, use and function, traditions and techniques, location and setting, and spirit and feeling, and other internal and external factors. The use of these sources permits elaboration of the specific artistic, historic, social and scientific dimensions of the cultural heritage being examined. (Article 13)

Despite its flaws, the Nara document on Authenticity unquestionably paved the way for rethinking 'originality' while also detaching it from 'materiality'.

To sum up, international official heritage discourses on originality and authenticity evolved from an over-emphasis on the truthfulness or genuineness of materiality to the truthfulness of intangible qualities embodied in heritage. However, authenticity in its 'tangible' and 'intangible' form is perceived as important for unveiling historic, aesthetic, artistic, social and scientific values of heritage. The question that emerges is to what extent do international discourses reflect national and local (unofficial) discourses on authenticity in the UK, Greek and Mexican discourse on listing where the case studies are located. As mentioned above, in conservation and World Heritage areas, such as the World Heritage Historic Centre of Mexico, official rhetoric on authenticity and heritage is ingrained into unofficial responses to heritage. In non-conservation areas, however, notions of authenticity are discursively manifested in the 'everyday' through associations with 'soul', 'aura' and 'sense of the past'.

'Unofficial' heritage discourses on 'originality' and 'authenticity'

Having briefly outlined the wider official heritage discourse on 'originality' and 'authenticity' at international and national level, I will now consider how residents value (or not) the 'originality' attributed to certain architectural features. As noted, I will argue that in some cases (especially in conservation and world heritage areas) the rhetoric of residents on 'originality' is guided by 'official heritage' discourses (Smith 2006). However, in most cases 'originality' is construed not as a distinct but rather as an 'interconnected' value. By this term, I suggest that 'originality' is dependent on 'heritage values' as well as conducing to them.

Such reconceptualisation of 'originality', and of heritage values more generally, as an 'interconnected', dynamic system of values will impact upon how heritage professionals discuss, communicate and 'manage' the 'heritage values' with which a place, site, object or practice is imbued. The idea of 'an interconnected, dynamic system of values' calls for a shift away from the classificatory and descriptive typologies of values. A values framework of 'how' 'heritage values' can be captured in the best possible manner is therefore more pertinent than a framework of 'what' values can be evidenced.

Table 3.1 Interconnections between 'materials' and 'values' extrapolated from NVivo analysis

MATERIALS/ Original features	→	VALUE Economic (property value)	●		
MATERIALS/ Original features	→	VALUE Rarity	●		
MATERIALS/ Original features	→	VALUE Historic	●	FEELINGS Homeliness, cosiness	●
MATERIALS/ Original features	→	VALUE Personality (character, soul)	●	VALUE Aesthetics	●
MATERIALS/ Original features	→	VALUE Aesthetics	●		
MATERIALS/ Original features	→	FEELINGS Awe	●		
MATERIALS/ Original features	→	FEELINGS Happiness	●		
MATERIALS/ Original features	→	FEELINGS Satisfaction	●		

In Table 3.1, I illustrate a snapshot extracted from the qualitative analysis software NVivo, mapping the 'cause and effect' of interconnected relationships triggered by 'original' features. The 'original' architectural features referenced by the respondents include windows, roofs, floors, fireplaces, high ceilings, plastering/cornices, fittings, construction materials, craftsmanship, light, feelings of spaciousness and layout (Fouseki, Newton et al. 2020).

As depicted by Table 3.1, the value of 'originality' engenders additional values such as historic, aesthetics ('character' of the place) and economic values (associated with higher values when the property is sold). Emotions such as happiness, overall satisfaction and awe are evoked as a result. The diagram shown here visualises a cross-tabulation between 'location' and profile of respondents in terms of ownership status carried out on NVivo (Fig. 3.1). It hints that the 'interconnectedness' of 'originality' with 'historic value' is primarily commented upon by respondents living in the World Heritage Centre of Mexico as well as inhabitants of Walthamstow. Similar visual cross-tabulations were performed on NVivo, revealing that for one property owner in Walthamstow the 'original features' of their home 'made them smile'. For property owners in Cambridge conservation areas, 'original features' were interlinked with the notion of 'aesthetics'. The linkage between a building's 'original' features and its 'personality/character' was stressed mainly by private tenants in Walthamstow and Cambridge.

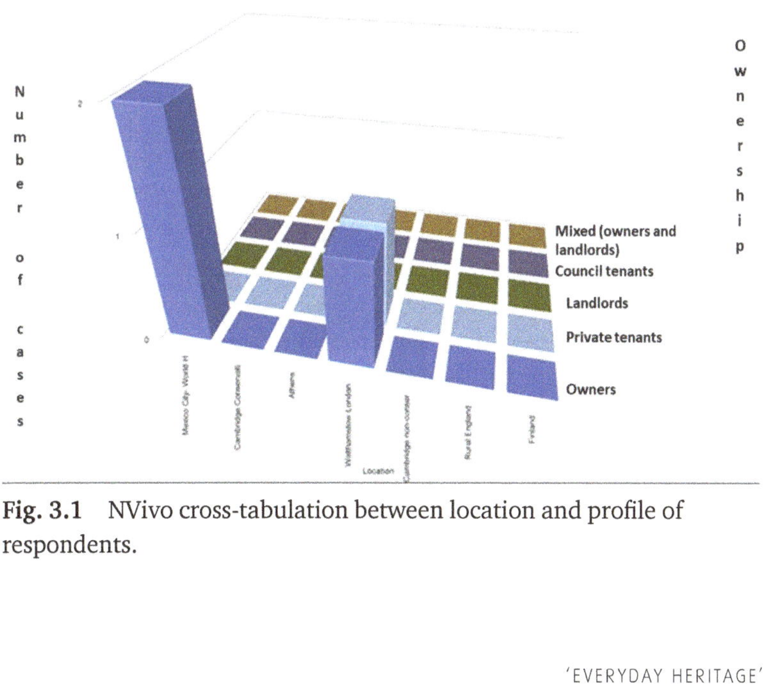

Fig. 3.1 NVivo cross-tabulation between location and profile of respondents.

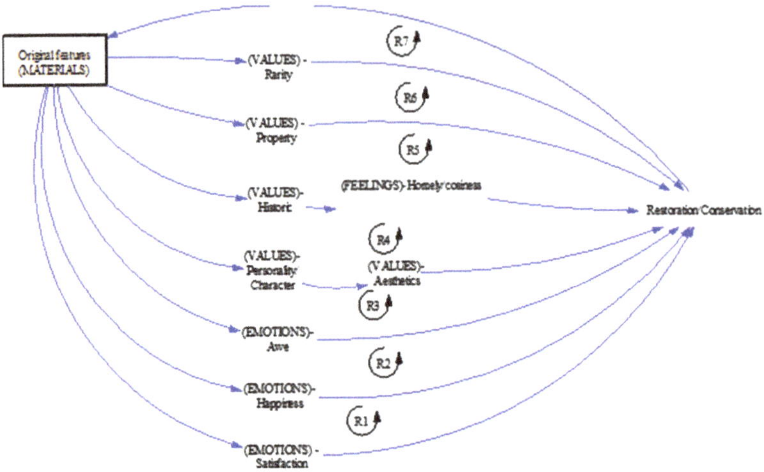

Fig. 3.2 Interconnectedness of original features, values and emotions.

Although these observations do not emerge from a statistically significant analysis, given the qualitative nature of the research, the identified diverse approaches are nevertheless notable and indicative of the complex ways in which people engage with notions of 'originality' in their everyday lives. 'Heritage values', like heritage itself, are socio-cultural, dynamic and systemic practices. As such, a 'heritage value' does not constitute a classifiable entity, but rather a dynamic process subject to interconnectedness and change. In the following diagram created on Vensim, I have sought to visualise the dynamic interconnectedness of heritage values and emotions triggered by 'original features' as a dynamic system (Fig. 3.2), subject to further analysis below.

'Authenticity', 'originality' and 'character'

> Apart from establishing a direct connection with its moment of birth (origin) when an object is translated from an idea into a physical manifestation, authenticity is also associated with the state of originality – the uniqueness that comes into being at the moment of conception when a particular unreproducible concatenation of materials and conditions come together to produce a sui generis creation. (Attfield 2020, 80)

I have noted above that official heritage management discourses and frameworks link 'authenticity' with 'originality' and 'genuineness'. The overwhelming emphasis until very recently has been on the 'integrity' or 'true' nature of objects defined in relation to their origins, fabric and the intentions of their makers (Jones 2010, 184). However, in recent years a general consensus has emerged among heritage scholars and professionals that authenticity is not inherent in an object. On the contrary: authenticity is culturally constructed and is therefore perceived in various ways depending on who is observing the object and in what context (Jones 2010, 182). When people experience and negotiate authenticity through heritage objects and places of practices 'it is networks of relationships between people, places and things that appear to be central, not the things in and of themselves' (Jones 2010, 189). Although the 'original material' is critical in signifying the 'real thing', calling to mind the sense of presence for which there can be no representation or substitute for the real thing (Attfield 2020, 81), ultimately what matters are the networks of relationships generated from the process of engaging with an 'original' object.

Jokilehto contends that authenticity 'is fundamentally understood as being true to oneself' (2006, 1). Thus by 'respecting' the 'genuineness' of an 'old building', someone is being true to themselves. Interestingly, elements of 'personification' can be traced in authenticity and originality discourses. For instance, the notion of 'character' – which occurs frequently in conversations around the value of 'old' buildings – is 'understood as an "authentic" tie between material and time: some element of the historic environment and a moment or period of origin' (Yarrow 2018, 338). None of the respondents in the current study explicitly used the term 'authenticity', but they did refer to the need to preserve 'original features' indicative of the 'character', 'personality' and 'soul' of the house. The 'personification' of an 'old' building expounds why a few residents expressed anger with hypothetical scenarios of removing certain original features, for example the fireplace.

> But I think **it would be absolutely criminal to remove these fireplaces** … A lot of people do, they just take them out, they just cut them off, they just break them up or whatever … **but that's a very nice feature of the house … It retains some of the history** and there are four of them in this house … **Well I mean it's a waste of space** but at the end of the day I think they look nice and there is no way over my dead body that they would be taken out … I like them all even though this one necessarily and the front room one are not my taste I can see there is something to it because even when you know if you look at some of the you know the brutalist stuff, you

> look at it and then 'Oh God! That's ugly!' but if you spend a bit more time looking at it, you then 'Ok there's actually something to it'... So yeah I mean there's, I see something to it ... **It's part of the history of the building. It comes back to, for me it goes back to when it was first put in,** you know there are various bits I, I mean that's an old chimney from the, probably a cooker, probably a coal cooker, that would probably be it. (W5)

Here the survey participant highlights the interconnectedness between 'aesthetics' and 'historic' significance, understood as the ability of an architectural feature to take someone back in time 'to when it was first put in'. The interviewee states that although the fireplaces do not comply with their 'taste', the fact that they are historic features 'makes them look beautiful'. The interviewee perceives the removal of fireplaces to be a 'crime', believing that it is everyone's ethical duty to sustain 'original' features of historic importance. Although he understands that fireplaces occupy valuable, much needed 'space', the historic significance is prioritised over this requirement.

'Character', 'personification' and 'continuity'

> Character, like so many of the central concepts we use on a daily basis in conservation, is a somewhat nebulous one. It is also one we rarely stop to think about in abstract. Not only is it hard to define but it shares with related concepts, such as integrity and honesty, a family resemblance by employing what Ruskin termed 'the pathetic fallacy'. That is to say, we apply concepts properly belonging to human beings to inanimate objects. Can a building really be 'compromised', its 'integrity' questioned, its 'character' altered? It all rather conjures up the image of a shy Edwardian bather embarrassed to be caught half-way through changing into a swimsuit in a bathing engine on the South Coast. (Holder 2001)

The notion of 'character' in the context of the historic built environment 'embodies these actions, ideas and intentions as an individuated essence, sometimes attributed quasi-personified qualities, for instance of "life" or "personality"' (Yarrow 2018, 341; see also Yarrow 2016). Like 'authenticity' and 'originality' – as with any 'heritage value' – the concept of 'character' is also one of interconnectedness. 'Character' as an interconnected concept is interlinked with 'authenticity' (Jive'n and Larkham 2003) 'integrity' (Jones and Mean 2010), 'honesty' (Yarrow 2018, 332), aesthetics (Urland 2016), function, material authenticity and physical structure (Yarrow 2018, 339).

In the case study discussed here, the notion of 'character' was specifically mentioned by respondents living in Walthamstow and in rural areas of England. For instance, one respondent living in a timber Swedish postwar house in rural England stressed that

> We would never wish to alter the exterior wooden appearance with cladding. This would change the whole character of the house. It would become nothing special.

The timber structure attributes to the distinctiveness and hence the 'character' of the house. This is prioritised despite the maintenance and financial challenges (for example, banks do not approve mortgages for timber buildings).

The desire of conservators and residents to sustain the 'character' of an 'old' building 'refracts a common commitment to continuity as a series of decisions about the intrinsic qualities of things, and of how best to retain them' (Yarrow 2018, 342). At the same time, while for heritage professionals 'character' echoes a specific historic period (Yarrow 2018, 338), for residents the past is conceived in more abstract terms.

For both heritage professionals and residents, however, 'character' is always a relation of continuity between past and present (Yarrow 2018, 340; see also Khalaf 2020). It is so because it allows for certain qualities to be preserved despite the change. For residents, preserving the 'character' of a domestic building is almost synonymous with preserving the 'soul', 'personality', 'feel' and 'atmosphere' (Fouseki, Newton et al. 2020; see also Yarrow 2019). The act of preservation of character and personality creates 'an ethical imperative that orients a series of decisions regarding the nature and scope of "appropriate" modification' (Yarrow 2019, 13). It implies a sense of moral custodianship and guardianship (Yarrow 2019).

The 'moral responsibilities' elicited by the notion of 'character' echo the work of social anthropologists in this area. Reed and Bialecki, for example, have argued that the concept of 'character' 'invites a convergence of ethical and aesthetic forms of practice, technique and judgement' (2018, 160). One consequence of this combination, as they stress, is a certain blurring of the divide between subject (human and non-human creatures) and things (Reed and Bialecki 2018, 160). Faubion affirms that the notion of 'character' should extend beyond the anthropic to include the artefactual – 'an extension that might best be understood as not really being an extension at all. We humans are, after all, ourselves artefactual' (Faubion 2018, 168). Reed and Bialecki further contend that the concept of 'character' in anthropological theory is often assumed to be associated with the fixing or stabilisation of a self (2018, 161). Indeed, much of the work concerning character in heritage and conservation is

> precisely about deciding what to take away, how to safely remove or discount attributes of the subject/object to render it characterful in the right way. Fixing then can be a purificatory action, and to the degree that character does stabilise the self, it can also enact a division or split of that envisaged self. (Reed and Bialecki 2018, 160)

For some residents, 'character' evokes feelings of 'cosiness' and 'homeliness' as one respondent explains:

> Yes, I think it's the typical English houses, [they] would have **fireplaces** … It adds a little **character** to the house, making it **English**, **original** and **cosy** because fire is always associated with warmth and cosiness … I think it's the character or the image of the house. For example, the window here and the plaster belong to a certain era and I think they go together. So, while improving some of the things, it would be best to preserve as much of that house as possible. (W2) (author's emphasis)

In this quote the 'cosiness' attributed to the existence of traditional fireplaces is interwoven with 'originality' and 'Englishness'. In a similar way, the survey participant W17 explained why they chose to purchase their flat in the first instance. Their decision was driven partly because of the presence of 'original features':

> This flat, it doesn't have all its original features but it still had some, so it felt like it had a little bit of character to it. So … it actually had that bit of character and history that we preferred so we definitely wanted this one.

As mentioned above, a dimension of 'personification' is inhered in the notion of 'character'. An 'old' house obtains 'personality' and 'soul' over time (see Fouseki, Newton et al. 2020; Yarrow 2019, 14). Another respondent, A2, asserted that the neoclassical houses in Athens 'have their own personality, and if you change that, they don't function in the same way'. Another survey participant, A6, emphasised that their neoclassical residence was 'built with love', having 'its own soul' and 'personality'.

> They are the human side of the city, they are closer to the earth and you have more sky visible. They make you feel peacefully, they have more windows. I would say that they have their own personality.

A resident in Walthamstow, W5, underlined how sash windows are

> part of the fabric of the house and it was nice to keep the house as it was, as it was meant to work, you know, it still had all the original weights and the cavities and, so yeah, you know, it was part of the soul of the house.

Responses related to the 'personification' of 'everyday heritage' are of great interest as it is mostly monumental and emblematic heritage that has been invested with 'personified' qualities. One of the most characteristic and thoroughly analysed examples is the Parthenon Marbles and Caryatids, which have been discussed as Greek exiles who are demanding their return to their homeland (Hamilakis 2007). In the context of 'everyday heritage', the building as a whole obtains attributes of a 'person' with 'distinct' features, personality and soul, which merit preservation through the maintenance of as many original features as possible. To sum up, an 'old' building, when inhabited, acquires 'character', 'personality' and 'soul' through the presence of original features. The presence of original features marks a sense of material continuity over time (Khalaf 2020).

The interconnectedness of 'aesthetics'

Out of the 214 cause-effect relationships mapped on NVivo, I extrapolated and further coded six reinforcing relationships (Table 3.2). Four core factors were identified as contributing to the 'perceived aesthetics' of an 'old building' including: character, age/oldness, original features (with special emphasis on fireplace and windows) and good condition/functionality.

The previous sections demonstrated how 'original features' contribute to 'character' and consequently to the 'aesthetic value' of an 'old house'. Korsmeyer (2016, 219) affirms that 'genuineness is a property

Table 3.2 Interconnected relationships between 'materials' and 'values'

Cause	Effect	Direction	Files	References	Type of relationship	Explanation
Character	Aesthetics	→	2	2	●	It has a character and therefore it is beautiful
Age value	Aesthetics	→	2	2	●	It is old and therefore it is beautiful
Original features	Aesthetics	→	3	3	●	It has original features and therefore it is beautiful
Fireplace	Aesthetics	→	2	2	●	It has an original fireplace and therefore it is beautiful
Original windows	Aesthetics	→	2	2	●	It has original windows and therefore it is beautiful
Good condition	Aesthetics	→	1	1	●	It is well preserved and therefore it is beautiful

that possesses many dimensions of value, including aesthetic value', attributing the 'aesthetic value' of artefacts to the sense of age that they have accumulated over time. For Korsmeyer, all 'artefacts possess at least one aesthetically significant property that is bound up simply with the fact that they are the very things that have survived the years' (Korsmeyer 2016, 219). In other words, the 'originality' and 'genuineness' of an 'old object' is 'aesthetically pleasing' because of the 'age' accumulated into it. Based on this, Lamarque (2016, 286) denotes that even if a replica produces 'a superficially similar appearance to the original ... there are well-rehearsed arguments in aesthetics that the two experiences cannot be identical'. This contention is maintained by Korsmeyer. He argues that no substitute or replica can possess an aesthetic dimension (Korsmeyer 2018, 23) although it is the encounter with the genuine – not the genuineness by itself – that contributes to the aesthetic dimension of heritage (2018, 29).

While the 'originality' has been proved important in the context of 'everyday heritage' for generating a sense of 'aesthetics', the replication of 'original features' in residences has evolved into a popular practice over the last years (as shown below). The practice of replication indicates that multiple factors can be combined in different ways while producing the same result. In other words, 'aesthetics' may or may not result from the presence of 'original features': replicas of such features can inspire similar feelings.

'Age value' also emerged via the coding analysis as one of the interconnected components of 'aesthetic value'. John Ruskin (1849) lyrically described the 'age value' with which 'old' buildings are imbued.

> For, indeed, the greatest glory of a building is not in its stones, nor in its gold. Its glory is in its Age, and in that deep sense of voicefulness, of stern watching, of mysterious sympathy, nay, even of approval or condemnation, which we feel in walls that have long been washed by the passing waves of humanity. (Ruskin 1903 [1849], 233–4)

The Austrian art historian Alois Riegl, in his 1903 study on 'The Modern Cult of Monuments: Its character and its origins', later identified 'age' as the clue to the extension of heritage into mass culture (Arrhenius 2004, 75). Riegl proposed that any artefact could gain an agevalue defining it as a monument, as long as it revealed to the onlooker that a considerable period of time had passed since it was new (Arrhenius 2004, 77). For Riegl, age value can manifest itself though a wide array of visible signs as seen 'in the corrosion of surfaces, in their patina, in the wear and tear of buildings and objects' (Ahmer 2020, 152). Riegl's approach to age value locates a monument firmly 'in the realm of the old, where it remains isolated from the functionality and use of the everyday' (Arrhenius 2004, 80).

For Korsmeyer, age 'engages issues of persistence over time that inevitably arise with artefacts, both metaphysically and practically' (Korsmeyer 2016, 230). While an 'aged' or 'aging' object, monument, site or building metaphysically signifies past, and as such is invaluable, practically it is at risk of permanent loss in the future (Korsmeyer 2016, 230). This implies an inherent tension in 'age value'. On the one hand, as a value 'age' needs to be 'sustained' because it signifies the historic significance of an object/site. On the other hand, an 'aging' object or building needs to be maintained, repaired and restored so that it continues to exist. While preservation and conservation may intensify the 'aesthetic properties' of an 'aging' heritage object, appreciation of age may diminish its value (Korsmeyer 2016, 320). Such decrease in 'age value' may also result in loss of 'aesthetics', as an element of aesthetics is often carried by the 'sense of decay and loss, of time and the fragility of human endeavour' (Lamarque 2016, 298).

In Riegl's conception, 'age value incorporates time into the aesthetic experience, evokes an emotional response to the life cycle of nature, to the inevitable flow of temporal and historical processes' (Lang 2006, 161). In other words, age value's importance depends on what it signifies for the viewer rather than on how 'old' an object may appear to be.

For the respondents of this study, 'age' was not mentioned specifically as a 'value'. However, as seen above, references to 'original features', as markers of the 'past', were common. Yet in contrast to 'official heritage' that is intended for 'viewing', an 'aging' object in the context of 'everyday heritage' has mostly negative connotations, since its functionality is affected.

Indeed, the 'everyday aesthetics' – and, accordingly, the 'everyday' perception of 'age' – can differ substantially in 'everyday heritage' from other forms of heritage. Saito (2007, 3) defines 'everyday' as the 'attitude that people take toward what they are experiencing'. She clarifies that while for some people everyday life looks like 'a dreary and monotonous routine', for others it may provide a 'familiar safe haven' (Saito 2007, 3). Therefore, the concept of 'everyday' is elusive as much as it is highly contested (Saito 2007, 9). For instance, we tend to experience 'everyday' objects and activities, whatever these may be, 'mostly with pragmatic considerations'. As a result

> Preoccupation with accomplishing a certain task often eclipses the aesthetic potentials of these 'everyday' objects and activities. These experiences are generally regarded as ordinary, commonplace, and routine. (Saito 2007, 10)

At this point I would like to delve into the interrelationship of aesthetics and material degradation in the context of 'everyday heritage'. This endeavour is driven by the following 'dynamic' question: at what point in time does an object or architectural feature squander its aesthetics due to its material degradation and loss of functionality? To answer the question I will draw on the notion of 'everyday aesthetics', which can enable comprehending the interrelationship of 'aesthetics', 'functionality' and 'state of condition'.

'Everyday aesthetics' shifts our attention from the world of art to everyday practices 'such as cleaning, homemaking, cooking, and wardrobe' (Melchionne 2011, 437). By reapproaching 'aesthetics' beyond the art world, our understanding of the pervasive role of the aesthetics in our lives is expanded (Saito 2007). In other words, 'everydayness changes how we apply conceptions of aesthetic value' (Melchionne 2011, 437). In a similar way to Melchionne, Naukkarinen's concept of 'everydayness' encompasses objects, practices and routines that are familiar, easy and obvious (Naukkarinen 2013). For him, the 'everydayness of the everyday' consists of

> certain objects, activities and events, as well as certain attitudes and relations to them. Everyday objects, activities and events, for me and for others, are those with which we spend lots of time, regularly and repeatedly. Most often this means objects and events related to our work, home and hobbies. (Naukkarinen 2013)

Naukkarinen moves beyond listing types of objects or practices that could be classified under 'everyday aesthetics' to the 'everyday attitude' which he believes to be

> colored with routines, familiarity, continuity, normalcy, habits, the slow process of acclimatization, even superficiality and a sort of half-consciousness and not with creative experiments, exceptions, constant questioning and change, analyses and deep reflections. (Naukkarinen 2013)

Arto Haapala (2005) emphasises an important difference between the aesthetics of art and of everyday life. Whereas in art the strange or innovative is often privileged as a locus of aesthetic interest, in everyday life the familiarity of an object or environment may contribute to its positive aesthetic character.

While Melchionne (2013), Naukkarinen (2013) and Haapala (2005) have adopted a 'restrictive' definition of 'aesthetics' encompassing what is ordinary, common and daily, Leddy advocates for an 'expansionist' definition which 'includes festivals, tourism and many daily activities of artists and other professionals, along with most ordinary and common experiences' (Leddy 2015, 1). Leddy has drawn on psychological studies of the experience of 'awe' and 'aura' to align the 'high points of everyday aesthetics more closely with the high points in the aesthetics of art and nature' (Leddy 2015, 1). Puolakka (2018) also adopts an 'expansionist' view of everyday aesthetics, arguing that the 'everyday' can – and should – be characterised by a mixture of old and new, routine and the non-routine, the familiar and the strange, the extraordinary and the ordinary. All these elements co-exist in human experience at almost every moment, sometimes interacting with, and even reinforcing, each other to generate improved everyday experience.

Dowling (2010) takes a step further to distinguish a 'weak' and a 'strong' formulation of aesthetics in daily life. According to the 'weak' formulation, 'the concept of the aesthetic at work in discussions of the value of art can be extended to include experiences from daily life' (Dowling 2010, 241). As for the 'strong' formulation, 'experiences from daily life can afford paradigm instances of aesthetic experience' (Dowling 2010, 241).

In both 'reductionist' and 'expansionist' approaches to aesthetics, what needs to be noted is that the process of appreciating 'something' as aesthetically pleasant is dynamic. As Lee has remarked (2010), in our habitual patterns of dwelling we draw together activities, people, ideas and places. By doing so, we make a house into a home and even more. We care for our homes, turning them into places of meaning and meaning making; our aesthetic sense of the home arises from this process (Lee 2010).

I mentioned above that as functionality of an 'aging' object declines, its 'aesthetic' value does likewise. Theories on 'functional aesthetics' can be useful here, helping us better to comprehend the above interrelationship. Scruton (2007, 245) has argued that when

> issues of function and utility have been fully addressed, appearance is all that remains, so that an attempt to close off redundancies must find a solution in the way things look.

When an object or architectural feature (in our case) which is fully functional and operational is viewed as 'beautiful', it consequently becomes meaningful. Indeed, a few respondents stated how much they 'liked the look' of original features. The 'look of something, when it becomes the object of intrinsic interest, accumulates meaning' (Scruton 2007, 244). To reverse this argument, if function and utility have not been fully addressed or become an issue, then the initial appreciation of aesthetics is jeopardised and may be lost entirely.

Saito has thoroughly analysed the close interlinkage between 'aesthetics' and 'functionality'. She has argued that for as long as an object remains functional, it can also be perceived as beautiful (2007, 8), describing the interrelationship between 'aesthetics' and 'functionality' as 'functional beauty'. The examples in this chapter make this contention evident in the case of original windows, most of which were replaced with UPVC versions when their functionality declined due to material degradation. However, this principle did not apply in the case of fireplaces. Most of these were preserved despite the loss of their original functionality.

Saito rightly points out that our 'aesthetic judgments regarding the appearance of objects as aged, clean, messy, and the like, are intricately intertwined with our moral assessment' (Saito 2007, 163). While some changes are welcomed positively, people more often 'lament the changes as things "age," "decay," "decline," "deteriorate," "wane," "decompose" or simply "get old"' (Saito 2007, 154). Again, the extent to which 'age' and 'decay' will be viewed as negative or positive qualities will depend on the context. An 'aged' object or monument may evoke a sense of nostalgia, the so-called patina of nostalgia (Bickford 1981), and may be preserved and sustained as such. However, in the context of 'everyday life' an 'aged' and 'decayed' feature has not only lost its functionality but may also be viewed as 'ugly'. This is because

> we seem to have constructed a life process for each material and object from inception to an optimal state, prime condition or peak, after which it is in steady decline. (Saito 2007, 150)

For Saito, what marks the decline is the decreased functionality, whether real or perceived (Saito 2007, 159). The perceived loss of functionality leads to actions (such as repairing, restoration, cleaning, replacement, disposal). Everyday aesthetics is thus diverse and dynamic, its examination requiring a non-art-centred approach to aesthetics (Saito 2007, 4).

According to externalist theories of 'functional beauty', 'the functional appropriateness of an object is a necessary but not sufficient condition for such an object to be considered beautiful (Sauchelli 2013, 42). However, internalist theories of functional beauty 'suggest that an object can also be judged as beautiful by virtue of the way it looks in relation to its function' (Sauchelli 2013, 42). According to another family of internalist theories, 'our perception of beauty related to function may also occur if we perceive that the non-aesthetic properties of an object contribute to the fulfilment of its function in a certain way' (Sauchelli 2013, 43). There is thus a high degree of subjectivity, with people's perceptions of aesthetics depending on expectations of functionality. This implies that 'visual tension' may occur if an object, albeit functional, 'fails to meet expectations regarding how certain elements should be arranged, given its expected function' (Sauchelli 2013, 49).

So far, we have seen that theorists of 'everyday aesthetics' are divided into two main groups. There is a group of theorists of reductionists who are searching for the extraordinary in the ordinary (such as Leddy and Naukkarinen) and others who emphasise the ordinariness of the ordinary (such as Haapala and Saito). To this end, Forss (2014) introduces the poetic aesthetics of dwelling as a bridging concept. The process of attaching to one's environment is a poetic process and therefore the 'dweller is a poet of homeliness' (Forss 2014, 186). Indeed, many respondents specifically referred to the 'sense of homeliness' which certain 'original features', such as fireplaces, evoked. Such a 'sense of homeliness' is interlaced with 'aesthetics' or what Forss would call 'attached aesthetics', representing an 'aesthetic relationship to the intimate environment in terms of habitual, animative and poetic characters of dwelling' with 'qualities of attachment to intimate places' (Forss 2014, 183). The 'intimate environment' is thus not extraordinary in nature, but rather ordinary, familiar and mundane (Forss 2014, 183). Therefore 'the aesthetics of dwelling is also an aesthetics of the familiar' that does not include the 'aesthetics of the strange' (Forss 2014, 183).

Dynamic interactions between interior environment and original features

This section unpacks in some greater detail the interrelationship of the 'intimate interior atmosphere' of a dwelling and the impact of 'original features', especially those linked to the interior space (such as high ceilings, sash windows). I will argue that interior environmental factors, such as light and ventilation, are critical factors in the creation of a sense of 'intimate atmosphere' and 'homeliness'. Decisions on preserving, replacing or restoring 'original features' will often depend on their ability to contribute to this sense.

I have shown elsewhere (Fouseki, Newton et al. 2020) that a reinforcing relationship between the size and number of original windows (materials) and natural light (environment) exists; this can be reversed over time, however, if 'thermal' and 'acoustic comfort' are negatively affected. Light provided through original windows and high ceilings has been highlighted by the interviewees as a contributing factor to the interior aesthetics and the thermal comfort, particularly during the winter. Shutters have been used in some cases for regulating light and thermal comfort in the summer months, but their use depends on affordability and required maintenance costs as revealed by one of the participants (W7):

> But then shutters … they are expensive to get nice ones, they take up room so they take up more room within the house as well, you know it's not that big a flat so we were kind of sorting you know the maximum light, maximum space.

Similarly another respondent (W2) declares a desire to use shutters but expresses a caveat:

> as long as they weren't on every single window, probably on the window which lets in the most light because sometimes that can be annoying on a really, really sunny day, when you are trying to have a lie-in but the curtains are too thin … but the only thing is that if they were wooden and if they got stuck on the window still and they made this creaking noise, I hate that.

The importance of shutters and ventilation at night, as well as increasing thermal comfort in summer, has been evidenced in quantitative studies by scholars (e.g. Caro and Sendra 2020).

Living in an environment that feels 'comfortable' is essential for appreciating the 'aesthetics of a dwelling'. Indeed, the 'interconnectedness of aesthetics' depends on the interwoven relationships of materials (such as original features), senses (such as thermal comfort) and space/environment (such as light and ventilation). In addition to this, the feeling of spaciousness, enhanced by the presence of 'original' sash windows and 'high ceilings', also contributes to the perceived 'aesthetics'. 'Spaciousness' is understood here as the 'feeling of openness or room to wander' (Herzog 1992, 238). The feeling of 'spaciousness' can be increased by lighting, with rooms receiving more light from open space and windows feeling larger, leaving inhabitants and users satisfied (Ozdemir, 2010).

From 'property' to 'home' and from 'home' to 'asset'

So far, I have approached the 'dwelling' as the vehicle that generates an 'intimate atmosphere of aesthetic homeliness'. In doing so I showed how a 'dwelling' was valued as a property with 'aesthetically pleasing' features before it was turned into an individual home. While the property was evolving into a home, a personal living space, dysfunctional architectural features lost their 'functional aesthetic' value; in most cases owners chose to replace them with modern materials and designs.

Over time, however, especially when the home was regarded a 'property to sell' (i.e. an asset), the market attitude towards architectural, original features in the wider area guided the preservation or not of the original features. If an area tends to attract property buyers who value 'original features', property owners intending to sell their houses will most likely opt for the restoration (in some cases replication) of original features for as long as they can afford such practices. This phenomenon tends to occur in conservation and designated areas (e.g. Sharpe 2006; Shipley 2000; Deodhar 2004; Degoulet et al. 2012) or in areas experiencing 'gentrification', as in the case of Walthamstow.

Replacing, restoring or replicating 'original features'

The interview data revealed an additional dynamic behaviour towards the treatment of 'original features', especially in non-conservation areas which lack the administrative framework and consequent restrictions. It was shown that while the replacement or removal of 'original features' (especially windows and fireplaces) had been a common practice in the past, over the last ten years a shift towards restoration, as well as replication, of 'original features' has taken place. This is particularly pertinent in areas undergoing 'gentrification', which attract a different population favouring original features. This change indicates the 'interconnected' aesthetic value with which 'original features' were associated at the early stages of inhabiting an 'old' property (Fouseki and Bobrova 2018).

Participants often commented on the 'age' of the building as being important and meriting respect and careful conservation (Fouseki, Newton et al. 2020). However, while 'age' is certainly worthy of respect, it has also been mentioned as a barrier for thermal comfort (Fouseki, Newton et al. 2020, 11). Therefore over time original materials are replaced by modern ones in order to improve thermal comfort. Given the cultural weight that 'aging' original materials have, however, it is not uncommon for some homeowners to reproduce original features. In so doing they signify the 'age' and 'originality', or a sense of 'pastness', that an object or site conveys: the sense that it is an enduring part 'of the past' (Holtorf 2017, 497). In other words, the value of 'age' or 'pastness' – to use Holtorf's term – does not relate to how old an object, building or site actually is, but rather to how old it feels. It is for this reason that the replication and reproduction of original features resulting from the replacement of old materials in order to improve thermal comfort is deemed to be of cultural as well as aesthetic value. In contrast to Korsmeyer's (2016) contention that a copy has no aesthetic value, in 'everyday heritage' a replica can be perceived to be as beautiful as the original; a replica can evoke the same aesthetic values as the original work. Therefore the experience of qualities such as 'age value' and 'authenticity' are fundamentally different in 'everyday heritage', where functionality needs to co-exist with aesthetics.

Conclusion

In this chapter I unfolded the dynamic interconnectedness of heritage values, and of 'original features' in particular, revealing how the interconnected values of 'originality' and 'aesthetics' link dynamically with the need to improve thermal comfort and energy performance. I argued that an 'old' building is a complex, dynamic system; valuing and inhabiting such a property is a social and cultural practice, with everyday tensions and dilemmas that require dynamic decision-making and choices to be made. I built my argument on the meta-interpretation of a dynamic study of rich qualitative data on which this chapter is based (Fouseki, Newton et al. 2020). The study explored how the 'aesthetic' value of 'original features' decreases over time, as functionality declines while the need for thermal comfort increases.

In this chapter I have delved into the interconnectedness of 'heritage value' in order to demonstrate that 'heritage values' are complex sets of interlinked values rather than a singular concept, quality or 'thing'. By drawing on theories of 'everyday aesthetics', I argued that original features serve to trigger an array of values that cannot easily be distinguished and classified into distinct types of values: one 'value' rather constitutes the cause of another (such as character, awe, personality, aesthetics). The idea that 'heritage values' constitute complex systems of interconnected values calls for a move away from classificatory and descriptive typologies of values towards the flexible, 'open-value' frameworks that guide heritage professionals in unpacking the complexity and interconnectedness. A values framework of 'how' such 'heritage values' can be captured in the best possible manner is consequently more pertinent than a framework of 'what' values can be evidenced. As a result, future guidance and policies on energy efficiency in historic buildings can move beyond the prescriptive listing of pre-assumed values to encompass guidance on how to capture the systemic, dynamic and interconnected heritage values.

4
Collection life cycles

Introduction

November 2015. As part of our annual project work with Heritage Malta, I visited the Marsa industrial area with my colleagues and Master students in Sustainable Heritage. Here more than one hundred traditional Maltese buses were stored, abandoned and awaiting a 'new life'. The site resembled a space 'in transition' – an interim storage that imposed a temporary pause in the usage of the buses until a new future is found for them. In a way we were experiencing the formation of a new heritage collection: a collection of 'objects' which once served a functional purpose – that of transportation – and which (or some of which) were about to be repurposed as a heritage collection. The large number of these 'large objects' meant that not all buses could be preserved, stored and displayed in a museum. A few buses could either be reused or even scrapped. This project made me wonder where the 'lifetime' of an object ends and/or begins again; does so-called 'scrapping' really mark the end of an object's lifetime? Or could 'scrapping' form a new life cycle, through the recycling of materials, for instance?

In this chapter I reaffirm the premise underpinning this book, according to which heritage in all its forms is inculcated by a 'circular life cycle'. This implies that the end of one life cycle marks the beginning of another. This premise prompts heritage professionals and scholars, especially those working in the field of collections management, to reconceptualise the concept of 'lifetime'. Collections management often revolves around the idea that a collection has a single, limited lifetime; one of the objectives of collections management is thus to predict and prolong this lifetime. However, if a collection is approached as having multiple, continuous life cycles, then collections management practices can move from a focus on predicting and managing a collection's expected lifetime to enabling scenarios for a collection's future uses.

To support this argument, I explore how a collection of 'functional everyday objects' evolves into a heritage and a collection management practice. In light of this, I examine the interactions between materials, competencies (skills), resources, values, space/environment, senses/emotions and time in the context of collections. I endeavour to establish at what point in time and under what conditions one social practice (i.e. that of 'bus' driving) evolves into a different social practice (i.e. heritage collection). To do so, I draw on the example of the vintage 'yellow' buses of Malta, replaced in 2011 by new, more environmentally friendly buses. The buses proved inappropriate for the size of Malta, with many Maltese now using their cars and with pollution levels rising (Pekkala 2015). The abandonment and replacement of the Maltese buses led to their material deterioration and the loss of skills associated with their decoration. At the same time, new values and feelings of nostalgia and pride, especially among tourists and bus drivers, were expressed, making the claim for 'heritagisation' a global one.

The 'heritagisation' of the buses signifies a new milestone, a new lifetime – that of a collection. However, only a small sample of the buses could form part of the collection due to lack of 'space' and 'resources'. This triggered 'new life cycles' for buses: a few were reused as souvenir shops or were acquired as items of nostalgia by private collectors and/or operators of heritage tours. By observing the life trajectory of these buses, we can detect the evolution of heritage collections practices and the factors which generate a circular lifetime.

Collections and collection management as dynamic, non-linear practices

A collection can be defined as a set of related elements (Pearce 2017). In view of this, a museum collection can be regarded as a structure consisted of related elements that depend on 'inner orderliness, inner malleability, the set of relations between parts of the unit, the form of the unit' (Dolák 2018, 25). Simmons and Muñoz-Saba (2003, 39) argue that a traditional approach to collections management is to retain the order by which a collection has been organised and as such to reduce the 'entropy' that causes disorder. For the authors, this order enables good financial and organisational management while disorder results in chaos. However, as I will show, behind a phenomenological 'order' in museum collections inherent 'chaos' lies, due to the dynamic, non-linear changes to which a collection is subject. Indeed, museum collections are dynamic in the present, representing a living, systemic context (Flexner 2016, 170), even as they were dynamic in the past. A collection may grow through the acquisition of new items or it may regress through de-accessioning or loss as a result of degradation. A collection can be formulated and grow through the acquisition of items that went through the process of 'heritigisation', as well as de-grow through disposal and deterioration.

The term 'collections management' has evolved from the need to 'organise, classify and control' a museum collection (Matassa 2011, 8). The systematisation of collections management is mirrored in the various national and international standards. In 2009, for instance, the British Standards Institution (BSI), along with Collections Trust, published a code of practice for collections management (PAS 197) (British Standards Institute 2009). Developed by a Steering Group of leading industry experts in consultation with 200 heritage practitioners, PAS 197 describes the framework of principles needed to manage cultural collections. It details the fundamentals of collections development, collections information, collections access and collections care and conservation.[1]

In this chapter, I argue that collections management is a dynamic, socio-cultural practice. As such it becomes evident that any attempt to standardise the process of 'organising, classifying and controlling' a collection is a very challenging task. This is due to the fact that personal and subjective biases and experiences will inevitably be at play during these interactions, for instance cultural 'values', 'senses', 'space' and 'environment'. Even if parameters of the systemic decision process – such as material degradation, available resources and environmental conditions – can be measured to some extent, the ultimate decision will result from the interactions of those somewhat objective and measurable parameters with those that are less measurable, for example values and senses.

Collections as dynamic assemblages

As already mentioned in Chapter 1, an assemblage can be defined as a 'non-essentialist, non-totalising social entity, constructed through specific historical processes and from heterogeneous parts' such as 'institutional organisations, norms and objects (e.g. laws and regulations) and normalised practices' (Pendlebury 2013, 710). Although the concept of 'assemblage' has been interpreted in multiple ways (Anderson and McFarlane 2011), I will use it here to connote the socio-technical and dynamic nature of a heritage system (here the system is the collection). Indeed, one of the strengths of this concept is

> its ability to co-join different actors (individuals or organisations) and their narratives and stories with other dimensions – for example legal and policy frameworks – and conceive these together as a definable and extremely complex and non-static social entity. (Pendlebury 2013, 711)

A distinguishing dimension of assemblage theory, along with related approaches such as the 'actors network theory', is the attention they give to non-human dimensions (Pendlebury 2013, 711). This aligns with the socio-technical nature of the proposed 'heritage dynamics' approach. Museums, after all, are complex, vibrant sites of original knowledge production, and their collections therefore

> need to be reconsidered as a mode of assemblage (and crucially re-assemblage) that remains fundamental to many archaeological projects and practices. (Wingfield 2017, 595)

Assemblages, understood here as systems that collect an individual set of practices into a set or collective whole, constitute a helpful concept for comprehending complex, dynamic socio-cultural spheres of activity. One system is in turn part of ever larger wholes, and a researcher can put several systems together to examine critically any number of social configurations or phenomena (Buchanan 2019). As outlined in Chapter 1, an assemblage is never static: artefacts, tools, individuals and social groups change over time and space (Srnicek 2007, 54). An assemblage reliably consists of heterogeneous elements that interact with one another as part of a system. Similarly, collections as assemblages can be seen as dynamically changing entities, with changes depending on external factors (environment, use) as well as internal impacts (material make-up) (Strlič et al. 2013).

Collections' 'lifetime'

As discussed above, one of the core objectives in collections management is to prolong the 'expected lifetime' of a collection (e.g. Bratasz et al. 2018). For collections managers, 'lifetime' is understood as the length of time for which a heritage item remains 'fit for purpose' (e.g. research and/or display) (Coppola et al. 2020; Verticchio 2021).

Attempts to model the 'expected lifetime' of a heritage collection have been made by heritage science researchers. An exemplary project moving in this direction is the 'Collections Demography' project funded by the Arts and Humanities Research Council. The project developed a general 'stock' (population) model, in which a collection could be defined as a group of objects to which a given set of management criteria is applied. This enables the usage of models for examination and optimisation of different management scenarios (with respect to the environment or use), as suggested in recent environmental management guidance (Strlič et al. 2013).

Modelling the 'expected lifetime of a collection' is not a straightforward process, however. Numerous factors can affect the perspective of a stakeholder (e.g. a curator or conservator) on the 'expected lifetime' of a collection including 'the age of the collection, the apparent deterioration rate of materials applied, how much time has been allotted to the job' (Lindsay 2005, 53). Although it seems that there is general consensus among museum professionals regarding the expected lifetime of a museum collection at around 100 years (see below), attitudes to the future are influenced by a diverse array of factors such as

> the value of spanning more than one generation; a measure of what can be achieved in one generation; the past history of the objects; available knowledge and practice; the nature of the objects; the age of the objects themselves. (Lindsay 2005, 59)

As mentioned above, the 'lifetime' of a collection is understood to be the length of time for which a heritage item remains 'fit for purpose' (e.g. reading or display). However, 'purposes' diverge from one 'user' to another, with the result that different purposes can imply different 'lifespans'. For instance, for a collections manager working at the National Archives the primary purpose of an archival collection is to 'be read' and 'researched'. For a museum visitor the 'purpose' of a similar collection may be to 'be viewed through display', while for a conservator the purpose may be to be 'stored' and 'maintained'. The 'expected collection lifetime' is consequently a relative and subjective concept. A discussion between the various stakeholders on what the 'expected collection lifetime' is should thus take into account resources, significance, use and material change (Dillon et al. 2012).

The 'expected collection lifetime' is an interesting concept emerging within collections management with which I will engage in detail below. For now, I would like to focus on the four elements underscored by current standards on collections management including 'resources', 'significance' (values), 'use' and 'material change' (materials) because, interestingly, they encapsulate four 'heritage dynamic elements' (i.e. resources, values/meanings, skills/competencies and materials). More specifically, the PAS 197 code of practice for cultural collections management advocates the development of a statement for the 'expected collection lifetime' which needs to take into consideration the synergy of the aforementioned factors: resources, significance, planned use and display, and expected rate of deterioration of materials. This is one of the first attempts to think of collections management as a systemic, synergetic social practice – one that takes into account multiple factors extending beyond the material objects. The notion of 'expected lifetime' presupposes constant change, but with a negative angle – in the sense that there is an anticipated end or change perceived to be at some point in time 'unacceptable'.

The 'Collections Demography' project aimed to delve into greater depth to consider the concept of 'unacceptable change' and 'expected lifetime'. It sought to do this by capturing the interrelationship between material change with research into what change is regarded 'unacceptable', leading to loss of value, projections concerning the 'future lifetime' and 'value' of that collection (Dillon et al. 2012; Dillon et al. 2013). The project demonstrated through extensive research with stakeholders and users of libraries, archives and museums that they hold certain views about what constitutes unacceptable change and what the expected lifetime of a collection is (Dillon et al. 2013).

In other words, the extent to which a decision maker discounts future outcomes and prefers positive outcomes to occur sooner rather than later is their 'time preference' (Dillon et al. 2012). Furthermore, the project demonstrated that decisions on collections management are influenced by a wide array of factors including the perceived future value of a collection, the perceived risk to long-term outcomes and judgements about the needs of current and future users (Dillon et al. 2012). The results of the project illustrated the impact of 'context' on what characteristics of a collection (e.g. information vs. materials) are considered most important to preserve, and therefore how lifetime should be defined for different contexts of use (Dillon et al. 2013, 46).

In 'heritage dynamics', the 'space and environment' reflect the context (both physical and symbolic). An additional interrelationship unveiled in the 'Collections Demography' project is the relationship between 'context of use' and 'attitudes towards the future'. The project concluded that visitors to historic houses exhibiting 'old' books in display cases expected a shorter 'lifetime' for the objects, whereas users at archives who read the books expected the collection to last longer (Dillon 2012; 2013).

The findings of the 'Collections Demography' project on perceptions towards expected (or desired) lifetime have the potential to challenge an expert's opinion (Strlič et al. 2015, 9). For instance, for a heritage expert, the desired lifetime of a collection in a historic house is longer than the desired lifetime as viewed from a visitor's perspective. Desired lifetime can be influenced by many characteristics, such as the age of a document, tears and missing pieces, but less so discolouration (Strlič et al. 2015, 9), possibly because the latter is associated with a patina of nostalgia.

The subjectivity with which concepts of 'expected lifetime' is imbued reveals that an object or a collection has multiple temporalities displaying new, alternating 'timescapes' (Loeve et al. 2018). In view of this, collection objects are not just artefacts, but can also be described 'in a worldly perspective as inhabitants of the planet' (Loeve et al. 2018, 10). Acknowledging the 'timescapes' of a collection is vital, since such acknowledgement can re-orientate the thinking of 'lifetime' as a linear, continuous process with an inevitable 'end date' into the conception of a non-linear, circular process in which the 'end date' of a life cycle marks the beginnings of a new life cycle.

Indeed, as can be demonstrated by the case of the Maltese buses in this chapter (as well as many other cases), the lifetime of collections is circular in that one life cycle can evolve into another under certain conditions. Consequently, the disposal of collection items does not signify the end of a collection's lifetime, but rather the beginning of a new life cycle. Moreover, even if an item is destroyed or vanished, it may have left digital traces or digital copies, which can in turn demarcate new collection life cycles. The time of a collection's life cycle is non-linear, indeed almost 'spiral', comprising sub-cycles, cycles and super-cycles (Singh 2020).

Therefore I would like to advocate for a change in language in the collections management field. It is more constructive to refer to the non-linear, 'spiral' life cycles of a museum collection rather than its 'expected lifetime'. A life cycle approach calls for museum collections to be regarded 'as eco-systems or habitats, which need managing, developing, sometimes growing and sometimes cutting back to prevent choking' (Merriman 2008, 18).

The idea that a heritage collection consists of non-linear, 'spiral' life cycles aligns with theories around the cultural biography of objects (e.g. Gosden and Marshall 1999; Kopytoff 1986). Kopytoff (1986), for instance, argued that 'things' could not be fully understood at just one point in their existence. This contention is further reaffirmed by Ingold (2010) who contended that people and buildings should be viewed as going through a process of ever new creative transformation, continuously re-born and constantly growing. He further pinpointed that such 'persistent' entities

> have no point of origin. Rather, they seem to be originating all the time ... The world we inhabit, they say, is originating all the time, or undergoing what we might call 'continuous birth'. (Ingold 2006, 3–4)

In other words, as Holtorf (2015, 418) stresses

> If each heritage object is considered as a process of becoming rather than a state of being, its meaning is not given but constantly evolving and the object can be expected to fulfil a valuable function in society even after being subjected to major alterations.

Accordingly, the disposal of objects is not just about questions of waste and rubbish; it is also implicated more broadly in the ways in which people manage absence within social relations (Hetherington 2004). The disposal is thus never terminal. It relates to issues of managing social relations and their representation around themes of movement, transformation, incompleteness and return (Hetherington 2004, 157). Since disposal is never terminal, alternative ways to manage the constant growth of collections should be explored (Morgan and Macdonald 2020).

Damage and 'unacceptable' change

Change is inherent in all life cycle approaches. Change is also a concept that underpins heritage and, in this case, collections management. 'Unacceptable change' is a standard term in collections management, where it denotes the end of a lifetime of a heritage collection. Yet this concept raises a few critical questions. First, at what point in time does change become 'unacceptable'? Second, is there such a thing as 'unacceptable change'? Third, if 'unacceptable change' is an acceptable concept, what makes a change unacceptable and what does that mean for a collection's future?

In the collections management literature, some forms of 'unacceptable change' are 'straightforward'. For example, the accidental breaking of a historic vase displayed in a museum into pieces is 'unacceptable change' (Blühm 2016). On the other hand, some forms of 'unacceptable change' are less visible and require investigation in a laboratory. For instance, the degradation of paper is a process of cellulose polymer chain oxidation – a process invisible to the naked eye but entirely measurable using appropriate instrumentation (Bicchieri et al. 2006). Broadly speaking, for conservators damage is defined as 'unacceptable change' if such change affects 'fitness for purpose', and consequently the possibility of a collection being able to yield future benefits in terms of significance and impact (Strlič et al. 2013).

However, for a 'circular life cycle' approach towards a collection, no change is 'unacceptable'. A change detrimental for the current use and function of collection may determine the end of a specific life cycle, but at the same time this may mark the beginning of a new life cycle. Even if 'unacceptable change' is accepted as a concept, it is worth noting, as with the concept of 'lifetime', that the 'unacceptability' of change is determined by people involved directly or indirectly in the management of the collection. The designation of something as 'unacceptable change' is thus a 'value-based decision' (Strlič et al. 2013).

'Unacceptable change' in heritage conservation has been translated through the so-called 'damage functions' (Rothlind 2021). A damage function can be defined as a function of 'unacceptable change to heritage dependent on agents of change' (Strlič et al. 2013, 80). As the authors observe

> Since there are a number of values associated with heritage, there can be a number of damage functions describing one and the same physical or chemical process of change. (Strlič et al. 2013, 80)

'Change', in the context of 'damage functions', connotes material change that can be described as a function of often numerous parameters referred to as stressors, agents of change or agents of deterioration (Strlič et al. 2013, 80). However, it may also denote change in use (for instance, a building first used as a place of storage and then converted into a domestic dwelling). In the context of collections, we may similarly witness the evolution of a collection from a fixed location and reference point to a travelling collection outside the museum doors, acquiring a different use in the process. Such a change can be more abstract and symbolic, of course, with the collection either acquiring a new meaning or losing a pre-existing significance. If then 'change' is multi-faceted (material, symbolic, context), it may be viewed as 'damage' by some users, even as others may see it in a more positive manner. Indeed, the concept of 'damage' is both observer- and context-dependent (Ashley-Smith 2013). It is thus defined not only in terms of material or systems change, but also in terms of human perception of how such a change affects the value of a historic object/building/site (Strlič et al. 2013, 85).

As mentioned above, in heritage science damage functions are defined as functions of unacceptable change dependent on agents of change (Strlič et al. 2013, 80) – including, among others, value change. Damage functions are thus conceptualised as a product of a value function and a dose–response (change) function, the latter depending on agents of change or stressors as shown below:

$$fD = fV\,fC\,p$$

It may be useful to think of the value function as a transformation function (fV) or matrix, applied to the change or dose–response function (fC) of a parameter (stressor) p. The correlation between 'value' and 'change' functions has already been stressed in risk assessment methods for heritage conservation (Strlič et al. 2013, 80). As early as in the late 1980s and 1990s authors began to write about risk assessment and conservation management, reminding the conservation world of the need to consider a wider range of agents of deterioration beyond temperature, relative humidity and light. These calls have encouraged conservators to adopt a holistic view of the causes of deterioration (Staniforth 2014).

Value, material change, context and 'expected lifetime'

I referred above to the 'Collections Demography' project, one of the first projects to investigate the interrelationship between 'values', 'material change' and 'context'. The 'Collections Demography' project focused on historic paper collections displayed or stored in various contexts including museums, where historic papers are displayed to be 'viewed' by visitors, and libraries or archives where historic documents are being used by visitors for research or other purposes. The project team of which I was a member concluded that for historic documents aiming to be 'displayed', it was the missing pieces rather than discolouration or tears that influenced readers/visitors' subjective judgements of fitness-for-use.

However, when a visitor/reader was prompted to think of a document in terms of its historic value, then change in a document had little impact on fitness for use (Strlič et al. 2015, 1). This observation proves that a context is value laden and that different values affect the perception of 'expected lifetime' in relation to 'damage' and 'physical change'.

As stated above, the 'perceived fitness of purpose' will determine stakeholders' attitudes towards the 'expected' or 'desired' lifetime of a collection. It becomes more and more accepted by 'cultural heritage guardians' that 'time-honored goals of eternity, stability, and permanence are nowadays increasingly discarded as unreachable', with an acceptance that 'things are in perpetual flux' (Lowenthal 2000, 20). As the comment that 'things are in perpetual flux' confirms, assessing the risks to museum collections is also a dynamic process. Risks themselves are necessarily future-focused in that the effectiveness of strategies employed to assess, mitigate or remove risks 'can only be judged at some future point' (Lindsay 2005, 51). They are also future-focused as 'they are very much influenced by our perspectives on time, and are also affected by disasters that have occurred' (Lindsay 2005, 52).

The findings of the 'Collections Demography' project suggest that attitudes towards the future vary according to the characteristics of a document (e.g. age and perceived significance). This in turn suggests that attitudes are likely to change over time, as both collections and their use change. In addition, different communities of stakeholders may have different attitudes towards the future care, condition and use of documents. Understanding potential sources of conflict and bias such as these may help to inform how the results of engagement with different groups of stakeholders are interpreted and used. The subjective and finite nature of the 'expected lifetime' of a museum collection is important

> when assessing the roles and responsibilities of conservation beyond material preservation. When it is recognised that objects cannot last forever nor be indefinitely maintained in a particular state, there is more room to consider the potential use of this life, i.e. there must be some other purpose beyond survival. (Saunders 2014, 2)

The growth and de-growth of museum collections through disposal

Disposal of collection objects was a not infrequent occurrence from the 1950s to the 1970s (Merriman 2008, 4). In response to concerns about government institutions selling off works of arts as assets, the 1964 Cottesloe Report on the sale of works of art clarified that museums could not sell an object unless authorised to do so by the Courts, by the Charity Commissioners or the Minister of Education on behalf of the Courts; they themselves had nothing to sell (quoted in Lewis and Fahy 1995, 134). This embargo shifted slightly in 1988, when the Museums Association Code of Conduct for Museum Professionals allowed for selective disposal under certain circumstances, usually by transfer to another museum. Where disposal is undertaken, the greatest number of artefacts are in the public domain (Lewis 1992). Merriman (2008) called for disposal to be used more frequently as a collections management tool, however, noting that museums often resist disposal even as they insist on continuing to collect, creating an unsustainable institution. He argues further that museums 'should be seen for what they are: partial, historically contingent assemblages that reflect the tastes and interests of both the times and the individuals who made them' instead of just 'repositories of objects and specimens that represent an objective record or collective memory' (Merriman 2008, 3).

How can resistance to disposal provide a sustainable means of collections management? Morgan and Macdonald (2020) draw on theories of 'de-growth' developed by the political economist Serge Latouche as a means of introducing a new constructive approach to the sustainable management of the constantly growing, accumulating collections. In a similar way to Merriman, Morgan and Macdonald (2020) discuss the resistance towards disposal of curators who view as their duty to collect and sustain for future generations. In a way, such resistance may be interpreted as a reluctance to 'lose' a particular object when their primary responsibility is to preserve an entire collection from 'loss'. For curators, disposal implies loss and end of lifetime. However, if a 'circular, dynamic' approach to collections management is adopted, the process of disposal can mark either the beginning of a new life cycle or the continuation of the previous one and a transformation to something else. This idea does not conflict with the curatorial duty and responsibility to 'preserve' and 'guard'. On the contrary: it provides a new form of 'creative management' and responsibility.

However, the fear of 'loss' remains more prevalent than the 'hope' for new uses through re-purposing among curators and collections managers. Indeed, the perception of risk and endangerment is a fundamental element in the production of heritage value (DeSilvey and Harrison 2020, 1). The consequence or driver of this perception is that heritage is perceived as a 'non-renewable' resource which merits institutional and legal protection from damage, decay and eventually loss. However, it becomes recently more and more widely acknowledged that 'loss' is inevitable; it should therefore be anticipated and accepted (see, for instance, Hambrecht and Rockman 2017; Fluck and Dawson 2021). To this end, strategies for management of loss should be developed (DeSilvey 2017).

Reconceptualising 'loss' as 'revival' or 'renewal' (or an acceptance that heritage is a 'renewable resource') will introduce a more constructive approach to collections management. In that respect, it could be contended that destruction and loss are constitutive of heritage, parts of its very substance (Holtorf 2006, 108) rather than something opposing heritage, in that destruction and loss of some heritage may lead to the creation of new forms of heritage (Holtorf 2015, 406). Or, as Holtorf puts it, 'Even preservation implies loss. Even destruction implies creation' (Holtorf 2006, 108). Similarly, DeSilvey comments that

> By accepting ongoing processes, we are not automatically triggering disposal and loss. Rather, we may in fact be opening ourselves up to a more meaningful and reciprocal relationship with the material past. (DeSilvey 2017, 179)

In view of this, heritage can be continually renewed even if the material fabric is altered or erased (DeSilvey 2017, 185), allowing new possibilities to emerge (Rico 2016). As a result, 'loss is potentially generative and emancipatory, facilitating the emergence of new values, attachments and forms of significance' (DeSilvey and Harrison 2020, 3). 'Letting go' of certain items can be a 'relieving' experience, particularly when 'retaining them could make matters worse' (Bendell 2018). Indeed, an 'increased ability to accept loss and transformation' can 'inspire people to embrace uncertainty and absorb adversity in times of change, thus increasing their cultural resilience' (Holtorf 2018, 639).

Accepting and 'curating' the 'loss' calls for the development of 'de-growth' strategies. So far, I have shown that 'heritage dynamics' is about the 'growth', 'de-growth' and 're-growth' of interconnected elements such as 'values', 'materials', 'place/space', 'effect', 'skills', 'time' and 'resources'. In this context 'de-growth' is not imbued with negative connotations. On the contrary, it calls for a 'simultaneous production of the present by the past and the future' (Kallis and March 2015, 361). De-growth signals a new socio-ecological imaginary that expresses features of spatio-temporal utopias (Kallis and March 2015, 361).

The Malta 'old' buses – a dynamic collection assemblage

Adoption of the theory that there are new, circular, continuing life cycles in a museum collection can contribute to 'optimistic' attitudes towards the disposal of museum objects, provided that the disposal signifies the start of a new life. Indeed, de-growth planning opens up a wide array of possibilities for new futures of museum objects once removed from collections. These include 'redistributing', 'reusing' and/or 'recycling' – even in some cases the 'using up' of an object's material, symbolic or other qualities (DeSilvey 2017; Morgan and Macdonald 2020, 62). As Bowell observes

> Instead of being relegated to the backs of cabinets and the bottoms of shelves, unloved collection pieces could be released, revitalised and reincarnated outside museums. (Bowell 2018, 154)

Such objects can be given back to communities or artists who could re-create them into something else (Bowell 2018, 158), be distributed to charities for teaching new skills (e.g. Mendoza 2017, 45–6) or reused for research and teaching by universities (De Clercq 2004). It is thus clear that 'letting go' should not be considered 'an ending of an object's lifetime, but perhaps a kind of rebirth, afterlife or "reincarnation"' (Bowell 2018 in Morgan and Macdonald 2020, 60). Accordingly, collections are no longer viewed as inherited 'inalienable assemblages', but rather as 'dynamic resources, which can be re-worked to suit contemporary and future needs' (Merriman 2008, 14).

This is clearly illustrated in the case of the 'old' Maltese buses which used to characterise the Maltese urban landscape. These 'old' coloured buses were replaced in Malta by new, environmentally friendly buses on 2 July 2011. A news item entitled 'Malta's Yellow Buses Retiring' encapsulates the reasons for the buses' obsolescence.

> It's about time these **old diesel-spewing decrepit traffic hazards (environment)** went off the roads. Far too many times I've seen accidents caused by their **overly-wide bodies squeezed into tiny streets** *(space)*. Sure **they look great as an icon** *(value)*, but in today's world completely impractical *(functionality);* and given the number of cars on the roads it's one less thing to worry about. (author's emphasis and additions) (Radzikowski 2011)

In sum, the environmental hazard, the space restrictions and the financial unsustainability were some of the factors that led to the discontinuity of such buses being driven. However, the article admits that

> In truth, I'd like to see one or two of the old buses **to stick around for history's sake** (*values*); and I can't deny – they look pretty good in photos. (author's emphasis and additions)

The seeds for a new 'life' were implanted by the 'aesthetic', 'cultural', 'emblematic' and 'historic' values, as well as the feelings of pride with which the buses were imbued.

However, discussions on the 'modernisation' of the new bus system began several years before 2011. Scenarios for the replacement of the old buses have been in existence since at least 2003. At that time, various possibilities were expressed regarding the future of the emblematic buses. They included selling the more modern buses to new operators; refurbishing and selling some of the vintage buses to operators, who would then provide heritage services for tourists (12 per cent of the bus fares derived from tourists) (Robbins 2003, 92); exhibiting some buses in a national transport museum; and/or selling a few buses abroad to foreign preservationists' collections, as the Maltese authorities considered lifting the ban on exporting older vehicles from the island. The remainder of the existing fleet would be scrapped (Attard and Hall 2003, 20). None of these initial scenarios included the acquisition of 127 buses by Heritage Malta at the time, in part a result of public outcry.

The yellow buses in Malta, formerly in various colours, had become 'one of the most recognisable sights on the island's roads'. The buses were initially imported in 1905, by 1920 the buses were manufactured locally 'with carpenters, mechanics, upholsterers and sundry decorators joining forces to produce coaches with a high degree of customisation for local use' (Chevron 2015). Here we have a list of competencies (skills) needed to drive the local manufacturing process, the implication being that the removal of the buses will result in the loss of such skills. Bus driving itself evolved into a dynamic social practice, the continuation of which depended not only on materials, competencies and meanings, but also on space/place, senses and resources. The continuation of this practice (i.e. driving the old buses) was threatened by new environmental values and urgent demands for more sustainable means of transportation, as well as the deteriorated materiality of the buses themselves.

However, while the material condition was decreasing, the vehicles' cultural and symbolic values were increasing. The yellow buses were attributed with personal and cultural values. This is due to the fact that ownership of the buses was transmitted from one generation to another (Grima 2011). Driving and maintaining the 'yellow' buses was a family business that passed down from one generation to another. At the same time the 'yellow' buses became a collective, cultural symbolic landmark of the Maltese urban landscape.

The personal (almost familial) attachment of the bus drivers to the buses became vivid during our two week fieldwork trip in Malta. During this we saw how the connection of the bus drivers with their buses

> resulted in a sort of love affair between the buses and their proud owners, leading to a high degree of individual decoration – not least what is locally known as 'tberfil' – a unique Maltese style of lettering/signwriting and decoration normally associated with buses, traditional boats, other vehicles and also shop signs. (Chevron 2015)

The unique appearance of the buses reflects this personal attachment, with 'bus bodies being built or reshaped in local workshops' (Grima 2011).

This illustrates once again how meanings (values) can dictate a unique material appearance which requires certain skills/competencies. However, while the drivers had this special connection with their buses the everyday commuters 'hated' them, as one revealed:

> After all, daily commutes on the bone-shaking behemoths with their rattling glass and lack of any air conditioning in the unmerciful heat of summer or on cold winter days does have its limits … Getting rid of the buses faced resistance from bus drivers. (Chevron 2015)

A few drivers ingeniously converted and upgraded their coaches to serve as tour buses for nostalgia-loving tourists. Cassar and Avellino (2020, 248–9) claim that taking a ride on 'Malta's grand old buses' fosters desire and longing in tourists seeking an escapist experience, by longing for a past and through a yearning for a colonial or Western influence. Indeed, this nostalgic attachment to the buses is reaffirmed by a study of tourists themselves on the island, most of whom liked the old buses because they had character. They fondly remembered their experience of journeys on board the bus as an adventure (Bajada and Titheridge 2017).

The disposal of the buses resulted in new life cycles. One ended up as a souvenir shop in the touristic area of Sliema. More than one hundred others were stored, temporarily at least, in the inner harbour area at Marsa – right next to where the also defunct Malta Shipbuilding used to be.

> They lie there derelict and forgotten with the occasional visitor coming for a closer look and perhaps take a few pictures. Mercifully

> some of the buses have been earmarked for preservation by Heritage Malta and will eventually feature in a proposed transport museum. (Chevron 2015)

The feelings (senses) emerging from the disappearance of the buses from the Maltese island (space/environment) were those of nostalgia (especially among people who travelled occasionally to Malta), as comments to relevant blogs reveal:

> I loved travelling on these buses when visiting Malta, they were part and parcel of Maltese life, they were so **colourful** the same as the drivers, with cabs decorated in holy pictures, swinging radio's, rosary beads etc, ok they were hot, sticky, rattled, but I loved them and so did my family and friends who visited Malta **renovate them, bring them up to date, put them back on the roads** … these buses were treasured by U.s. (author's emphasis) (Chevron 2015)

This blog entry calls for the renovation and reuse of the buses, not as static museum objects, but as mobile 'emblems' of Malta's urbanscape. Despite their material degradation, the public (especially tourists) viewed them as aesthetically beautiful, an aesthetics derived from their colours and art decorations. For another blogger the buses were 'lovely', albeit 'ugly' and 'rattled', and iconic: 'they were the character of the island' (Chevron 2015).

Another commentator, John, mentions how some tourists call for a number of buses to be preserved for tourism:

> As a tourist I loved them but I can well understand how the **locals** wanted something **more practical** and 21st century. They were still in service when I was last in Malta and I suppose I will miss them when I invariably return but it's the residents of Malta who dictate its transport system not 2 week tourists. Please keep a few as **tourist buses.** (author's emphasis) (Chevron 2015)

This blogger acknowledges that functionality can (and should) be a priority; if the buses were not 'fit for purpose' for the local population, therefore, they should change. Lillian Holland (in Chevron 2015) who has fond memories of Malta, also hopes that 'some of the old mustard buses will be kept for posterity'. She recalls:

> I was born in Malta and clearly remember the old system of different colours for different areas. When I got married, I took my

> husband for his first visit to Malta and he **immediately fell in love with the island and its old 'bone shaker' buses**. After that first visit we visited Malta every year since 1970, in between other holidays, we made so many friends who we are still in touch with today. Malta is my 'little island in the sun' and I'm so proud to say I was born there. (author's emphasis) (Chevron 2015)

Discussions on the future usage of the 'vintage' buses took place as early as in 2003. A government subsidised tour bus service, the 'Visit Malta bus', was set up by the tourism and transport ministries using traditional Malta buses. This initiative was abandoned in April 2005 due to several political and economic obstacles.

This event indicates that the 'heritagisation' process had started prior to the acquisition of the buses by Heritage Malta. The 'scrapping process' (the loss) triggered the 'heritagisation' by linking the buses with heritage sites – a 'product' aimed purely at tourists. Thus the initial socio-cultural practice of driving for anyone was replaced by a new socio-cultural practice of driving for tourists. However, this practice discontinued – not because the link between 'competencies', 'meanings' and 'materials' broke, but because there were too many parties with conflicting interests involved.

Resources and materials proved to be two of the main critical factors. A revised transport plan, publicised in 2006 and based on a report carried out by Halcrow, stated that the bus operation proved financially unsustainable from a business point of view due to the high rate of car ownership on the island.

Heritage Malta had stressed the unique significance of several Maltese buses years before their replacement by the new bus fleet. Following these concerns, in 2010, Transport Malta passed on to Heritage Malta ten old Maltese buses retired from service in 2003. As soon as the government announced the withdrawal of the old buses, the plan to save a number of Maltese buses for the National Collection, maintained by Heritage Malta, was drawn up. A total of 127 buses out of the 299 of the old bus fleet were selected. The selection was based on the different Maltese coach-builders, their former route colours, notable chassis and a selection of British imports from the 1980s to the 2000s. The buses intended to be scrapped were documented from 7 to 14 July 2011; 'iconic' items and spare parts were removed from these vehicles, which were then scrapped at a Kirkop scrapyard. Buses not on the original Transport Malta list came in as a second thought by their former owner after they had been intended for scrapping. A handful of these examples were considered worth keeping and replaced others that were originally chosen, but which were therefore removed from the retention list and eventually scrapped (Heritage Malta 2011).

> The entire operation turned out to be a very rewarding and **emotional matter**, as many owners and their families **cried their hearts** out while taking the last photographs with the bus before handing it over. **Buses were often considered effective members of the family**. (author's emphasis) (Heritage Malta 2011, 73)

This personal attachment on behalf of the drivers rendered the heritagisation process even more complex as the nationalisation of the bus collection distanced the owners and disassociated their personal values. By the end of the 'salvage operation' – as it was called by Heritage Malta – 95 buses had been acquired. Of these, 84 were stored at an open storage space in Marsa while the remaining 11 were given on loan to the Malta Historical Vehicle Trust. The trust was established in 2007 with the aim 'to acquire, restore and exhibit to the public vehicles that have a historic and social significance to Malta' (Historic Vehicles Malta n.d.). An additional 32 buses were disposed of and 172 were scrapped. It is worth noting that the storage of the buses was not properly secured. Since their acquisition, several iconic items and fuel have been stolen from the collection.

Robert Cassar, the conservator in charge of selecting and protecting a sample of the buses for Heritage Malta, stated that 'A lot of the owners thought their buses were going to be scrapped, so they took all the little badges and the chrome parts to keep them'; this made the work of Heritage Malta more complex as it was precisely the chrome and badges that made the buses unique (Schembri 2011a). However, he also noted that

> once drivers realised that the buses wouldn't be scrapped, a lot were very happy to give us the badges back. Others even gave us spare parts. (Schembri 2011a)

The buses were imbued with personal and collective value. Assessing the values and what the buses mean – and for whom – might have initiated a dialogue for co-deciding on the future of the buses. This example demonstrates that the bus drivers were willing to collaborate as soon as they were reassured that the selected buses would not be scrapped.

An additional challenge relates to the long-term maintenance of the buses. Since owners, understandably, were reluctant to spend money on the maintenance of vehicles that were intended to be abandoned, paint and mechanical parts were showing signs of wear. The generated fear of 'loss' among the community prompted Malta Post to issue a set of 20 postage stamps to commemorate the withdrawal of service of the traditional Malta buses on 2 July 2011, a day before the restructure. The stamps showed Maltese buses in the different colours that had existed for the different routes. The commemoration process began just before the withdrawal and is indicative of the buses' emblematic character.[2]

A few buses were re-purposed for sightseeing tours,[3] Red Cross Mobile clinic, souvenir shops[4] or for preservation and future display in a museum managed by Heritage Malta, as mentioned above. In 2012 'space constraints' led Heritage Malta to sell a number of old buses out of the '140' salvaged. This operation was described as a 'salvage operation' by Heritage Malta's chairman Joseph Said, who stressed that the guardianship role of Heritage Malta was 'to safeguard Malta's history'. He recalled the loss of the old trams that also used to be present in Malta and which 'don't exist anymore because these were scrapped, and we couldn't afford a repeat scenario with the buses'.

Preserving 140 old buses proved a challenge. It was thus decided to sell identical examples, with the income generated covering the conservation of the other buses. Mr Said recounted how former bus owners

> shed tears of happiness when, last summer, they found out their buses were among the few that would be saved from the scrapyard. They brought parts of the bus which they had kept to give back to us to use when restoring them.

In the cases of buses that were 'scrapped', Heritage Malta kept some 'iconic' parts such as grilles and bumpers, which were made specifically for a particular vehicle, or a 'holy picture that was displayed on a dashboard' (Ameen 2012).

The selection process by Heritage Malta took into account what could be the minimum number of buses needed to represent a storyline of local bus body-builders and other examples which retain their original foreign body but were modified to the local owners' requirements. As a result of this study 27 of the most representative old buses were retained for the national collection. Once these were transferred from the Malta Shipbuilding storage to a recently rented warehouse at Ħal Far, Heritage Malta published an Expression of Interest whereby interested parties could bid for a bus and thus secure its preservation by local enthusiasts and foreign transport and other museums. Two other buses were also transferred to the Health Promotion Department and the Office of the President respectively, for alternative public use. The Expression of Interest reads as follows (Heritage Malta 2016):

> Advt. No. HM28/01/2012. Expression of interest for the acquisition of surplus legacy buses.
>
> Upon the launching of the reform of the public transport system, Heritage Malta, in collaboration with Transport Malta, salvaged a number of legacy buses from being scrapped. Heritage Malta has now conducted a thorough exercise and has established which buses are to be preserved as part of the **National Collection**. Consequently a limited number of surplus buses may now be disposed of since their types (i.e. model, body-builder, workmanship involved etc) are better represented by other identical examples which have been preserved. **Nevertheless Heritage Malta feels that these surplus buses are not to be scrapped and in this respect is inviting offers from those who would be interested in acquiring one or more of these buses.** Vehicles will be sold *tale quale* ['as it arrives'], and all necessary permits, licences, etc would need to be sought by the prospective purchasers. Heritage Malta reserves the right to refuse the best offer. **All proceeds will go towards the conservation of the preserved buses**.' (author's emphasis) (Heritage Malta 2016)

This public call for expression of interest to purchase one of the buses highlights a few issues of note. Firstly the operation, as mentioned above, is seen as a 'salvage operation', aimed at 'saving' the buses from disposal and 'scrapping'. 'Scrapping' in this context marks the end of the lifetime of an object while preservation and reuse is a 'salvage'. Second, the status of the buses retained by Heritage Malta has evolved to a 'national' one since they constitute part of the 'national collection'. Their 'nationalisation' does not necessarily eliminate (at least not completely) the individual character with which they are imbued on a personal or familial level by the bus owners. Indeed, a sensitive balance between the two spheres, 'public' and private', is sought. The 'new' privatisation status emerging from the sales denotes a 'new' life and purpose for the buses while securing funds for the sustainability of those retained by Heritage Malta (Xuereb 2016).

A local enthusiast, Peter Skerry, undertook the task of documenting the old buses before the start of their 'new future' life. The images available on his website illustrate all buses transferred from owners to local authorities, including the delivery of those to Ħal Far and Malta Dry Dock Yard in Marsa. He concludes by stating that

> other than those buses purchased from owners direct (and therefore not traded), no buses would have been saved at all had it not been for the interest and flexibility of certain individuals at Heritage Malta. July 2011 saw a major victory for the enthusiast, but the war continues, and all could be lost at the stroke of a pen. For those with longer memories – it has happened before.[5]

A newspaper article published in 2011 by the *Malta Independent* and entitled 'Nostalgia versus efficiency' discusses an alternative scenario (*Malta Independent* 2011).

> In hindsight it is easy to say now that perhaps something could have been done to preserve the character of the buses from the outside while ensuring that the inside was clean and comfortable, and changing the engines so that they could be run in an environmentally friendly way; but for whatever reasons, this compromise was never reached.

Would this compromise have prevented the 'heritagisation'? (Schembri 2011b). This retrospective proposal reveals that, at the time of replacement, the 'heritage value' was not recognised *per se*. However, as soon as the buses stopped operating in the Maltese landscape, they obtained a heritage dimension in that their loss provoked nostalgia and sorrow.

The 'heritagisation' of some buses which led to their inclusion into the 'national collection' imposed a freezing, albeit temporarily, of their status; the vehicles had to be left standing in an open space till their relocation to a museum materialised. On the other hand, other buses acquired a new life as soon as they were used for commercial, touristic functions. A newspaper article published in 2013 (see note 5) highlights how an 'old bus gets new lease of life as souvenir shop', an example of reuse that is of interest. The article informs us that the bus 'retains its old colours and original features, including a statue of St Mary above the windscreen'.

Norbert Abela, the owner's 22-year-old son, explains that this bus was known as L-Iskafi and had been built in Malta from the chassis up. His sister Dorianne said that it was heart-breaking to see the bus withdrawn from service, but that it had been given a new lease of life in tourist hotspots such as Sliema, Vittoriosa and Valletta. The adaptive reuse of this old bus may perform a 'therapeutic' role for the former owner who found its withdrawal so distressing.

Not all 'adaptive reuses' through sale proved sustainable in the long term. A Facebook page entitled 'Our Maltese Vintage Bus Project' outlines the trajectory of an old bus which was purchased by a private owner in 2016 with the intention of restoring and reusing it. Transport Malta's advice not to drive the bus caused initial disappointment, but in 2018 they did give a green light for the registering of the bus for 'PRIVATE USE', although this excluded the opportunity of having any paying passengers. However, the project did not prove sustainable, and in 2019 the bus was sold to a buyer from the UK who converted it into a camper van/bus.[6]

Tourists on 'Trip Advisor' are looking nostalgically for the old buses. A commentator on the site is asking **'Old buses – have any been preserved?** While the current bus service is pretty good, we'd love to see some of the original buses. Is there a local museum or preservation society we could visit?'[7] The commentator does not necessarily desire to use the 'old bus' as a vehicle of transportation but rather as an object to 'view'. Such 'viewing' will act as a memory mechanism, recalling the experience of using these buses in the past. The touring companies intend to revive what has now been transformed into a 'heritage experience'. 'Supreme coaches' and 'Koptaco' are two of the main companies reusing the old bus for tourist tours. Koptaco's website is of particular interest:

> Vintage Maltese buses have been used on the island since 1905. These **classic buses** have become **tourist attractions** in their own right, due to their **uniqueness**, and are depicted on many Maltese advertisements to promote tourism. However, these old buses have been replaced by a more modern fleet. At Koptaco we are still catering Old Buses to our Clients. Please contact us for more information and prices.[8] (author's emphasis)

The appropriation of the buses for 'touristic' purposes might have caused strong reactions, especially by private owners who treated the bus as one of their 'family members'. However, the reuse offered a better alternative than scrapping, as the buses are still 'alive'.

Moveable memorabilia from the 'scrapped' buses was kept in 2017 and relocated, alongside the 'preserved' buses, from the former Malta Ship Building to warehouses in Ħal Far. Here a number of other buses within the collection were relocated to outside storage pending the construction of another store (Heritage Malta 2017). In 2018 covered storage to the remaining buses pertaining to the national collection was provided; some of the buses needed repairs due to the fact that they had been stored in the open air (Heritage Malta 2018).

Interestingly, the presence of 'old buses' extended geographical boundaries, with some 'yellow buses' appearing in London and bringing 'a fresh wave of nostalgia whooshing back!' The site 'GuidemeMalta' clarifies that the 'Maltese buses' were used in London and now 'served actually a ride between Ashurst Station, South London [actually in Kent] and Hartfield, East Sussex in the summer months of 2019'. The commentary ends: 'Ain't they beautiful!'[9]

'Everyday heritage', as shown in Chapter 3, is 'beautiful', but with 'everyday heritage' 'aesthetics' are powerfully linked with functionality (functional aesthetics). If functionality is compromised, then the 'functional aesthetics' decline. The 'old' Maltese buses lost their original functional purpose. Even when some of them were reused for touristic purposes, their new function is to be present in the Maltese landscape and 'adored', 'admired' or simply 'experienced'. The 'functional aesthetics' have shifted into 'aesthetics of nostalgia'.

The example of Koptaco was followed by the 'Malta Bus Coop' company in 2019. What differentiates this company from other tour companies is not only the fact that the buses are 'the old traditional Maltese buses', but also that the drivers are those 'who wanted to stick with their old rides'. The Malta Bus Coop website states that the buses 'have served as a means of income for some families for decades', highlighting the personal significance of the buses. They were restored with environmentally friendly systems and a fresh coat of paint before starting their new lives as tour buses.

> You can also check out the fleet and request your favourite bus. Each of the buses has been given a fresh coat of paint, and has had detailed work done by Ġużeppi from San Ġwann – a passionate artist renowned for his tberfil work, and who has been personalising buses for decades.[10]

This statement unveils the systemic nature of heritage. The 'safeguarding' of the 'old buses' through adaptive reuse was succeeded by the 'safeguarding' of the art and crafts needed for the personalisation of the buses. Indeed, the 'material loss' often implies a loss of 'immaterial heritage', such as the craftsmanship and skills associated with it. To this end, a novel project intends to create a new electric bus fleet while retaining the craftsmanship of the old buses. This project is described as a 'rebirth' of the old buses by the Mizzi studio, the architectural firm responsible for the new design:

> Joey is Malta's main tberfil artist, a dying craft that implemented itself as part of our Maltese culture ... His **tberfil** can be seen all over our old Maltese buses and has now been fused onto our new design of The **Malta Bus Reborn zero-emission** electric fleet![11] (author's emphasis)

Besides the *tberfil*, the chrome bumper adopts the form of angel wings, often seen on traditional buses, to symbolise victory and flight. Another traditional feature, an abstract Maltese cross, was carved into the rear of the bus as a symbol of national pride. This new design also includes badges of a Maltese cross, along with horseshoe badges traditionally fixed to the buses to ward off evil spirits.[12]

Conclusion

This chapter argued that a collection has circular, almost spiral, life cycles. By approaching collections as renewable processes, disposal may transform from being a 'difficult' process into a 'creative practice' that opens up unimaginable future uses. Using the example of the 'old' Malta buses, I showed how the social practice of driving discontinued as a result of 'material degradation', 'environmental hazards' and 'space constraints'. The discontinuation of driving proved temporary, however, since touristic companies did reuse a selection of buses for tours. In addition, a 'new life' was attributed to some buses, which became part of a collection or were reused by other private owners. Dormant or new heritage meanings emerged. The personification of the buses is of particular interest here. The 'Maltese buses' were regarded by their owners as family members. The owners attributed an individual character to their bus through craftsmanship, memorabilia, holy pictures, etc. This rendered each bus unique and irreplicable, from a material as well as an emotional and symbolic perspective. The 'official' and 'unofficial' rhetoric around the future of the buses revolved around the need to provide 'a new lease of life'. The appropriation by tourists may not have been an ideal outcome for private owners, but it did provide a means to extend the 'lifetime' of their buses.

What is of additional note here is the 'speed' with which a 'new life' was attributed to the buses that were 'salvaged'. The buses retained by

Heritage Malta are still in the 'awaiting' phase while a proper place for display is found. On the other hand, buses that were privatised by companies are up and running. This indicates the potential of public-private partnerships in providing more sustainable approaches to adaptive reuse of heritage.

'Scrapping' was regarded as the end of the lifetime of a bus, although its memorabilia were kept. However, if the materials emerging from scrapping can be reused for different purposes, then 'scrapping' becomes just one more spiral in the continuous life cycle of objects. By thinking of collections as assemblages of continuous, 'spiral' life cycles, collection management practices can move beyond the risk assessment procedures and restrictive standardisation that determines an 'expected lifetime'. Instead, such practices can encompass scenarios for future alternative uses without excluding partnerships with public and private institutions. I would therefore like to advocate for a change in language in the collections management field. In other words, it is more constructive and, ultimately, practical to focus upon the non-linear, 'spiral' life cycles of a museum collection rather than upon its 'expected lifetime'.

Notes

1. https://www.bsigroup.com/en-GB/about-bsi/media-centre/press-releases/2009/3/New-guidance-for-protection-of-heritage-and-culture/.
2. https://www.wopa-plus.com/en/stamps/product/&pid=70101.
3. https://www.transport.gov.mt/land/bus-service/special-vintage-bus-services-775.
4. https://www.facebook.com/ItTortTaLArriva/photos/?tab=album&album_id=640078859338980.
5. https://maltabuses.piwigo.com/index?/category/702-route_buses_1955_2011.
6. https://www.facebook.com/OurMalteseVintageBusProject/.
7. https://www.tripadvisor.co.uk/ShowTopic-g190320-i895-k9477407-Old_buses_have_any_been_preserved-Island_of_Malta.html.
8. http://www.supremecoaches.com/the-fleet/13/39_seater_traditional_maltese_buses.
9. https://www.guidememalta.com/en/is-that-malta-s-traditional-yellow-bus-we-spot-on-london-s-roads.
10. https://lovinmalta.com/sponsored/watch-the-iconic-traditional-maltese-bus-is-here-to-stay-thanks-to-this-new-initiative/.
11. https://www.mizzi.co/malta-bus-reborn.
12. https://lovinmalta.com/news/news-human-interest/watch-unsung-hero-of-maltas-iconic-buses-set-to-make-a-grand-comeback/.

5
Museum exhibition dynamics

Introduction

August 2007. While I was working towards the submission of my doctoral thesis, I started work in a post-doctoral research position at the University of York associated with the '1807 Commemorated' research project funded by the Arts and Humanities Research Council. The project aimed to investigate public responses to a series of museum exhibitions organised as part of the bicentenary of the abolition of the slave trade. I recollect travelling prior to the submission of my thesis on an August weekend, in order to join the project team at the International Slavery Museum in Liverpool. Here we conducted more than a hundred semi-structured interviews with museum visitors.

The museum engaged with a wide range of audiences but, more importantly, it provided the space for critical dialogue and reflection on the legacies of the 'dark' and 'unspoken' history of enslavement today. Fourteen years have passed since this bicentenary of the abolition of the slave trade. I would thus like to revisit two of the London-based exhibitions investigated at the time as part of the project: the 'London, Sugar and Slavery' exhibition at the Museum of Docklands and the 'Atlantic Worlds' exhibition at the National Maritime Museum.

What is a museum exhibition? Most textbooks and handbooks on museum exhibitions approach such events in phases, considering exhibition development, museum audience engagement, museum design, museum environment, evaluation and digital interpretation (see, for instance, Dean 2002; Bogle 2013). Exhibitions are often presented as a 'process' or 'product', the development of which is linear and consists of a beginning, middle and end. However, I contend that museum exhibitions are social, dynamic practices; as such, they consist of non-linear, dynamic interrelationships which are subject to change even after the exhibition's launch. This contention assuredly applies to 'permanent' exhibition galleries, but temporary exhibitions also often leave an outlasting 'permanent digital trace' of a continuous, dynamic 'life'. A museum exhibition is also a complex system that involves multiple agents, among whom curators may be imbued on occasions with power in dictating the nature of exhibitions (e.g. Wilson 2011) and multiple media utilised in the process of representation and communication.

If we affirm that a museum exhibition is a non-linear, dynamic process, we can also assert that a museum exhibition is a dynamic social practice. It is the aim of this chapter to unfold the complex, non-linear dynamics of a museum exhibition at the respective stages of conceptualisation, development and visitation. To do so, I will draw on the 'Atlantic Worlds' of the National Maritime Museum and the 'London, Sugar and Slavery' of the Museum of Docklands – two permanent museum galleries in London launched in 2007, the bicentenary of the slave trade's abolition in Britain. Commemoration of this abolition prompted the design of numerous, mainly temporary, exhibitions, which involved African and African Caribbean communities in the development process to a greater or lesser extent (Fouseki 2010; Fouseki and Smith 2013; Smith et al. 2014).

As noted above, this chapter was triggered by my participation in '1807 Commemorated', a two-year research project at the University of York funded by the Arts and Humanities Research Council. Assisted by the project team, we carried out 1498 semi-structured interviews with visitors at seven exhibitions commemorating the abolition of the slave trade. These included the 'Equiano exhibition' at the Birmingham Museums and Art Gallery, the 'Inhuman Traffic: The Business of the Slave Trade' exhibition at the British Museum, a small exhibition illustrating the association of Harewood House in Yorkshire with slavery, the 'Breaking the Chains' exhibition at the British Empire and Commonwealth Museum of Bristol, the 'International Slavery Museum' in Liverpool, the 'London, Sugar and Slavery' exhibition at the Museum of Docklands and the 'Atlantic Worlds' of the National Maritime Museum (Smith et al. 2014).

In addition to the visitor surveys, we conducted 54 semi-structured interviews with museum staff from the partner museums, 37 interviews with curators and other museum professionals from 24 regional or local museums and galleries, 6 interviews with policy-makers and academic consultants and 24 interviews with members of 'community consultation groups' actively involved in the development of exhibitions. This last included a focus group discussion with 11 individuals who participated in a day-long workshop, held at the Museum of Docklands in May 2008 (Fouseki 2010).

Despite the richness of the project's data and subsequent analyses, however, there are still unexplored areas that I hope to address. Firstly, what exhibition elements contributed to the dynamics of visitor experience? Secondly, how did the participation of external stakeholders influence the exhibition dynamics? In other words, can we observe distinct models of communication dynamics and, if so, how do these models align with models of 'community participation'? Thirdly, what changes, if any, have occurred since the launch of these exhibitions? If we acknowledge a museum practice to be a dynamic social practice, the continuation of which depends on the interconnected non-linear relationships of materials, spaces, feelings, values, skills, time and resources, which of those elements or chains, if broken, threaten the existence of a museum exhibition or mark its rebirth?

By drawing upon the two permanent galleries of the Museum of Docklands (LSS) and the National Maritime Museum (NMM), I will argue that a museum exhibition is a socio-cultural, dynamic and systemic practice. As such, its development and continuation depend on the interconnections of materials, values/meanings, space/place, skills/competencies, resources, time and senses/feelings. I will evidence that 'senses/feelings' and 'space' constitute the most critical components for demarcating the life cycle of a museum exhibition. In terms of 'senses' and 'affect', the emotionally engaging 'London, Sugar and Slavery' gallery has not dramatically changed. This is partly due to the fact that the gallery has embedded a fluid exhibition space which changes periodically, in consultation with different community groups. On the other hand, the 'Atlantic Worlds' faced the urge for change when 'feelings' of anger emerged, especially among African Caribbean communities. The current 'Work in Progress' exhibition section illustrates this shift.

I will also demonstrate that each gallery is characterised by a disparate model of communication. The National Maritime Museum (NMM) exhibition is an example of an object-oriented, academic exhibition aimed at portraying 'historic facts'. It is an object-driven gallery, in that it allows the availability of objects to dictate the narrative. The objects also become the centre of the exhibition rather than the medium of the narrative. As such, the exhibition display does not contain any dramatic 'peaks' but is rather presented as a static, flat narration. However, the flat, static narrative does not necessarily mean that it results in 'emotionless' engagement or disengagement (disengagement is itself a form of emotional reaction).

Our visitor surveys disclosed that emotions of anger and frustration were experienced either by those who came across such an exhibition unexpectedly or by those who felt that their history was not properly represented. On the other hand, the LSS exhibition uses dramatic language and imagery aimed at emotional engagement; it seeks to create dramatic peaks throughout. The LSS display is not so rich in objects as the NMM collection – a fact which, in a way, afforded scope for alternative interpretation.

The distinctly different communication styles reflect the different 'consultation' models. At NMM the role of the consultative groups was, as evidenced by the name, consultative; at LSS external participants had an active role in all exhibition phases, even during the last stage of text writing and editing. We can thus observe that prioritisation of objects over the narrative can alienate external participants, while prioritisation of narrative over objects can make external participants experience a sense of ownership. The level of participation can also dictate the degree to which a gallery follows a local, national or international focus. In galleries with high levels of 'community involvement', such as the LSS gallery, the geographical focal point tends to be local. At LSS, for instance, there is insistence on the legacies of the 'slave trade' for contemporary London – especially around the Docklands area – despite international references to the Caribbean and Africa. At the NMM, by contrast, the focus of the gallery is national, reflecting the status of the museum. Nevertheless, as noted above, a curatorial shift can be perceived at the NMM. A recent 'Work in Progress' section indicates a change from a 'factual' exhibition to an interactive and emotionally engaging gallery, featuring connections to the local, surrounding area. Finally, it should be noted that discussions on developing these galleries pre-dated the bicentenary of the abolition of the slave trade, even though the commemorative occasion afforded the momentum and funding resources to materialise the exhibition plans. The fact that there were earlier discussions may partly explain why these galleries have become 'permanent', 'integral' components of their museums, in contrast to most of the commemorative exhibitions which were temporary.

It is thus evinced that museum exhibitions are 'something' far more than the display of objects and stories. They have been described as 'publicly sanctioned representations of identity, principally, but not exclusively, of the institutions which present them' (Ferguson 1996, 126). The ways in which an exhibition has been developed or engages audiences is a tell-tale sign of a museum's institutional culture. Exhibitions may provide 'the central speaking subjects in the standard stories about art which institutions and curators often tell to themselves and to us' (Ferguson 1996, 126). A participatory approach to exhibitions alleviates the curatorial voice, telling more stories relevant to different 'communities'.

Therefore, exhibitions are the 'material speech' of what is essentially a political institution; what they do and in whose name are thus 'important to any sense of a democracy, especially a democracy of representations' (Ferguson 1996, 130). Indeed, museums 'do not simply issue objective descriptions or form logical assemblages' but rather serve to 'generate representations and attribute value and meaning in line with certain perspectives or classificatory schemas which are historically specific' (Lidchi 2001, 160). Deconstruction of the dynamics of an exhibition can therefore not only unveil how visitor experience is shaped, but also reveal the ideological, political and other dimensions of a museum as a whole.

Methodology – how to deconstruct the dynamics of a museum exhibition

In this section I introduce a framework of 'reading' and deconstructing the dynamic structure of a museum exhibition. The proposed framework brings previous scholarly work on systematic exhibition analysis together with the theoretical framework of this book. The framework establishes the 'contextual framework' (that is, the academic, institutional, marketing and political dimension) within which the exhibition dynamic analysis can be situated. I then proceed with analysis of the individual components and their intersections.

The 'contextual framework' is inspired by the work of Geerlings et al. (2015), who developed a historic critique framework for exhibitions. The authors identify six dimensions for exhibition analysis. The 'academic dimension' contributes insights on how current debates in academia or 'out-dated historical views' are incorporated into an exhibition. The 'political dimension' refers to implicit or explicit historical references about political entities of belonging, such as nation, region, locality, transnational or imperial links. It also links to the ways in which an exhibition construes notions of gender, race, religion and identities (Geerlings et al. 2015). The 'institutional and intra-institutional dimension' denotes the relationship of a certain exhibition with other exhibitions in the same museum, as well as the impact of institutional practices, discourses, traditions and policies on shaping exhibition narratives. The 'marketing dimension' is associated with the written and visual information produced 'about' the exhibition and its supporting media (such as the catalogue, press release, educational resources and websites). It also refers to the target audience the exhibition is addressing and the extent to which the exhibition confirms or disturbs visitors' tacit expectations and view of reality. The authors also distinguish two additional dimensions, 'narrative' and 'material', which I will retain as the critical components of the chain of continuity and change. The academic, institutional, marketing and political dimensions thus formulate the contextual framework within which our exhibition dynamic analysis is located.

The 'narrative dimension' mentioned by Geerlings et al. (2015) for the purposes of this analysis cross-cuts the 'heritage dynamic' elements of 'materials', 'meanings', 'space', 'skills' and 'time'. Questions relevant to the narrative are 'what narratives does the exhibition construct, what visions of the world does it convey, what idea of narrativity is being represented or what notion of authorship are relevant to this dimension?' (Geerlings et al. 2015, 3). The 'narrative dimension' is dynamic. Not only was the narrative as a *process* created over a period of time, possibly with a long-lasting effect once the visit is over, but also the narrative as *experience* depends on the dynamic interconnections of exhibition materials, values conveyed through them, the space and place of display, the emergent feelings, the skills and knowledge required for its development and the time and resources needed. The 'narrative' is thus the 'output' of the dynamic interconnections rather than the context.

Exhibition narratives are 'located in the world', 'crafted by emotionally situated agents' and 'embedded in the corporeality of their lives' (Munroe 2016, 115). The process of narrative-making is consequently intersected by a matrix of emotional and affective entanglements with human and non-human elements such as texts, people, discourses, objects, practices and spaces (Munroe 2016, 115). Since narrative is a human construct, a process of exclusion and editing is required. This serves to perpetuate exclusionary narratives of the past, underpinned by intensely held attachments that feel 'emotionally authentic' to dominant groups in society (MacLeod et al. 2012, xxii).

'Heritage dynamic' elements in exhibition dynamics

As noted above, Geerlings et al. (2015) have identified 'materials' as one of the dimensions of their proposed 'contextual framework' for exhibition analysis. For the purposes of this analysis, however, 'materials' have been recognised as one of the core 'heritage dynamic' elements. In the context of exhibitions, materials form the medium by which the narrative is constructed. Several questions can be asked in relation to materials – for example, whether the objects are replicas or original; what materials are used for interpretation in terms of colours, sounds, lighting; how are the objects displayed in showcases or the museum space, etc. (Geerlings et al. 2015).

An exhibition provides the medium to convey meanings and emotions through something 'tangible' – whether that is the objects in display showcases, text panels, graphics, monitors, screens, etc. An exhibition consists of a wide range of material things and the interplay between them. The role of the designer is critical in assembling 'material things'; we could indeed argue that all the above are exhibition objects. Photographs displayed in a showcase, for example, are 'both images and objects that exist in time and space and thus in a social and cultural experience' (Edwards and Hart 2004, 1). Thinking materially about everything displayed in the gallery space encompasses processes of intention, making, using, distributing, consuming, discarding and recycling (Edwards and Hart 2004, 1). Materiality in this context is 'concerned with real physical objects in a world that is physically apprehendable not only through vision but through embodied relations of smell, taste, touch and hearing' (Edwards and Hart 2004, 2).

'Meanings' and 'values' around the 'exhibition things' are changing and re-changing. An object may acquire a 'new life' and meaning when it becomes part of a larger assemblage or may gain a new set of meanings over time. The exhibition development requires a wide array of skills such as historical knowledge, research, curatorial expertise, design, interpretation and communication. For exhibitions that involve participation, additional competencies, such as negotiation skills, are also needed. Questions such as who has written the text or provided input into the text (Moser 2010, 27) and other phases of the exhibition are therefore important to ask. As to 'resources', in addition to the financial and human resources needed to materialise an exhibition, objects can also be regarded as 'resources', especially by object-centric institutions. 'Time' is also a resource, as well as a construct connoting the ways in which time is conceptualised in an exhibition context. 'Space' and 'place' prompt us to reflect on how the museum space is designed as well as the location of the museum itself, including its surroundings and their relevance to the exhibition. Finally 'senses' and 'emotions' provoke questions on what mechanisms an exhibition employs to trigger emotional responses, as well as on the emotional impacts that an exhibition may have on visitors.

The 'heritage dynamic elements' can be deduced even further, generating specific questions about the architecture, display, design/colour/light, text, forms of display and exhibition types during an exhibition dynamic analysis (for a detailed list of questions see Moser 2010, 25). Table 5.1 presents a few questions alongside the individual 'heritage dynamic elements'. It was used as an 'exhibition dynamics' tool for the two cases under examination.

Table 5.1 Guiding questions for mapping exhibition dynamics

Exhibition dimension	Materials	Values/Meanings	Space/Place	Senses/ Feelings	Skills/ Competencies	Time	Resources
Museum architecture	Is the architecture an object of display?	How does the architecture relate historically and culturally to the display? Does the style of the museum building emphasise a cultural contrast between the host or custodian of the collection and the objects in display?	How does the surrounding landscape align or contrast with the exhibition?	What feelings does the architecture evoke?		Does the architecture evoke certain time periods?	
Space	What are the predominant design materials in the museum space? How do they change across the exhibition, if they do?	What is the meaning or symbolism of the chosen materials?	What is the size and shape of the gallery and of the individual sections? Where is the gallery located? Is the gallery easy to find?	What feelings does the gallery evoke? What feelings does the adopted spatial organisation evoke?	What skills and competencies have been utilised to create the space?	Does the spatial organisation follow a linear timeline?	How was the design of the space funded? Are funders mentioned in the space?

	What materials have been used to demarcate the zones?		What is the spatial organisation of the displays (i.e. lined up on the wall, set out less systematically in a circular way, etc.)?				
Design	What display materials are used? What colour are they? How are they illuminated?	What meanings do the chosen display materials evoke?	What does the design of the space look like?	What feelings does the design evoke?	Who worked on the design? Were 'communities' involved? How inclusive is the design?	Does the chosen design evoke certain time periods?	What proportion of the budget was attributed to the design?
Colour	What is the predominant colour in exhibition materials such as panels, captions and walls?	What meanings and values do the chosen colours represent?	Does the colour vary across the exhibition space or is it the same throughout?	What feelings do the chosen colours evoke?	Who decided on the colour design?	Are different time periods indicated in different colours?	

Table 5.1 (cont.)

Exhibition dimension	Materials	Values/Meanings	Space/Place	Senses/ Feelings	Skills/ Competencies	Time	Resources
Lighting	Are certain objects lit in a different way? Which ones and why? What is the effect of the chosen lighting on the objects?	What lighting has been chosen and why?	Does the gallery use artificial or natural light? How is the space lit? How is the lighting in the exhibition space arranged? Is there a difference between how showcases and free displays are illuminated?	What feelings does the lighting provoke?	Who was responsible for the lighting?	Does the lighting reflect certain time periods?	What proportion of the budget was dedicated to lighting?
Text	What materials have been used for text panels? To what extent has text been used in the exhibition?	Is the style of text academic, factual or neutral? Or is the style engaging, emotional, reflective and interactive?	Where is text displayed and how?	How does the text set the mood? How does the text differentiate the space in order to arouse different emotions?	Does the choice of text presuppose certain exper-tise? Have 'communities' or organisa-tions external to the	Do introductory panels establish a chronological, thematic or circular order? At what point in time was the text prepared?	How much time and resources did the text preparation require?

					museum's staff been involved in the writing of the text?		
Layout	How are the surfaces of the room (ceilings, walls and floors) used?	What particular meanings/values do the alignment of the objects evoke?	How are the displays arranged within the room? How are the objects displayed? What arrangements have taken place?	What particular feelings do the alignment and layout of the objects evoke?	Were 'communities' involved in the layout design?	Does the arrangement of the objects follow a chronological or a thematic order?	
Display types	What types of display materials are used (e.g. audio-visual, graphic, etc.)?	What values/ meanings are implied by the choice of certain displays?	How have images or other display materials been used across the space?	What feelings do certain types of display evoke?	Did 'communities' have a say in the selection of certain displays?	Are different types of display used to signify different time periods?	What resources were required?
Exhibition style	Is the exhibition object-centred or people-oriented? Are certain materials associated with certain exhibition styles?	Is the exhibition style didactic or one of discovery? How does the exhibition style confer meaning upon the objects?	What exhibition style(s) are adopted throughout the space? How does the exhibition style change, if at all?	What feelings and senses does the exhibition aim to address? Is this an interactive exhibition?	What was the involvement of 'communities' in the determination of the exhibition style?	Does the exhibition follow a linear narrative? As such, does it follow a certain exhibition style?	

Exhibition dynamics – the 'Atlantic Worlds' exhibition

What are the exhibition dynamics of the 'Atlantic Worlds' gallery? In other words, how was the exhibition developed over time? How does the display unfold throughout the gallery space? What significant changes, if any, have occurred since the exhibition's opening and why? Which 'chains of what elements broke', demarcating a new life for the gallery? In order to answer these questions, I will begin by unfurling the 'contextual framework' dimensions.

Contextual framework

At this point, it is worth pointing out that the dynamics of an exhibition commence before even its conceptualisation. This is certainly the case with the 'Atlantic Worlds' gallery at the National Maritime Museum (NMM) which opened in 2007, the year of the bicentenary of the abolition of the slave trade in Britain. This gallery constitutes a development of the former 'Trade and Empire' exhibition, which formed part of the re-launching of the museum in 1999. The 'Trade and Empire' gallery and its approach sought to reflect new thinking about what was meant by 'maritime history' (Longair and McAleer 2013). It was provocative at the time as it aimed to explore the history of the empire 'not just in relation to commerce and maritime power, but also with reference to issues of post-colonial knowledge and identity formation, raising public critics [*sic*]' (McAleer 2013). The exhibition was 'accused of mounting a politically correct travesty of the empire that will mislead thousands of millennium tourists next year'. Critics saw the display as aimed 'at depriving the British people of any aspect of their history in which they can take justifiable pride' (Ezard 1999).

Following partial financial support from the Heritage Lottery Fund, which enabled the acquisition of a major collection of objects linked to slavery, the Michael Graham-Stewart collection, the 'Atlantic Worlds' gallery opened in 2007 (McAleer 2013, 79). The acquisition of the collection in a way imported several constraints in terms of what narrative could be adopted – although, as several of the community group members argued, an object need not itself provide a constraint since imaginative ways for interpretation and re-interpretation can always be used. One of the 'constraints' imposed is the fact that this particular collection lacked 'objects that could illustrate the lives and cultures of the enslaved and convey their agency and resilience' (McAleer 2013, 79), a reflection of the historiographic trends of the time (Hamilton and Blyth 2007). However, even more strikingly, it lacked a focus on today's contemporary legacies of the history.

The political dimension of an exhibition display is interwoven with its economic dimension. At the time there was not only a political emphasis on social inclusion, but the funders' expectations were also for museums to engage with a diverse range of groups, particularly when dealing with a hidden and unspoken history. The 'Atlantic Worlds' team thus initiated a series of consultation meetings with several museums (although individual levels of participation varied) (Fouseki 2010). The 'Trade and Empire' history combined with the type of collection to cultivate a certain 'academic discourse': authoritative, factual and 'neutral' (if such a thing exists). The language is primarily factual and academic, with 'peaks' of dramatisation and emotion in the exhibits related to enslavement. This may be due to feedback received by participants who were consulted during the process as explained below.

External environment

An exhibition gallery needs to be reviewed within the context of its wider location. A gallery space is part of a larger museum building, in turn part of a landscape with underlying connotations that can potentially appear under certain conditions. The 'Black Lives Matter' movement, for instance, vividly exposed the strong connections of the surrounding local landscape with each of the museums under examination and the resulting need for re-interpretation or action, as explained below. A starting 'loop' in deconstructing the exhibition dynamics is thus formulated by the interconnection of 'social change' (values/meanings), 'relevance of the surroundings to the exhibition theme' (place/space) and the 'associated external museum activities' (resources) (Fig. 5.1). This reinforcing interrelationship may lie dormant for a while until it becomes visible. At the National Maritime Museum this relationship can be showcased through the 'Work in Progress' section (see below), which outlines the contemporary legacies of the slave trade and their permanent presence in the local surroundings.

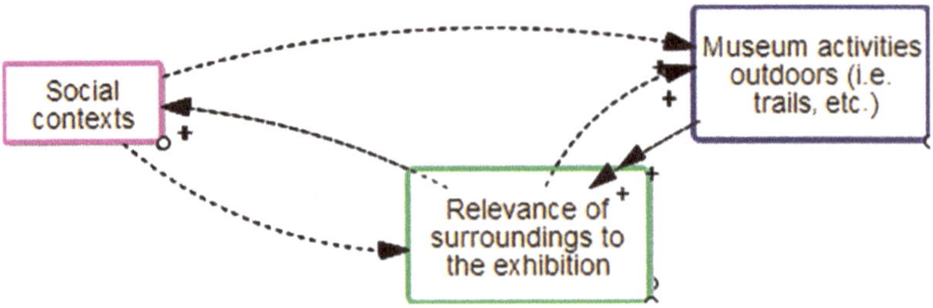

Fig. 5.1 'Loop' formulated by the interconnection of 'social change' (values/meanings), 'relevance of the surroundings to the exhibition theme' (place/space) and the 'associated external museum activities' (resources).

Museum building

The next layer of dynamic relationships under examination is the extent to which the museum building is acknowledged as an integral part of the exhibition narrative. If the museum building is perceived as an indivisible component of an exhibition, then the museum itself becomes both an object and an exhibit. The focus of the gallery inevitably becomes local. While this relationship is clearly apparent in the case of the LSS gallery, the NMM building functions mainly as a building envelope. However, its architecture unavoidably carries values associated with national pride for the Royal Navy and British Empire. The museum per se does not constitute an 'exhibit' per se, however (as it does in the case of LSS), possibly the result of its 'national focus' (Fig. 5.2).

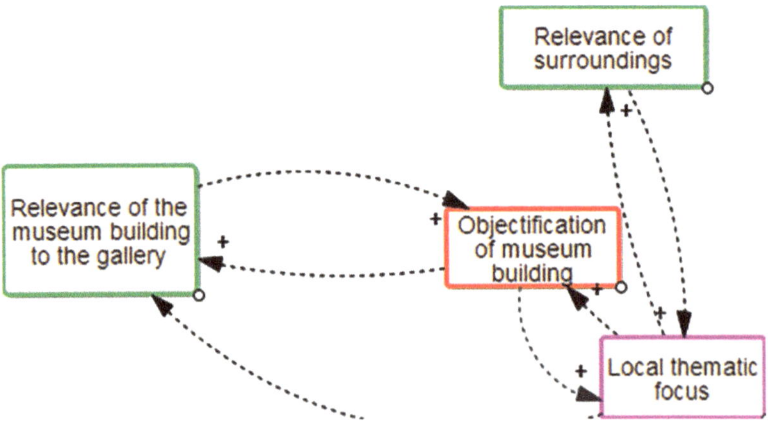

Fig. 5.2 Snapshot of the exhibition dynamics illustrating the conditions under which a museum is 'objectified'.

The NMM has been exhibiting the history of the British Empire since opening its doors in 1937. As McAleer observes, the museum was founded at a specific historical moment, when its supporters believed that the establishment of such an institution and the consequent instilling of 'legitimate pride', and perhaps even the determination to emulate 'past endeavours', in its visitors might help to stem the decline in Britain's political fortunes in the period. (McAleer 2013, 76)

The museum has thus from its establishment 'collected, displayed and interpreted Britain's intertwined national and imperial history', as well as reflecting on changing attitudes to, and understandings of, the country's place in the world (McAleer 2013, 77). As a result, the NMM was relaunched in 1999 with new galleries including the 'Trade and Empire' gallery, the predecessor of the 'Atlantic Worlds' exhibition discussed below.

When first visiting the exhibition, a visitor will inevitably encounter the building. The architecture of a museum building and its location undoubtedly serve to influence the ways in which an exhibition will be experienced (Moser 2010, 24). This is mainly due to the fact that museum buildings are an integral part of the wider complex socio-economic, cultural and political societal system (Jones and MacLeod 2016, 207) within which they were constructed and are experienced. As such, museum architecture is a social process undergoing constant change

> a dynamic space that is made meaningful through the interactions of space, objects, sociality and the very meanings that flow from that interaction. (Jones and MacLeod 2016, 207)

In this light, museum buildings of neoclassical architectural style may 'imbue displays with a degree of authority or influence' (Moser 2010, 24), given that throughout the Western world museums in the mid-nineteenth century were 'regarded as institutions of authority and knowledge, and their classical architecture was designed to reflect this' (Messham-Muir 2002, 74). Indeed, the NMM is housed in the former 'Royal Hospital School', built in the eighteenth century (Littlewood and Butler 1998, xvi). Its architecture connotes 'imperialism' and colonial power, reminding visitors how much wealth was built on human exploitation and enslavement. Despite these connotations, however, the building does stand separately from the exhibition itself.

Narrative-making

Based on the '1807 Commemorated' interviews and the wider literature on the subject, it can be concluded that the gallery was object-driven, dictated largely by the availability of objects acquired in the Michael Graham-Stewart collection. In a curator-driven gallery, the objects for display are pre-selected, the design of the layout is pre-defined and it is only at the last stage of text finalisation that external groups to the museum may be consulted. In such a situation, the narrative is dictated by available objects and available historic knowledge around the objects. 'Objects' and 'knowledge' are both the 'materials' and 'skills' viewed as 'resources'. In this curator-led approach, the sequence of exhibition development will imply the selection of the objects first, followed by the appointment of the exhibition's designer and specification of the layout in the space; both interpretation and text are left towards the end. The first two stages are pre-decided prior to the involvement of the 'community groups'. The nature of narrative is somewhat pre-decided too; it is 'historical', 'distanced from the present' and 'academic' in tone.

As is shown below, however, specific exhibitions around enslavement and resistance tend to utilise a different language tone. The adoption of a 'historic', 'academic' narrative emphasises the need for text to fit into 30–50 words of a caption – the priority, after all, is the display of objects. This leads to plain 'factual' captions that do not contextualise the objects they describe. However, the digital space is offered as a platform for multivocality and comments or additional descriptions (as seen below) (Fig. 5.3).

Locating the 'Atlantic Worlds' gallery in the museum proved complex. The pandemic imposed a one-way orientation system which involved passing through the ground floor and going straight to the second floor before taking the stairs down to the first floor where the 'Atlantic Worlds' exhibition is located. A visitor thus crosses the 'Tudors', the 'Nelson' and the 'Polar Worlds' galleries before accessing the 'Atlantic Worlds' exhibition. It is worth mentioning too that the gallery can easily be skipped; the visitor can simply follow the staircase to the second floor instead of opening the side doors of the gallery, unlike the galleries mentioned above.

Grever et al. (2012) describe the narrative of 'Atlantic Worlds' as a 'zig-zag' movement from decline to progress, 'presenting history both as a "rise-and-fall" and a "fall-and-rise" narrative'. In view of this, the narrative represents a non-linear, dynamic recycle of decline and growth. It does so by first describing the travels of European explorers across the

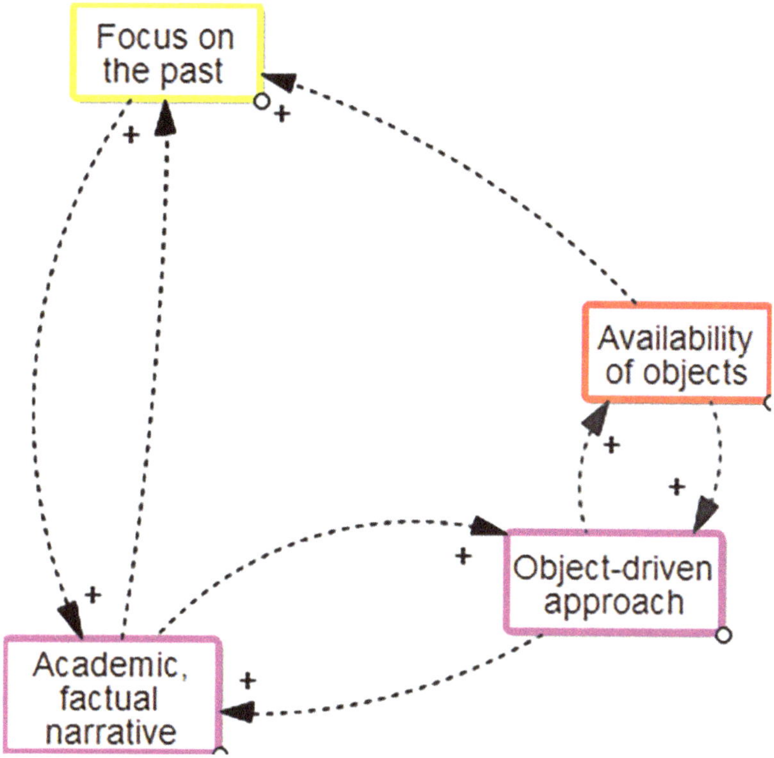

Fig. 5.3 Dynamic interrelationships between 'objects', 'values' and 'skills'.

Atlantic Ocean and the expansion of British trade and empire before turning to movement of people through migration or the transatlantic slave trade. Towards the end the gallery focuses on the abolition of slavery and the growth of British maritime power (Grever et al. 2012). Analysis of the language used through the gallery demonstrates that the exhibition is past-oriented; it lacks references to the present, with the exception of the recent 'Work in Progress' section. It is also Euro-centric; African countries only come into play 'when Europeans encounter them through their explorations for resources' (Grever et al. 2012, 883) (Fig. 5.4). Moreover, 'in the sections preceding the resistance and rebellions of slaves, the passive tense dominates when enslaved people are mentioned' (Grever et al. 2012, 882). However, the 'Work in Progress' section adopts a fundamentally different approach that addresses these aspects.

Let us now see how these general trends manifest themselves in the exhibition space.

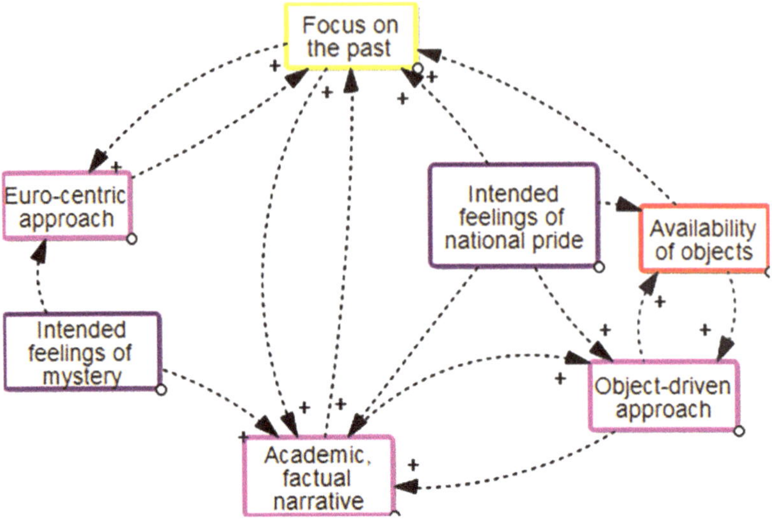

Fig. 5.4 Dynamic interrelationships between 'narrative' and 'objects'.

Materiality and space

The 'narrative design' is thematic: it neither follows a chronological order nor dictates a linear path since the themes are organised in a circular manner. This is of interest since, despite the focus on the past, a linear, chronological outline has not been chosen. The background walls are grey and the light is low with some audio/video props in the middle of the gallery where the new re-interpretation takes place. The gallery contains a rich collection of objects, mostly consisted of paintings along with some objects associated with the 'transatlantic slave trade'. Just outside the entrance to the exhibition a transparent glass panel prompts visitors to 'discover the troubled history of the Atlantic Ocean'. Above the text, the image of a head drum obtained by Admiral Sir Frederick Bedford (1838–1913) during his naval excursion in West Africa is portrayed. On the side of the entrance (place) is displayed an assemblage of text panels and images which can provide a more representative picture of the gallery's content. Three texts and images are arranged vertically, implying some form of hierarchical order.

The image on top depicts a brown single head drum (materials) on dark red background. The caption in small font reads: 'Single head drum obtained by Rear Admiral Sir Frederick Bedford (1838–1913) while on Royal Navy operations in West Africa'. This short caption is of significance as it pinpoints a time (end of the nineteenth century), a place

(West Africa) and a culture/value associated with African civilisation. It hints at the appropriation of cultural items through imperialism and war. However, the plain, factual character of the caption, as well as the location of the image on the side of the entrance, means that it can easily be skipped.

The object also has a digital presence, however, containing a much more detailed description.[1] The first part of the description focuses on the material and typological description of the object. Only five lines later is contextual information provided and a much more sophisticated explanation given:

> It [the drum] may have been taken during the action against Nana Olomu in September 1894, or during the Brass River expedition of February 1895, where British military action far inland was undertaken on the pretext of anti-slavery enforcement. It reflects European interest in African artefacts at the end of the 19th century, many of which were collected as a result of military action.

Although space restrictions may have imposed the inclusion and exclusion of information, the digital space seems to be perceived as a safer space for critical engagement than that of the gallery.

The caption is followed by text of larger font: 'Discover the troubled history of the Atlantic Ocean'. This prompt explicitly states that the history of the Atlantic is 'troubled' – this combined with the 'African obtainment' above can easily connote, although still implicitly, the transatlantic slave trade. The senses/emotions generated are those of mystery rather than of fear or pain.

Senses, feelings and space

A mood of 'mystery' and 'exploration' is set by the low lights and the introductory panel which reads:

> ATLANTIC WORLDS
>
> This gallery is about the movement of people, goods and ideas across and around the Atlantic Ocean from the 17th to the 19th century. The connections created by these movements changed the lives of people on three continents, profoundly affecting their cultures and societies and shaping the world we live in today.

The introductory panel does not make explicit reference to the slave trade. However, a recently installed panel just after the introduction indicates the museum's shift towards community consultation. If we approach an exhibition as a 'beat sheet' of a screenplay, then this moment is the first 'beat' that disrupts the factual presentation given up to that point.

> This gallery no longer reflects the approaches and ambitions of the National Maritime Museum. It opened in 2007 but many visitors and staff are offended and hurt by the language used, the interpretation of objects and the lack of Black voices. Work to change the space began in 2019. You can see the new 'Work in Progress' section at the centre of the gallery. COVID-19 meant further projects were paused. These are now being revised to reflect the events of the past months. You can help shape the next steps by sharing your thoughts on the comment cards.

The statement opens with the identification of 'space' and 'time' – the spatio-temporal statement locates the visitor in time and space. It continues by explaining how certain 'materials' and 'meanings' generated certain feelings before concluding with another spatio-temporal statement (Fig. 5.5). The visitor experience begins with a prompt to participate through comments cards.

A comparison of this new text with the former introductory text can easily showcase the shift.

Let us compare the first two lines:

> Former text: 'This gallery is about the movement of people, goods, and ideas across and around the Atlantic Ocean from the 17th to the 19th century'.
>
> Recent text: 'This gallery no longer reflects the approaches and ambitions of the National Maritime Museum'.

The original text introduces what 'this gallery' is about, while the new text states what 'this gallery' is not about. The original text provides a factual statement about the theme, specifying the geography and time with which the gallery objects are associated. It explicitly states that it is a gallery about the past, not about the present, while the movement of people is portrayed as equivalent to the movement of goods and ideas.

The second sentence elaborates the first sentence in both texts. The old text expands upon the past-oriented approach highlighted in the first

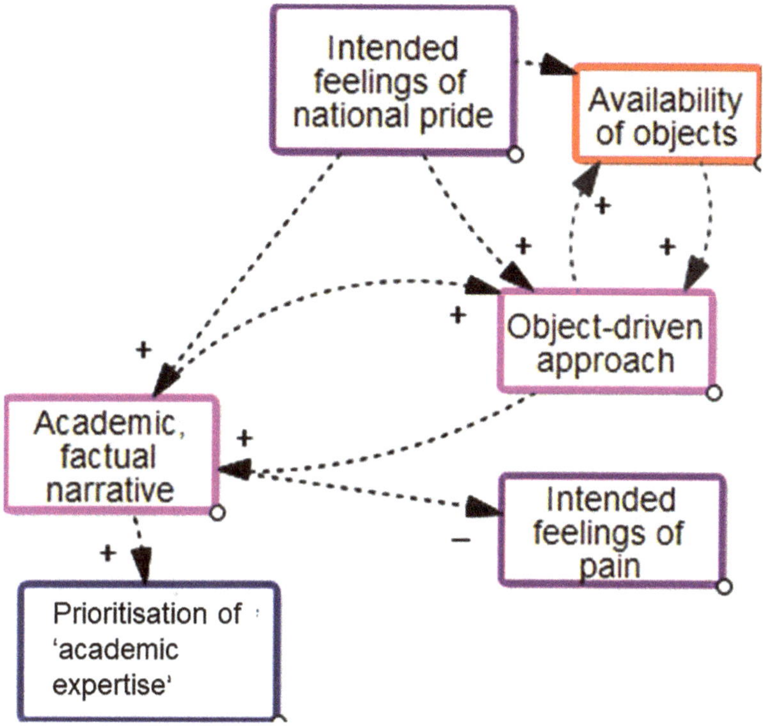

Fig. 5.5 Dynamic interrelationships between feelings, materials and values.

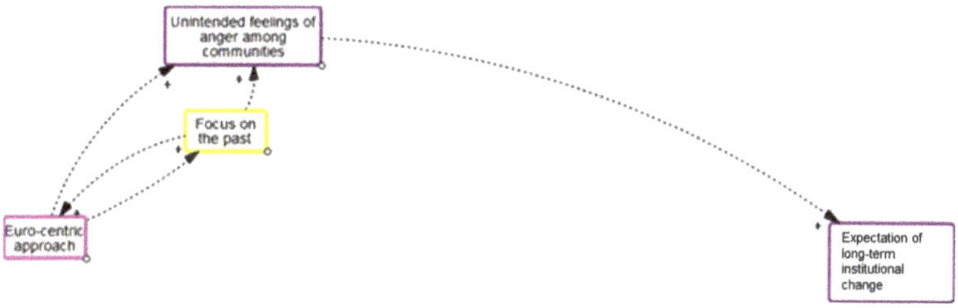

Fig. 5.6 The dynamics of community expectations.

sentence by clarifying how these movements affected three continents and shaped the world we live in today. It does not provide information on how the world was shaped – it may be in a negative or positive manner, or in both. The second sentence in the recent text explains why new work is under way. It discloses the feelings experienced by visitors and staff as a result of the narrative, materials and lack of representation (Fig. 5.6).

The gallery opened in 2007, but the text explains that many visitors and staff were and are offended and hurt by the language used, the interpretation of objects and the lack of Black voices. The text finishes with the engaging pronoun 'you', prompting people to provide feedback and ideas for the new 'Work in Progress' gallery.

The opening statement of this panel begins with a time dimension statement – that is, the gallery **no longer** reflects the approaches of the museum. A shift in the approaches and ambitions of the museum driven by reactions of both visitors and staff towards the use of language, the interpretation of objects and lack of Black voices is implied in this statement. In other words, it was not the absence of objects (materials) but the absence of meanings and representations, complemented by the presence of 'offensive' language and 'inappropriate' interpretation, which caused reactions. The lack of representation of meanings thus encourages new (re)interpretations and new 'materialities'. Another driving factor for the 'Work in Progress' section is described as the 'events of the past months', a reference to the 'Black Lives Matter' events in 2020. Following the temporary closure of the National Maritime Museum due to Covid-19, visitors are encouraged to share their thoughts on visitor comment cards (Fig. 5.7).

The panel constitutes both a response and a promise to critiques raised mainly by African Caribbean communities. The panel is displayed on different material to the original plexiglass. It is a brown panel, aligned

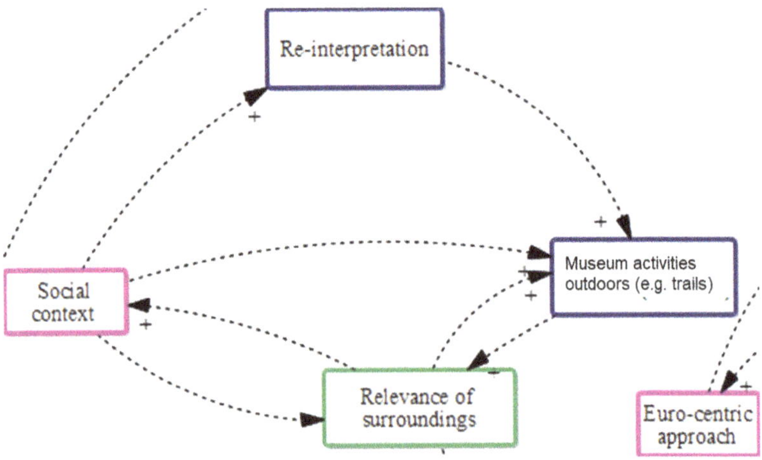

Fig. 5.7 Dynamic interrelationships between external forces, values and skills.

with the texture of the new section with which it is associated. The mood here changes from one of a 'neutral factual statement' that invites exploration to one that 'invites curiosity' but also promises the adoption of a radical approach to the gallery. The tone of the museum changes from an authoritative, impersonal one to one of confession and collaboration. However, the effect of this 'beat' panel is temporary as we move in the space returning to the 2007 gallery.

The 'Work in Progress' panel reads:

> This gallery no longer reflects the approaches or ambitions of the National Maritime Museum. It opened in 2007, the 200th anniversary of the Act for the Abolition of the Slave Trade in the British Empire. However, the legacies of the transatlantic slavery are noticeably absent and Black voices are not well represented in the space.
>
> Changing this is a work in progress.
>
> These three walls are the first stage of an ongoing project responding to the existing gallery, using it as a **catalyst for change** and **more transparent museum** practice. They were developed **in partnership** with a small, intergenerational team of people from the African diaspora including Pamela Franklin and Adam Terrelonge, who can be seen in the film nearby. This space foregrounds **human stories** and considers the **local landscape of Greenwich** and surrounding areas of this history. We hope this will improve the gallery and inform how the Museum presents this history and legacies of transatlantic slavery in the future. Please **use the comment cards to provide feedback** about the gallery or reflections on the themes raised. (author's emphasis)

The 'Work in Progress' section emphasises the need of museums to be transparent and co-creative. The former object-oriented approach is replaced by a desire to display human stories and local connections. The exhibition encourages interactive dialogue with visitors who can record their comments on visitor cards.

This section lies at stark contrast with the rest of the gallery. Overall the language is 'markedly dispassionate and neutrally descriptive', with the exception of the panel on the 'Middle Passage'. This does resort, in a limited way, to emotional and intensifying language, with references to the 'harrowing voyage', 'appalling' conditions, families 'torn apart', bodies 'unceremoniously thrown overboard' (**beat 2**). In a slightly similar way, the panel dealing with resistance to slavery in the Caribbean uses a more direct language of active agency (the enslaved 'resisted from the moment of capture onwards'; 'they broke tools'; 'they made bids for freedom', etc.) than is usual in the other panels. Such a choice presumably seeks to avoid the commonly noted danger of reducing enslaved people imaginatively to the status of passive victims and passive beneficiaries **(beat 3)**.

Where visitors are presented with a form of emotional engagement or subjectivity within the text panels is through the inclusion of personal narratives or accounts at the end of the panel. These provide a means not only of reinforcing the account presented in the main body of the text, but also of supplementing that text's usually neutral and 'objective' style with a human and personal tone. This may be due to feedback provided by community members who were consulted in the process, as can be evidenced from the interviews (Fig. 5.8).

I should note here that although the language is factual, it does not lack ideological underpinnings. Words such as 'naval power of the British' connote a strong sense of 'imperial power'. The slave trade is placed on the same level as 'other lucrative commerce'.

A comparison between the physical and digital space is illuminating. The colours of the paintings displayed at the 'Exploration and Trade' thematic section, for instance, are more vivid online than in the actual gallery. As before, the online description at the 'War and Conflict' section of the painting displaying the island fortress of Goree on the west coast of

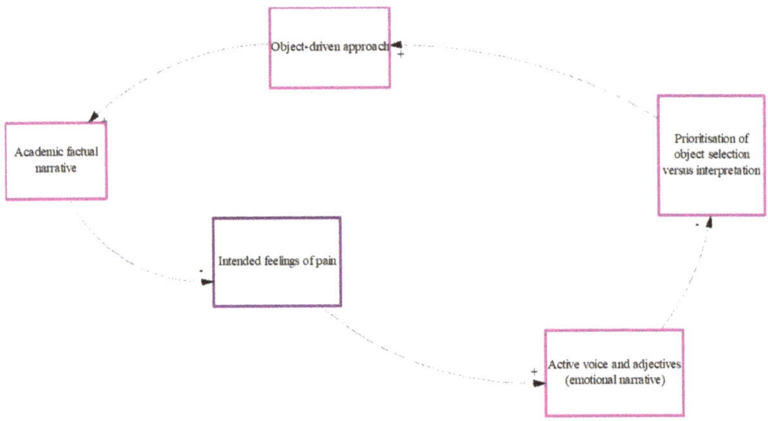

Fig. 5.8 Interrelationships between mode of consultation, senses and values.

Africa makes reference to John Paul Jones, who 'served briefly on slaving ships in 1766 but quit in disgust'. This painting functions as one of the 'exhibition beats' since it depicts the psychological and physical suffering endured by enslaved Africans on board ships during the Middle Passage. The text reads:

> Focusing on this aspect of transatlantic slavery was a tactic employed by European abolitionists who attempted to evoke sympathy for enslaved Africans and their plight through images and evidence of the misery of the Middle Passage.

Towards the end of the visit the visitor reads the following:

> The items shown in this gallery come almost **exclusively from the collections of the National Maritime Museum** (NMM). They have been chosen to illustrate specific aspects of Atlantic history as well as possible, given that the Museum's **holdings are a legacy of earlier collecting**. Much else was not collected or is not available. Moreover, **the complete history of the Atlantic Ocean is both complex and particularly difficult to reconstruct**, not least in any practical museum display. The Museum's collections also reflect this difficulty, both in what they hold and what they do not. (author's emphasis)

This rhetoric and tone of this panel stands in contradiction to the panel mentioned above. It reflects the original intentions of the gallery and the original object-driven approach, adopting a defensive tone in response to anticipated accusations by segments of the public on the lack of specific objects or interpretations. The first sentence inhibits the power of collections – in contrast to the Museum of Docklands – as the NMM used its own collections. It states that it is based on earlier collecting, although a new collection was purchased with HLF funding that constituted the basis of the new gallery (McAleer 2013, 79). An additional reason provided for the lack of representation of meanings is the complex history of the Atlantic Ocean, which cannot be fully represented in a narrow space. What has changed since then? The 'space' has remained the same, as have the 'objects', but attitudes associated with them have changed, leading to new interpretations.

The available objects demarcated the boundaries of what 'will' or 'will not' be depicted. This object-driven approach may lead to the under-representation of meanings and values with negative consequences for the sense of ownership (as it happened). In other words, a negative (balancing) relationship exists between objects (materials), space (both physical and metaphorical), representation of values and sense of ownership. This relationship is evidenced at the Museum of Docklands where the lack of available objects provided the space to represent the values of those consulted, enhancing a sense of belonging and ownership.

Participation dynamics

The emphasis on the academic/factual narrative meant that in the original version academic expertise was prioritised over community voices (Fig. 5.9). In fact, the consultative panels were divided between the 'cultural' and the 'academic' consultative panel. This reduced the possibilities of multivocality as the different types of expertise and approaches were not expressed and exchanged in the same room. This separation also led to feelings of anger among the communities.

This distinction hinders and jeopardises the sense of trust and shared sense of ownership. The acceptance of the invitation was due to knowing or having worked in the past with either the museum and/or the community members – so networking is clearly important here. The challenge is to maintain and strengthen the trust. Personal communications with NMM staff highlighted the challenges of bringing together an academic group with a 'cultural' group in order to reach a consensus. The reality is that the involvement of a diverse group of consultants requires the 'space' and 'time' to negotiate before consensus may be reached.

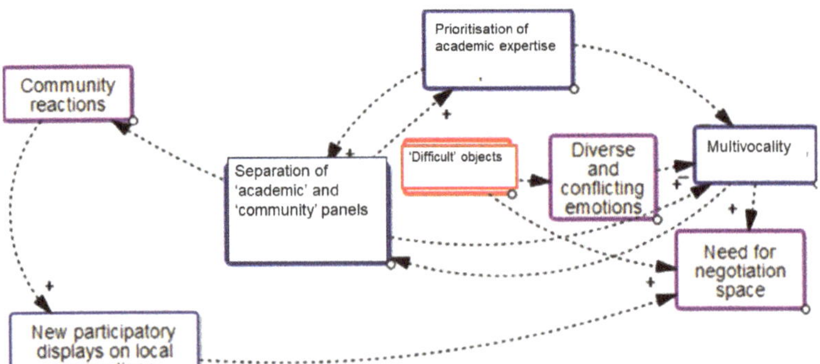

Fig. 5.9 Impact of participatory style on skills and competencies.

Exhibition dynamics – the 'London, Sugar and Slavery' exhibition

The 'London, Sugar and Slavery' exhibition was inaugurated on 10 November 2007 at the Museum of Docklands. It is a permanent exhibition, a section of which is dedicated to hosting temporary, smaller-scale exhibitions co-created with local communities. The notion of fluidity, transformation and change is thus integral to the permanent character of the exhibition. This section of the gallery is considered a 're-interpretation' gallery space (pers. comm. with a museum staff member in January 2008), a location where new interpretations can be shaped over a period of time in partnership with various groups.

Contextual framework

The Museum of Docklands has always focused upon the social history of London, and in this case on the working conditions around the docks. The available expertise of the first director, Chris Ellmers, on the working history of the river determined the nature of the first exhibition (skills/expertise). However, in 2005, in the light of the forthcoming bicentenary of the slave trade's abolition in Britain which opened up funding opportunities (resources), the new gallery was brought into being. As explained by the curator Tom Wareham, in his interview as part of the '1807 Commemorated' project, the idea of the museum of Docklands was first conceived in the 1980s.[2]

> At a time when the big issue in the East End of London was the **closure of the Docks**, which was the major employer in the area and the closure of the Docks brought huge financial disruption and disadvantage to the East End of London, also at that time **staff at the museum of London were collecting material** with the view to recording the history of the port and the docks from that point of view, so over a 20 year period and that's how long it took, the collection and the whole concept of the museum evolved along that basis. So that in 2000, when the funding actually came in from HLF and the plans all went forward and the idea, the conception was put into paper and design, it kind of became rather an industrial museum, erm, and the time the museum had been completed and opened in 2003, er, **what we began to realise was that things had changed over the 20 year period** and in fact the real story was not

> so much about the closure of the docks but **was actually about the people in the area and how they had related to the port and the river.** So really from the point of view, [from] the point [of view of] at which the museum opened we were looking at putting the people back in the story, and that was 2003. And in 2004 we realised that, erm, the bicentenary of the abolition of the slave trade was coming up and that triggered a thought process because the building that we're in was actually built by, basically the committee, the London Committee of West Indian Merchants and Planters to take the produce of the slave plantation, so the building itself had this huge story and we hadn't made enough of that story in the museum; it was there but it was very poorly told. So we thought that really the first thing that we should do as a museum is to adjust that element of the story so there is the bigger story about the port and east London and its people and there's the specific West Indies trade story. So the West Indies trade story, in a sense we thought that would be the best place to kick off a change for the whole museum, so that's really where that change first starts. (Interview with Tom Wareham (Wareham 2007))

This quote encapsulates the seeds of the birth of the Museum of Docklands, and consequently the birth of the 'London, Sugar and Slavery' exhibition. The 'threat of loss' of social history associated with the working history of the docks after their closure led to the substantial collection of associated materials and stories. However, from the time of collection in the 1980s to the time of opening in early 2000s (time) things had changed so much that the focal point had become about the people living in the area rather than the story of the docks. The forthcoming bicentenary provided an additional boost to rethink the gallery, given the building itself.

In 2004, prior to the 'London, Sugar and Slavery' exhibition, 'there was only a small display in a corner of the museum' on slavery (Spence 2011, 150). As Spence explains, this was due to the limited existing research on the role of the West India Docks in the slave trade and the first museum director's expertise on the working history of the river and the operation of the Port of London. In 2005 the museum decided to expand the interpretation of the slave trade because of the relevance to the building and the wider West India Dock environment (Spence 2011, 150). Although the bicentenary offered new funding opportunities (resources), it was clear that the initiative to create a new gallery was not simply because of this event.

The gallery was funded by several organisations, including the Heritage Lottery Fund, and co-shaped through debates and discussions with various African Caribbean organisations such as the Tower Hamlets African Caribbean Mental Health Organisation (THACMHO). The gallery displays a wide array of audiovisual materials including images, copies of paintings, films, music, maps and interactive displays, as well as 140 objects (Araujo 2012, 26).

The surroundings

Upon arrival, visitors to the museum experience the docks area. Although currently gentrified, it has plenty of reminders of the work and trade that once took place on the site. The building itself is a former sugar warehouse (No. 1 warehouse). The West India Import Dock, of which No. 1 warehouse is part, was opened in 1802 by the West India Dock Company. The first dock in London designed and built for trading, it remained in use until 1980.[3] Consequently, 'the building is a unique historic artefact that is testament to a crucial chapter in the history of Britain as well as the African Diaspora' (Spence 2011, 149). The displaced, now removed statue of the slave owner Robert Milligan shows the impact of the recent 'Black Lives Matter' movement, a movement relevant to the exhibition. While entering the museum, unlike the National Maritime Museum, the 'London, Sugar and Slavery' exhibition is the first that visitors will encounter; the lift takes them straight to the third floor where the exhibition is located.

The museum has developed walking tours to highlight surrounding landmarks associated with the British slave trade (Araujo 2012, 26). The tours emphasise the legacies of that history on contemporary London, a message conveyed through the exhibition. The tours mention the headquarters of the Corporation of London, for instance, which during the eighteenth and nineteenth centuries included shareholders of the Royal African Company. Other references include the life-size statue of Sir William Beckford (1709–70), a plantation owner and former mayor of London. It is located in Guildhall, at the east end of the south wall of the South Sea House building that housed the SSC (South Sea Company), crucial for the city's role in the Atlantic slave trade.

One of the most indicative examples illustrating the interrelationship between 'social change', 'museum activities' and 'relevance of exhibition to the surroundings' is the removal of the statue depicting Robert Milligan. The statue was commissioned by the West India Dock Company in 1809, but Milligan's associations with the slave trade were hidden till recently (Araujo 2012). The bicentenary prompted David Spence, then director of the museum, to call upon the community to reinterpret the statue of Robert Milligan. In the appeal, posted on the museum's website, it was stated that

> the wealth Milligan and his colleagues enjoyed was directly related to the suffering of many thousands of enslaved Africans who were forcibly removed from their homes in West Africa to work and die on the plantations. (Araujo 2012, 30)

Connections with the surrounding landscape are made on several occasions within the exhibition itself. For example, the panel that accompanies the reconstructed portrait depicting Lloyd Gordon as Robert Wedderburn (the son of an enslaved woman and slave owner James Wedderburn) reads:

> Wedderburn was distantly related to Andrew Wedderburn, Lord Loughborough and Chancellor of the Exchequer, whose name is inscribed on the foundation stone of the West India Dock. This monument can be seen at the exterior west end of this building.

The building

The very first text panel that a visitor encounters when entering the 'London, Sugar and Slavery' exhibition is an information panel about the building, which constitutes the number 1 object of the exhibition. The panel reads:

> You are standing on the top floor of one of London's oldest dock warehouses. A warehouse is a special type of building designed for storing goods.

The language is 'motional' in that it describes scenes rather than providing facts about specific dates and specific names; the emphasis is placed on 'people' and less so on time, facts or objects.

The significance of the surroundings and the building made the museum realise that it 'ought to be having something which permanently related this place to the subject, and as that became refined it was to concentrate very specifically on London and this location's involvement with transatlantic slavery' (interview with David Spence). He continues

> We are in a sugar warehouse built by the West India Merchants Committee built, erm … not just from the profits of the sugar i.e. the slave trade, but built specifically as part of the mechanism of the triangle. So we know from the CUP slaver data base records the names and dates and owners and captains of the slavers that left from the dock water not more than fifty metres from where we're sitting, we know where they sailed to West Africa, we know where they sailed to in the Caribbean with their cargo, the enslaved Africans, we know you know the CUP data some of the details about how many Africans were transported and how many survived, and those then goods primarily sugar here, but also sugar and rum which were loaded in the Caribbean and then moved back here in this dock. And because of the terms of the West India Committee investment building, it meant from its opening in 1802 until abolition of the trade or its enforcement in 1808 that erm there was a monopoly of the trade, so every single London slaver came in and out of this dock; we know that. So our research to date indicates that there are no other surviving buildings in the UK that have that relationship with the trade. There are plenty of buildings that can be built with profits from the trade but not specifically created by West India Committee merchants, who were absentee landlords, who also owned shipping interest and who also controlled the price of sugar from the home market in the UK in London. (Interview with David Spence (Spence 2007))

Spence thus describes the building occupied by the Museum of Docklands as 'a unique historic artefact that is testament to a crucial chapter in the history of Britain as well as African Diaspora' (Spence 2011, 149). This quote reveals how a museum building can potentially act as both an object (artefact) and a place (space). Emphasis is given on the 'past' temporal dimension – as the words 'history' and 'historic' stress – as well as the 'unique', national, international and 'evidential' (testament) value of this artefact. Spence further contends that the building also 'provides a means to examine the history of the city', expanding the spatial dimension to encompass the local, not just the national and international significance. From a 'dynamics perspective', the building fulfilled a certain purpose – that of storing products transported through the slave trade – from its construction. As soon as the slave trade was abolished, the building continued to serve as a storehouse since the dockyard only ceased operations in the 1980s, a change that led first to the abandonment and subsequently to the revitalisation of the area. The process of regeneration and development meant that the building was transformed into a piece of heritage, the difficult aspects of which were only explicitly acknowledged and displayed in 2007.

The building is part of a series of warehouses which received Grade I listing in 1950. The early date of their listing derives from the fact that out of the initial nine warehouses only Nos 1 (where the museum is located) and 2 survived the bombing of the Second World War. During the process of regeneration, No. 2 was converted in 1998–2000 into a mixture of apartments, restaurants and shops. No. 1, built between 1802 and 1804, was converted to become the Museum in Docklands in 2003. The buildings are part of the West India Dock conservation area, designated in 2007.[4]

The warehouse building constitutes a clear example of 'circular heritage'. It was converted from a warehouse to a Grade I listed building, then to a museum and finally to an 'exhibit' as well as a museum. Indeed, as reiterated in Chapter 4, each object/exhibit has its own life cycle – an exhibition is the amalgamation of the many life cycles of an object. The bicentenary provided a chance to recognise and promote unspoken values associated with the building. In the lead up to the opening of the museum, the warehouse's architectural value was prompted in the publicity materials, which praised it as a 'great monument of European Commercial Power' (Wemyss 2009, 42).

Narrative-making

One of the first objects encountered is a painting by Huggins, dating from 1827. The descriptive caption of the painting does not contain details about the art (as is the case at the NMM), but on the connections that trade and merchants had with the slave trade. At NMM there is only a minor reference; here the caption emphasises the fact that a 'ship of this size would also have carried around 500 African men, women and children into slavery per voyage'. At NMM a dehumanised approach is taken, epitomised by equalising enslaved Africans with trade products, while the 'London, Sugar and Slavery' narrative emphasises the human dimensions. The connections of the ships' names with enslavement are made clear. The dramatic tone of the 'London, Sugar and Slavery' gallery is exacerbated by the display of hundreds of names of enslaved Africans next to the titles of the exhibition, establishing a 'somber mood' (Danbolt 2019, 68). Interestingly, while the path is less flexible than that of the NMM, a delineated structure enables navigation.

A comparison between the introductory panels that feature in the two galleries is of interest here.

> Behind the growth of London as a centre of finance and commerce from the 1700s onwards lay one of the **great crimes against humanity.** In the **unprecedented rush to accumulate huge wealth,** societies and tribal communities throughout West Africa were **disrupted beyond repair; tens of millions of people were displaced and transported; millions were exploited, tortured and killed.** At the heart of these developments, London became a locus of numbers of Africans caught up in the tumult. (author's emphasis emphasis)

The introductory panel at 'London, Sugar and Slavery' makes a direct link to the legacies of the history that explain London's wealth today. The language is 'emotional' in that it uses adjectives and expressions articulating the pain and suffering of 'enslaved Africans'. Danbolt notes how 'reproductions of paintings of Africans in London in the eighteenth and nineteenth century, as well as contemporary photographs presenting Londoners of African descent today, dominate the panel'; together with video screens from the streets of London and beaches of Ghana and Barbados, they combine to indicate this intimate relationship between past and present (Danbolt 2019).

Overall the gallery consists mostly of panels with printed quotes from poems and speeches by historical figures and image reproductions 'that are enlarged, cropped and magnified' making 'the panel visually dynamic and give it a collage-like nature' (Danbolt 2019, 68). The story is global, but the geographical focus is local. On the other hand the 'old' gallery at the NMM highlights the power of the British Empire, generating feelings of national pride.

The exhibition did not have many objects and thus relied on the reproduction of images. This, in a way, provided the freedom to choose objects or images of objects depicting the intended narrative and messages. At the NMM the opposite occurred, with the available objects dictating the narrative. We see, for instance, the reproduction of imagery of former enslaved men who thrived once they gained their freedom or elsewhere. The focus is not so much about the past (as at NMM), but more on the impact of the past in the present. The African presence is stressed from the eighteenth century until the present; the impact of stereotypical imagery and inequality are also highlighted.

Although the gallery is dramatic throughout, a few 'beats' can be detected. One such 'beat' is the picture of the 'Gate of no return!' Language was discussed thoroughly between the curatorial team and the consultation panels and an entire panel is dedicated to terminology. It stresses the need to avoid the dehumanisation of enslaved Africans:

> We have tried to be careful in our use of language in this gallery. In particular we have tried to avoid using terms that strip individuals of their humanity – since this was a tactic central to the imposition of slavery. The word 'slave', for example, implies a thing or commodity rather than a human being. We have used the term 'enslaved African' wherever possible. In the main we have avoided using the terms 'Black' and 'White', preferring 'African' or 'European'. But in the Legacies section of the gallery we engage with the term 'Black' as it is used to refer to the non-White post-war migrant settlers in Britain.

It could be argued that 'the use of the first-person plural here creates a kind of intimacy' (Pillière 2018), as if the museum is explaining its actions and implicitly asking the visitor too to reflect on the use of language. At the same time there is a marked attempt on the part of the museum to separate itself from previous events and attitudes, as the conscious choice of the term 'enslaved' as opposed to 'slave' illustrates (Pillière 2018). The visitor is also invited to reconsider and reinterpret this history by understanding its relevance to contemporary London.

> Londoners are proud of the fact that their city has always been a diverse city. Our urban landscape with its galleries, museums and monumental buildings bears witness to the millions who sweated, both here and around the world, to make it the great city it is.
>
> It was not only bankers, shippers and insurers who grew rich off the back of enslaved labour. Today we all benefit from the commercial and material success developed on that historical base.
>
> In our everyday lives do we think about this, and remember that Africa beats in the heart of our city?

Contrary to the exclusive *we* used at the beginning of the gallery to refer to the multiple actors involved in the writing of the interpretative labels, the inclusive *we* at the end of the gallery clearly appeals to Londoners and residents in the UK: 'our urban landscape' … 'we all benefit' … 'our city' (Pillière 2018).

The way in which language is used to describe certain objects point towards the same direction. For instance, one emotional object was the description of the sugar cane. The description is not factual; it rather focuses on what it meant to work on a sugar cane plantation: 'However, the cane has sharp-edged leaves and those harvesting it by hand often sustained painful cuts and injuries'.

From a 'dynamics' point of view, the text initially constitutes a narrative that emphasises that this story is a global story as much as one about London. Towards the end of the gallery, the narrative message has evolved to highlight that this 'story' is in fact a story with which each of us relates: 'this is your story as much as it is my story'. The 'space' is utilised to reinforce this connection as much as possible:

> Some of these slaving ships sailed from the dock outside this museum. The sugar and rum they carried back was stored where you are now standing.

The history related to the abolition of the slave trade also endeavoured to provide an inclusive picture of the story, highlighting the role of women and other lesser-known abolitionists. Before the story of the abolition the visitor has the chance to engage not only with the resistance of enslaved Africans against the slave trade, but also with contemporary exhibitions co-created with African communities.

Unlike the NMM exhibition – based on chronological and spatial elements to produce an exhibition narrative that aims to 'inspire and mobilise cohesive societal commitments based on the dynamics of recognition, identification, affirmation and judgment' (Bonnell and Simon 2007, 65), the 'London, Sugar and Slavery' exhibition

> seeks to do the exact opposite, that is to use the dynamics of recognition and identification to unsettle received narratives about the past and/or to produce new forms of subjectivity. (Witcomb 2013, 255)

It does so by 'modeling the process of historical inquiry through the use of affective strategies of interpretation' (Witcomb 2013, 256).

Affective exhibition assemblages

How is affect being created at the 'London, Sugar and Slavery' exhibition? The process of affect is dynamic and systemic. At LSS the combination of objects, language and other interpretation media aim to generate feelings of sorrow, pain and even guilt as the gallery reminds us that this history belongs to everyone. The affective nature of exhibition narratives is the result of the intersection of 'emotional and affective entanglements with both human and non-human elements: texts, people, discourses, objects, practices and spaces' (Munroe 2016, 115). In other words, each of the above components cannot trigger emotional responses alone; it is the *interaction* of all the elements that results in an emotional response. An exhibition that uses affect in their interpretation strategies works

> poetically to provoke unsettlement in their viewers by playing with their collective memories about the past, challenging them to rethink who they think they are and who they think they are viewing. (Witcomb 2013, 256)

This contention can certainly be validated by the visitor responses to the 'Atlantic Worlds' and 'London, Sugar and Slavery' exhibitions. The latter uses affect through combining texts, objects, sounds, lights and spaces to reflect critical thinking in the visitor responses (Smith et al. 2014).

If affective assemblages derive from the interconnections of texts, objects and space, it is no wonder why the design – and community participation in it – is critical. The design of an exhibition serves as the 'social glue' that connects the assemblage's components. Objects have the capacity to influence the text and tone of the museum, turning something which at first glance appears fairly neutral into something that conveys a vastly different meaning (Munroe 2016, 127).

However, objects by themselves are not enough. In the 'London, Sugar and Slavery' gallery a number of items had the capacity to affect the tone and trajectory of the narrative. In particular, the consultative group highlighted the affective weight of images and texts of brutality, punishment and torture of enslaved people. The curator stated:

> One of the issues that we were made aware of is that some of these items have different significances for the African Caribbean community. If you put a slave collar up, for example, it is seen in a different way [by them]. They made us aware that these relics had a very different emotional impact [for them].

As mentioned above, the African Caribbean group expressed concerns that an emphasis on pain and suffering as demonstrated through objects and images of torture would undermine the narrative on resistance. Moreover, the group was anxious that the display of such objects might reinforce the status of the enslaved as dehumanised, helpless victims. Because of this, the LSS gallery has a limited number of images and artefacts concerned with brutality. Indeed, the group had diverse and often conflicting opinions regarding the imagery, objects and text; some group members stressed the significance of clearly demonstrating the brutality and suffering, but others felt that such a portrayal would cultivate images of victimisation and stereotypes, diverting from the message of resistance and rebellion (Bressey and Wareham 2010; Fouseki 2010, 184). Two of the community representatives, for instance, emphasised that:

> **We started with the narrative**, what is it that we want to tell … there was a big debate and [Name of participant] was saying 'I want the pain, there is this pain that I am carrying and my people are carrying that we need to tell. London needs to know about this pain and it's one of the main problems of many of my people'. There was an immediate resistance from [Name of participant 2] … 'No, this [exhibition] will be about the untold history of [Place of city where museum is located]'. (07comM106 2008 in Fouseki 2010, 184)

Similarly, another respondent mentioned:

> I would like to mention that I am a bit disappointed with the exhibition because … I felt that … the space is … very white and clinical … and when you speak about slavery … you should try to make the viewer see how horrible it was. (07ComC1022008 in Fouseki 2010, 184)

David Spence acknowledges the tensions and conflicting voices among the group.

> How, for example, to reconcile the conflicting views from a black mother who didn't want her son to grow up with negative stereotypical messages about black people being the subject of oppression but wanted positive messages and role models, and the black older who wanted the whole terrible truth of enslavement, whips, chains and instruments of torture to be present in the gallery? (2011, 158)

To address this challenge, it was decided that the gallery should have two 'show states' (the exhibition itself is dynamic). The first – more conventional – would comprise a normal gallery visit with text on walls, objects in showcases, touch screen interactives and so on. The second state would be a *son et lumiere* experience that transformed the gallery. Every 20 minutes the gallery lights would be lowered and a sound and light show lasting three minutes provide a dramatic intervention; powerful images would play over walls and showcases, including the Buxton table (that is the table on which Buxton, William Wilberforce and other abolitionists drafted the 1833 bill to abolish slavery throughout the British Empire), with the voice describing what happened to enslaved Africans. 'Your children will be taken away from you; you will be beaten; you will not keep your name'; 'you are to be stripped of your name, you are to be taken from your loved ones, you are to be brutalised' (Spence 2011, 158). The show provokes a form of 'empathetic unsettlement' that can make people think that enslavement could happen to anyone (LaCapra 1999). Danbolt observes that

> not without pathos, this direct address calls us to reflect on the unimaginable violence of being reduced to property, while also asking us to remember the continual history of resistance, of people surviving against all odds. (Danbolt 2019, 71)

So far, I have shown that the interpretation strategies mounted by the two galleries are in opposition. While the National Maritime Museum adopts a one-dimensional, standardised approach (with the exception of the 'Work in Progress' section), the London, Sugar and Slavery gallery has a multi-layered narrative consisting of a 'standard' form of exhibit, a rotating 'sound and light show' and a 're-interpretation' gallery space. In addition, the affective techniques employed are different. For instance, one of the typical objects displayed in many galleries at the time was 'shackles', an object that many African Caribbean visitors find disturbing. It is worth comparing the captions accompanying the same object to comprehend the different intentions better. A display showcase at the National Maritime Museum with multiple shackles is accompanied by this caption:

> On board slave ships, captive Africans were kept below decks for most of the time. Men, women and children were segregated. Men were usually kept shackled, handcuffed in pairs by their wrists and iron leg-rings inverted to their ankles. Frequently, they had so little

> space that they could only lie on their sides and could not sit or stand up.

This caption is certainly less factual, possibly as a result of the consultation, although this description depicts enslaved Africans as passive victims overshadowing the resistance and battle against the slave trade and enslavement. At the Museum of Docklands, the display case displays one object (a punishment collar) accompanied by the following caption:

> This **horrific** object would be placed around a man or woman's neck to discourage any attempt to run away. The arms of the collar extended overhead to snag in sugar cane or low foliage.

Likewise, the curators were also divided, with one curator mentioning that

> We didn't want this to be a story about Africans being tortured and beaten. We wanted to make it clear it happened, but we wanted to concentrate on a positive story of Africans resisting. (07ComM122007 in Cubitt 2014, 236)

The visitors also received the display of atrocity materials generated in different ways (Cubitt 2014), with one visitor commenting that the physicality of the objects makes the concept real:

> For example, the display unit you have over there that shows the neck brace, things like that, it does make you very emotional, because it does make you see it existed, it's not that something that is being talked about, it really did exist, you can physically see it, and that does make you quite emotional. (Cubitt 2014, 254)

Participation dynamics

One of the most critical aspects in the dynamics of participatory exhibitions is trust (e.g. Fouseki 2010; Lynch 2013; Lynch and Alberti 2010). The degree of trust and ownership is reflected in the language used. One of the main factors determining the degree of acceptance of an initial museum invitation by community participants is that of pre-existing 'positive collaborations' with museum staff or panel members (see Fig. 5.5). An additional factor is the involvement of the director. Interestingly, while the trust at the National Maritime Museum gradually deteriorated because the physical and metaphorical space to affect the narrative was declining, the reverse occurred at the Museum of Docklands. Here trust increased, especially after the director's suggestion that the curators should co-author the text with the consultative panel. We therefore see a strong connection between offering the space to negotiate and co-decide and the experience of trust; mixing abilities and skills was an additional factor to this.

The findings support Lynch's analysis of how trust in participatory exhibition projects develops. Providing the space for dialogue and negotiation (see also Fouseki and Smith 2013), being brave with conflict and debate (Lynch 2013; Lynch 2011) and sharing authority between museum staff and consultative groups (Lynch and Alberti 2010) are only some of the techniques to employ in developing a mutual relationship of trust between museum staff and consultative groups. Or, as Lynch and Alberti argue,

> Museums must develop a new form of trust. This radical trust is based on the idea that shared authority is more effective at creating and guiding culture than institutional control. (2010, 15; see also Lynch 2013)

Radical trust implies that the museum cannot control the outcome (Lynch and Alberti 2010, 30).

'Time' is also a critical factor in sustaining trust and collaboration. Time is a constraint for any single involvement in the delivery of an exhibition project. However, there is a reinforcing relationship between 'trust' and 'time': the more time communities are given to collaborate with the museum staff, the stronger is the feeling of trust and ownership. The opposite is also true: the stronger the trust, the more willing a community group is to dedicate time to the project.

The notion of trust was critical in the sustainability of the consultation. The director's personal involvement in the London, Sugar and Slavery exhibition conveyed the message to the consultative group that this project was of strategic significance. 'The dynamics of the consultative group were to prove critical to the success of the project' (Spence 2011, 152). Spence attended and chaired every single meeting, indicating that this exhibition was a personal and institutional priority.

> The gallery project became a transformative agent for the museum and became in many ways synonymous with the organisation's

aspirations to become a more diverse institution. (Spence 2011, 152)

A participatory process is not easy. It requires time for negotiation, dialogue and co-creation. One of the greatest challenges in the consultation process was the finalisation of the text panels. When the first text panels were presented to the consultative group, nine months after the initial discussions, 'the museum hit a serious problem' (Spence 2011, 158). The text written by the curators was 'simply not recognised by the group as being their own' (Spence 2011, 158) because the text did not contain the urgency of the group's desire to convey that this was a new history that had not been heard before. This only occurred two weeks before the deadline. It was at this stage that the director proposed for the group to nominate a member to work closely with one of the curators and rewrite the entire text.

Therefore, in exhibition projects where participation remained at the level of consultation, the process of community involvement declined as the time of the opening approached. On the other hand, in museums such as the Museum of London, Docklands, the process of participation was increasing. To this end there was a lack of objects and possibly prior extensive experience.

One dynamic loop that is of significance is that the more active the participation the more space is needed, since the voices involved are more diverse (see Fig. 5.5). There is also a reinforcing relationship with time – the later designers get involved, the later the space to exhibit is allocated. One of our interviewees who had worked closely with the communities underscored the negotiation processes undertaken for securing a sufficiently large space for the re-interpretation section. The 'physical' space would ultimately determine the 'symbolic' space attributed to a community group for co-creation.

The fact that a gallery is co-created does not necessarily imply that it will not be controversial. On the contrary: the gallery is likely to be subject to stronger reactions in comparison with galleries that adopt a 'neutral' approach (if such a thing exists). Indeed, one visitor wrote a letter of complaint, copied to the Mayor of London, demanding changes: this was 'a reaction to the terminology' (Spence 2011, 158). As Spence rightly puts it, a museum may not be a neutral space, but it is a 'safe space' in which to debate differences and similarities, a location that allows individuals to abandon their 'comfort zones' and to leave written comments.

The fluidity of permanence

The 'permanence' of a gallery does not imply that it is stagnant. In the case of the Museum of Docklands a temporary, fluid exhibition space has been dedicated to co-created work with communities, allowing periodic reinterpretations (Fig. 5.5). The panel introducing the space reads:

> **VIEWPOINTS**
>
> This space is for small, changing displays that complement the **London, Sugar and Slavery** gallery. We work with experts to present the latest historical research and with Londoners of all ages to explore issues covered in the gallery.

David Spence has argued the importance of the fact that 'the gallery continues to change and develop' (Spence 2011, 161). In addition to the 're-interpretation wall', a meeting was recently organised to explore the gallery's future. The meeting concluded that in terms of 'time' there is need for permanent as well as temporary events that allow multivocality; in terms of 'space' there is need to spread the story across both museums (i.e. Museum of London and Museum of Docklands) and the future relocated museum. In terms of 'values', however, there is a need to include more digital means to enable people do their own research.

The dynamics of the surroundings

The 2020 'Black Lives Matter' movement led to the removal of the statue of Robert Milligan, a prominent British slave trader, that 'had stood uncomfortably outside' the museum for years[5]. The museum staff were keenly aware of the statue's problematic background, but the momentum of the protests gave the museum the agency to act. The removal of this statue was just one of many that occurred after the removal of the statue of Edward Colston in Bristol. Robert Milligan was hooded at the opening of the new London, Sugar and Slavery gallery at the Museum of London, Docklands in 2007. The Museum of London recognised

> that the monument is part of the ongoing problematic regime of white-washing history, which disregards the pain of those who are still wrestling with the remnants of the crimes Milligan committed against humanity.

The statue of Robert Milligan was covered with fabric and a 'Black Lives Matter' sign before its removal. As the museum's statement read:

> The statue of Robert Milligan has stood uncomfortably outside the Museum of London Docklands for a long time, one of only three museums in the UK to address the history of the transatlantic slave trade ... At the Museum of London we stand against upholding structures that reproduce violence, and have previously engaged in interventions that critically engage with pro-slavery lobbying.
>
> We are committed to the processes of learning and unlearning as fostered in our London, Sugar & Slavery gallery, which opened in 2007 at the Museum of London Docklands ... The museum, being another physical manifestation of slavery situated in an old sugar warehouse, constantly challenges the contentious nature of this history.
>
> Now more than ever at a time when Black Lives Matter is calling for an end to public monuments honouring slave owners, we advocate for the statue of Robert Milligan to be removed on the grounds of its historical links to colonial violence and exploitation.

The statement indicates the dialogical interrelationship between 'social change', surroundings and museum space (see Fig. 5.1).

The National Maritime Museum took a different approach, announcing that it deliberately did not

> issue a statement in response to the Black Lives Matter movement because we believe that change in society will only come through committed action and consequently we look to our work as a museum in contributing to that change.
>
> RMG holds a significant collection in relation to the Trans-Atlantic Slave Trade, and we have contributed significantly to research, learning materials and exhibitions (ref the Understanding Slavery Initiative), which we regularly update. Indeed, we have just

completed an intervention in one of our galleries to bring a more current perspective that was planned over a year ago; this is currently viewable in our 'Atlantic Worlds' gallery. We will do more.

Nelson is celebrated in two galleries dedicated to him at the Museum. Nelson's enduring appeal is his complexity as both vulnerable and heroic, weak and strong, clever and naive. We have no plans to change our presentation or interpretation of him at present, but inevitably will do so in the future, to ensure his continuing interest to future generations.[6]

However, the Atlantic Worlds gallery contains a panel related to the removal of the figure head of the *Royal George*. It reads:

Removal of the figurehead of the Royal George

For many visitors and staff its imagery of a powerful white king with two subservient black men is a hurtful reinforcement of enduring racial stereotypes. ... Monarchs are typically portrayed as the dominant figures, with others shown in a secondary and more deferential stance. However, this figurehead is often seen as celebrating the role of White people in ending slavery. Such images overshadow the determined actions and huge sacrifices of Black people to achieve this goal.

The events of late spring and summer 2020 lent further urgency to the ongoing programme of changes in this gallery. In August the figurehead was removed and placed in storage.

The caption below the picture of the figurehead reads:

The gold-painted figurehead from the Royal yacht *Royal George* (1817) shows George III with two kneeling African men on either side. He wears a laurel wreath, the emblem of victory.

Even if the figurehead is absent from the gallery space, however, it is still visible in the digital space:

The figurehead of the Royal Yacht 'Royal George' shows George III in the guise of a Roman emperor, wearing a laurel wreath, a signifier of victory. On either side are **two kneeling African men with hands clasped** (although the arms of the figure on the king's right have been damaged) ... The stance of the African men has drawn obvious comparison with the famous kneeling figure on Wedgwood's anti-slavery plague, which was produced in the late 1780s with the motto 'Am I not a man and a brother?' This powerful and highly adaptable piece of abolitionist propaganda became the symbol of the Society for Effecting the Abolition of the Slave Trade ... **It is tempting to suppose that the imagery of the figurehead might allude to the abolition campaign or be a commentary on the fact that the British trade ended during George III's reign.** But it is very unlikely indeed that such an overt political statement, seemingly a direct alignment of the monarch with the abolitionist cause, would be incorporated into the iconography of a royal yacht. Moreover, although the figures kneel in a similar imploring gesture, they are not a direct copy of the Wedgwood design, where the beseeching African is clearly enslaved and bound in chains. However, given their immediate proximity to the king, it would be perfectly appropriate for any figure – human, animal or mythological – to be depicted in a deferential stance. **It is, therefore, a distinct probability that any resemblance to the abolitionist emblem is coincidental.** All of this makes the celebration of national victory a far more plausible interpretation. **The interpretation of the object certainly does not reflect the views of the African Caribbean community but rather the curatorial.**[7] (author's emphasis)

The fact that the online descriptions are more detailed, reflective and, possibly, more dynamic than the ones in the gallery space is indicative of the huge potential that digital interpretation has to foster multivocality and interactivity, in conjunction with and beyond the 'physical' gallery space.

Conclusion

In this chapter various aspects of 'exhibition dynamics' were analysed, including aspects that correlated with the dynamics of participation of exhibition development, the dynamics of exhibition narrative and the dynamic change of exhibitions after their inauguration. I drew on two London galleries exhibiting the hidden and difficult history of 'transatlantic slave trade' – the 'London, Sugar and Slavery' exhibition at the

Museum of Docklands and the 'Atlantic Worlds' exhibition at the National Maritime Museum. I argued that museums should not be seen in isolation from their local and social context. Even 'national museums', such as the National Maritime Museum, are an integral part of their local surroundings – a connection that local communities expect to be portrayed in the gallery. I alleged that while the two museums adopted a fundamentally different approach in constructing the exhibition narrative, the 'Atlantic Worlds' ultimately embraced a similar approach to that of the Museum of Docklands, as shown in the 'Work in Progress' section.

Both galleries were destined to be 'permanent' fixtures in their respective institutions. Both were planned prior to 2007, the bicentenary of the abolition of the slave trade in Britain and an occasion that secured funding from Heritage Lottery Fund for both galleries. However, the narrative development was radically different between the two sites. The 'London, Sugar and Slavery' exhibition endorsed an emphasis on local (London) and the contemporary impacts of the transatlantic slave trade today. Housed in a former sugar warehouse, the building itself was 'objectified', becoming part of the exhibition. The language is emotional, dramatic and personal. The exhibition is narrative-driven, underpinned by multivocality that represents the diverse voices of the participants. 'London, Sugar and Slavery' thus relies more on audiovisuals and text panels and less on objects to convey its message. The participation itself proved to be a challenging but rewarding process. Towards the end of the project the 'consultation panel' worked more intensively with the curatorial teams to finalise the text.

On the other hand the 'Atlantic Worlds' exhibition, mounted by a national museum, maintained a 'distanced', less empathetic language. Its factual, academic and at times Euro-centric narrative revolved around notions of national pride. The gallery is object-driven in that the available collection shaped the narrative. The 'consultation panel' was divided into two sub-panels, an 'academic' and a 'cultural' panel. As the gallery development progressed, participation was diluted and multivocality decreased. Figure 5.10 provides a holistical portrayal of the exhibition dynamics as a systemic practice; segments of this diagram have already been discussed in the sections above.

Finally, I demonstrated that the dynamics of an exhibition do not end at the time of its inauguration. In both cases it became apparent that the galleries and their surroundings were subject to constant change. The LSS had already embedded a changeable exhibition wall

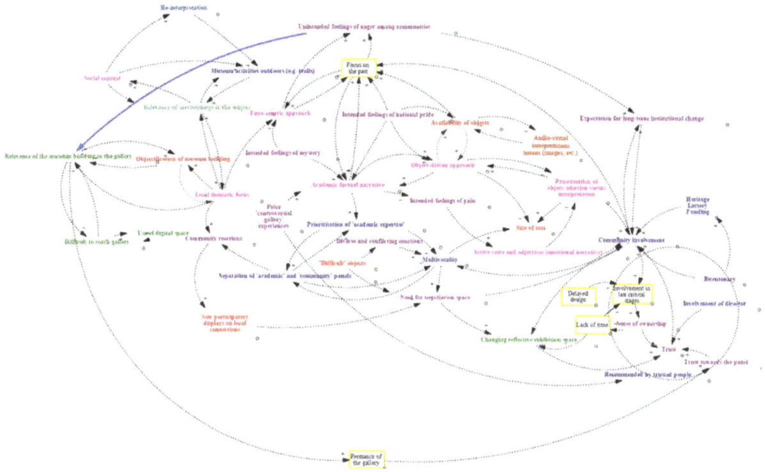

Fig. 5.10 Exhibition dynamics.

(re-interpretation wall) dedicated to periodically changing, co-created exhibitions. The 'Black Lives Matter' movement led to the removal of the statue of Robert Milligan that stood in front of the Museum of Docklands. Yet the 'Atlantic Worlds' exhibition did not remain uninfluenced. A 'Work in Progress' section now acknowledges the significance of connecting the gallery with the local history and legacies of this history today. It remains to be seen what further changes this section will inspire in the rest of the gallery.

In taking an 'exhibition dynamics' approach, it is important to think of an exhibition not just as a project with a fixed starting and completion date, consisting of linear steps and milestones along the way, but rather as a complex, socio-cultural, dynamic practice inseparable from the social and geographic context. A continuous reflective approach before, during and after the exhibition can underpin its development process, making exhibitions more responsive, relevant and engaging to the wider communities of which they are part. A systemic approach to exhibition development also calls for the various departments of a museum institution, especially of large museum institutions which are compartmentalised in distinct departments, to work together as one aspect/dimension is immediately interconnected with another. The involvement of the museum director in participatory exhibition projects is recommended as a means of generating trust and commitment among participants.

Notes

1. https://collections.rmg.co.uk/collections/objects/6280.html.
2. https://archives.history.ac.uk/1807commemorated/interviews/wareham.html.
3. https://historicengland.org.uk/listing/the-list/list-entry/1242440.
4. https://www.towerhamlets.gov.uk/Documents/Planning-and-building-control/Development-control/Conservation-areas/West-India-DockV1.pdf.
5. lr-misc-docks-milligan-statue.pdf (museumoflondon.org.uk).
6. https://www.rmg.co.uk/national-maritime-museum-response-weekend-news-articles.
7. https://collections.rmg.co.uk/collections/objects/18805.html.

6
'Dissonant heritage' dynamics

December 2000. I have just embarked upon my first 'proper', 'paid' job as an archaeologist at the then Organisation for the Construction of the New Acropolis Museum. My first task may not have been as exciting as I had possibly hoped (I was collating and organising photographs from the ongoing archaeological excavations on the Makriyianni plot where the museum was built). However, the fact that I was working on the slopes of the Acropolis Hill still seemed to me like a dream. A few months later, this 'dreamscape' was disrupted by 'screams' and 'shouts' from outside the temporary storage room where we used to work. Apparently, as I was informed, this was not an infrequent phenomenon. The residents of the surrounding blocks of flats that were scheduled to be demolished to enhance the museum's surroundings were reacting strongly against the decision.

That incident was a turning point for my future studies. After four years of studying archaeology and art history, it was only then that I realised archaeology is as much about the present as it is about the past. I decided to pursue a postgraduate degree in Cultural Heritage Studies, a degree that fundamentally changed my way of thinking about archaeology and its relevance to the present. Now, 20 years later, the New Acropolis Museum has been built and the surrounding blocks of flats demolished; the museum is globally admired and attracts large numbers of visitors. However, most of them are not aware of the lengthy, controversial debates with which the museum construction was associated. Although this recent dissonant history is an integral part of the Acropolis's narrative, it is largely an invisible story.

Heritage is inherently dissonant (Fouseki 2008; 2015; see also Smith 2006, 82). This is because there are multiple, and often conflicting, values attributed to heritage (e.g. Ashworth et al. 2007, 3). As a result 'heritage dissonance', as a condition of discordance or lack of agreement as to the meanings of heritage (Tunbridge and Ashworth 1996, 21), is often inevitable. Although this is widely acknowledged in heritage literature, how 'heritage dissonance' manifests itself as a 'social practice' is less discussed or known.

This chapter aims to investigate the dynamics of 'heritage dissonance'. It does so by an in-depth exploration of one of the most contested museums in the world – the New Acropolis Museum in Athens, Greece. The construction of the Acropolis Museum located on the 'Makriyianni plot' beneath the slopes of the Acropolis Hill underwent a remarkably lengthy history of controversies and delays. While the seeds for constructing a new, 'modern' museum for the Acropolis and its monuments were planted in 1976, the museum was only inaugurated in 2009, due to contestation and disputes. By drawing on this controversial museum project, I attempt to explore a series of critical questions: Why did the construction of the museum lead to such lengthy debates? What contributed to the dissonant nature of the museum construction? How did this dissonance evolve over time? What new insights about 'dissonant heritage' can we gain by examining this case study? What are the implications of deconstructing the mechanisms of 'heritage dissonance' for heritage management?

Through the meta-interpretation analysis of 356 newspaper articles and personal communications that I have analysed elsewhere (e.g. Fouseki 2006; 2008; 2015), I will demonstrate that the nature of the core 'heritage dynamics' elements (i.e. values/meanings, materials, skills/competencies, senses/emotions, space/place, resources, time) is fluid and hybrid. For instance, one of the main elements in the emergence and evolution of opposition to the construction of the New Acropolis Museum was the 'visual contact' of the modern museum building with the Acropolis Hill monument. This, according to the museum's opponents, would affect the aesthetics of the 'sacred' historic urban landscape. On the other hand, for the supporters of the museum, the 'visual contact' was a prerequisite as it would allow the 'reunification' of the Parthenon Marbles, displayed abroad away from their original context, with the monument they originally derive from. Initial discourses on 'visual contact' revolved around 'aesthetic sensory perceptions', merging senses and values together. However, over time 'visual contact' was associated with place and space. The 'visual contact' of the museum with the Acropolis Hill meant that the two sites would be united. One site was meant to function as the projection of the other. Ultimately, the architect approached 'visual contact' almost as a 'material' in the museum's design.

In what ways is the deconstruction of the mechanisms of 'heritage dissonance' significant for heritage theory and heritage management? On a theoretical level, although the dissonant nature of heritage has been discussed and analysed through case studies, the ways in which it manifests and evolves remain unexplored. It is therefore essential to unpack the mechanisms of heritage dissonance in order to 'deal' with the concept in a more effective manner. As mentioned above, heritage is inherently dissonant; it is imbued by a wide range of values which often stand in conflict with each other. Such an acknowledgement should form the foundation of any heritage management plan or project. In other words, any disputes or conflicts should not arise as unexpected, nor should they be a surprise. Once this is recognised, a 'dispute management' section could be incorporated into any heritage management plan.

By 'dispute management' I do not imply that disputes and controversies are a negative aspect that needs to be prevented or resolved. On the contrary: with dissonance recognised as an inherent element in heritage, I would like to stress the importance of accepting it and, by doing so, allowing time, resources and space for negotiation, dialogue and participatory planning. What I propose extends far beyond the standard, short-term, top-down consultations that we often see occurring in heritage management. I contend that 'embedding' a 'dispute management' strategy into the broader heritage management framework will underpin the entire duration of the heritage project (see also Fouseki 2008; 2015). By doing so, on a practical level, huge delays in implementing a project can be avoided. More significantly, if we accept that heritage is a 'common good' (Silverman and Ruggles 2007), integrating a dispute management strategy into heritage management will enable a heritage project properly to reflect the multivocality of opinions.

The New Acropolis Museum as a contested arena – a historic outline

Disputes around the construction of the New Acropolis Museum emerged back in the 1970s, as soon as the then Prime Minister, Konstantinos Karamanlis, approved the construction of a new museum on the 'Makriyianni plot', beneath the Acropolis Hill. The museum construction plans constituted part of a wider restoration programme on the Acropolis monument which was instigated in 1974, the year that marked the end of the seven-year military dictatorship in Greece (Fouseki 2006). The construction of a 'new' museum on the Acropolis

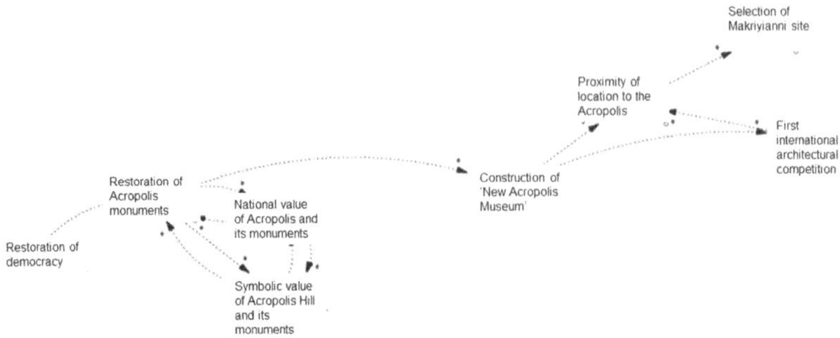

Fig. 6.1 The dynamics of the early stages of the New Acropolis Museum's construction.

slopes generated accusations that the new building could not be aesthetically integrated into the surrounding 'sacred' and 'emblematic' Acropolis landscape (Hamilakis and Yalouri 1999). Despite these initial concerns, two national architectural competitions were announced, in 1976 and 1979 respectively, in which proposals were invited for a new museum on the Makriyianni plot. None of the competitors was successful, however. Instead the judging committee concluded that the architects had not provided adequate information regarding the stability of the building and its aesthetic integration into the historic landscape (Fouseki 2006; see also Ntaflou 2012) (Fig. 6.1).

The architectural competitions proved to be challenging, in that they were governed by national law yet were endeavouring to resolve a local problem. This focused on the specific needs of the Parthenon Sculptures in terms of space and light implemented in a small plot (Kontaratos 1978), located in a densely inhabited historic core. The solutions submitted were not regarded as satisfactory and thus did not lead to any results (Filippides 1992).

So far, the dynamic interplay between the 'space/place' of the historic landscape and its projection into the future museum can be noted (Fig. 6.2). The Acropolis Hill and its surroundings are imbued with national emblematic and aesthetic values (referred to as 'aesthetic sacredness' by Yalouri 2001). The new museum is aimed at enhancing the 'national' value by providing a suitable **space** for the archaeological objects (**materials**) of the site, but it is viewed by a few architects as an 'aesthetic sacrilege' for the surrounding landscape (**place**). Therefore, although **symbolically** the museum is in harmony with the Acropolis, **spatially** it antagonises the surrounding landscape.

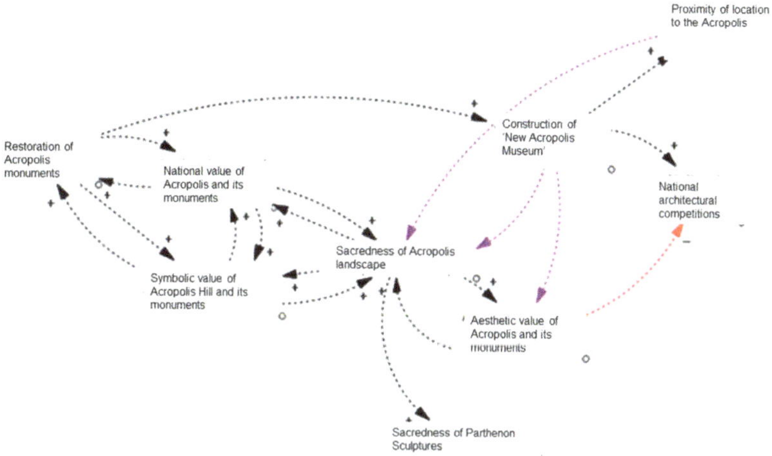

Fig. 6.2 Interrelationships between 'national' and 'sacred' values on the Acropolis Hill.

The early oppositions are 'aesthetic-oriented' in that they revolve around the 'sacred' and 'symbolic' aesthetics of the surrounding historic environment. The figure indicates an inherent dissonance. While the 'new' museum is intended to enhance the national, aesthetic and symbolic values of the Acropolis objects and monuments (hence the stress upon the need to locate it in the proximity), this is materialised, according to opponents of the museum, at the expense of the aesthetic and symbolic values of the surrounding landscape. The nature of dissonance is two-dimensional. Firstly, there is conflict between the 'new materiality' of the museum building and the 'ancient, symbolic' value (as expressed by the Acropolis). There are consequently two contested spaces and two contested sets of materialities and values that need to co-exist. Secondly, there is conflict between the values of the symbolic space (Acropolis) and its material objects, with the latter benefiting from a large museum. To put it simply, the museum construction appeared within an already 'contested' environment. The word 'antagonism' used in newspaper articles at the time is characteristic of the contested nature between the two spaces. Later architectural designs aimed to instigate a dialogue between these two spaces.

What later seems to alleviate this antagonistic relationship is the rising claim for the 'repatriation' and 'reunification' of the 'Parthenon Sculptures' with the Parthenon Temple through the new museum. The claim for the 'repatriation' of the 'Parthenon Sculptures' was led by

Melina Mercouri, an internationally renowned actress who undertook the leadership of the Ministry of Culture in the 1980s. In 1984 Mercouri filed a restitution request with UNESCO's Intergovernmental Committee (Kynourgiopoulou 2011, 158). Certainly the construction of a 'new' museum would invigorate the repatriation claim, since the old Acropolis Museum on the Acropolis Hill had already been proved inadequate. On 16 May 1989 an international architectural competition for the construction of the New Acropolis Museum was announced. The legal claim for 'restitution' evolved gradually to a 'political' and 'symbolic' claim for 'repatriation' and 'reunification' (Fouseki 2014).

For this international competition three possible locations were proposed. The options consisted of the Makriyianni area, the site of the Dionysos Restaurant and the Koile site, to the west of the Philopappos Hill. The Makriyianni plot is occupied by non-listed and listed buildings with a distinct set of values, from the architectural and historic to the religious and symbolic (Fouseki 2006). The 'visual contact' of the museum with the Acropolis Hill, a key concern for the selection of the most appropriate site, was guaranteed by all three locations. However, all sites ran the risk of new archaeological discoveries being made, which would inevitably delay the construction of the museum. This was soon proved.

The winning design of the 1989 international competition was awarded to the Italian architects M. Nicoletti and L. Passarelli, whose design was located in the Makriyianni area. Their design proposed an interior space organised by the dimensions and visual relation with the Parthenon Temple, symbolised by a big window ('the open eye onto the Acropolis'), thus creating a continuous relationship with the Acropolis's presence. The intention was that the Parthenon Sculptures could be viewed 'in the same spatial relations' they had on the original building.

Both the competition and the successful design provoked criticism. The project was criticised for a lack of integration into the surrounding local urban landscape (Filippides 1992). Others criticised the process of selection and the jury's inability to generate further refinement of the ideas of the first phase (Paisiou 2012). In addition it proved hard to keep transparency and anonymity, crucial elements of every competition process, in the judging (Kontaratos 1992). Finally, the selection of the Makriyianni site was a point of constant debate, especially by the Greek Architects Association; they were joined by local inhabitants whose flats were at risk of expropriation and demolition.

As a result, the museum construction was referred to the Supreme Judicial Council. In September 1993 the Council decided to cancel the project (decision no: 2137, 24-09-1993) (*Ta Nea*, 25/11/93; *To Vema*,

03/11/1996; *Eleftherotypia*, 10/03/2002). The decision was based on the argument that the competitors' submissions were opened by the Greek Technical Committee rather than the International Evaluation Committee, as the guidelines of UNESCO (1956) regarding the conduct of international competitions require (*Ta Nea*, 25/11/93; *Eleftherotypia*, 10/03/2002). This appeal was just one of many that followed, causing severe delay to the project.

The construction of the museum was to prove even more complex. As soon as the archaeological excavations on the Makriyianni plot began in 1997 (Fig. 6.3), a uniquely well-preserved early Christian settlement dating to the seventh century AD was unveiled, along with other archaeological remains (*Ta Nea*, 14/05/1998; *Ta Nea*, 18/08/1999). The archaeological discoveries reignited opposition against the construction of the museum on this plot. The Central Archaeological Council (CAC) therefore decided on 12 October 1999 that the new archaeological finds should be integrated into the new museum, constituting as they did

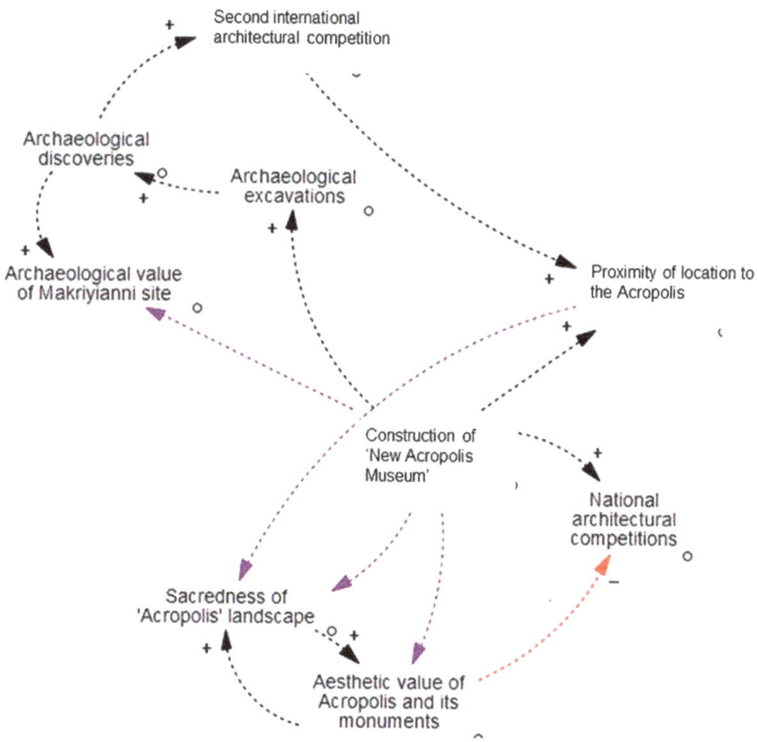

Fig. 6.3 The impact of archaeological discoveries on the construction of the New Acropolis Museum.

unique remains of the seventh century AD (Papachristos 2004, 446; *To Vema*, 25/07/1999; *Ta Nea*, 18/08/1999; 14/10/1999). To achieve this, a new international architectural competition was announced. It sought to design a museum building that could integrate the archaeological remains while retaining the visual contact of the 'Parthenon Sculptures' with the 'Parthenon Temple'.

The creation of an 'in-situ museum' was promoted by Professor Dimitrios Pandermalis, the president of the then Organisation for the Construction of the New Acropolis Museum (OANMA), as an effective way of linking the past with the present and of integrating the archaeological remains and the historic buildings of the Makriyianni area into the museum complex. His assertion at the time reinforces the hypothesis that the New Acropolis Museum was meant to act mainly as the 'Parthenon Museum', implying a hierarchical process of valorisation among the antiquities.

> The visitor will pass through the remains of the daily human life of the Byzantine and Roman periods and eventually will be elevated to the godly world of the archaic and classical periods. (*Eleftherotypia*, 18/07/2002)

Opponents of the museum construction did not favour the proposed solution (*Ta Nea*, 02/06/2000; *Eleftherotypia*, 20/04/2002; *Ta Nea*, 17/07/2002). Despite their resistance, the new, international architectural competition was held and completed. The successful architects were Bernard Tschumi and Michalis Fotiadis. Their design proposed a glass gallery (the so-called 'Parthenon Gallery') on top of the museum, following the dimensions and orientation of the Parthenon Temple. This would enable the displayed Parthenon Sculptures to be viewed in conjunction with the Temple, lit naturally by the 'Attic light'. The new design built thus upon the conceptual design of Nicoletti and Passarelli.

'Visual contact' in the 'Attic light'

At this point, it is worth reflecting in some detail on the 'visual contact' element, a prerequisite for the 'new museum'. One of the first questions that emerges is whether 'visual contact' is a component of a social practice or a social practice itself. If 'visual contact' is a component, is it a 'sense', a 'value', a 'material', or a mixture of all these elements? Clearly some components cannot be distinctly demarcated and classified into categories. In the case of the construction of the New Acropolis Museum, 'visual contact', as will be discussed, evolves from a 'sense' to a 'value' to 'material'. At the same time ensuring the 'visual contact' of the 'Parthenon Sculptures' with the Parthenon Temple is both a desired goal and a political action. The achievement of the goal is obfuscated by the 'restricted space', 'presence of historic buildings' and potential presence of 'archaeological remains': in other words, material as well as symbolic constraints inflicted by the symbolism of the location.

'Visual contact' and 'Attic light' go hand in hand in the discourse around the reunification of the marbles and the museum. The creators of the new museum emphasised how the new display allows the viewers to enjoy the exhibits under the 'natural light of Attica', as they were originally viewed (Plantzos 2011). According to Tschumi

> the light of Attica is different from the light elsewhere in the world ... Only under this light may one **view** the Marbles **properly.** Indeed, one sees the Marbles differently as one would if they were still intact on the Parthenon. (author's emphasis) (Tsiros 2009, 20)

For Plantzos (2011, 619), such views align with environmental determinism by which culture and environment are organically tied. The adverb '**properly**' is indicative of the expected respect with which visitors, almost as pilgrims, should view the museum. The museum, a project of the 'sacred Acropolis Hill', is also a projection of the same sacredness; as such, it too is a 'sacred space', with its guardians demanding respect and awe.

I queried above whether the 'desired goal' for 'visual contact' is a 'sense', a 'value', a 'material', a 'spatial' factor or a mixture of all of these. Indeed, as Gazi argues (2019), visual practices extend far beyond one's physical ability to see. Far more than a natural process and physical operation, vision is subject to the dynamics of social forces. Consequently 'seeing' is always shaped by a broader set of cultural assumptions and frameworks (Gazi 2019). The visual has always served as a powerful tool in the service of identity politics whereby certain aspects of heritage are emphasised and others silenced (Waterton and Watson 2010). In this sense, visuality is not simply an act of observation (vision) or a simple, unmediated visual experience, but a culturally and socially mediated act, a cultural construct (Bryson 1988, 91–2). Within the heritage discourse specifically, visuality assumes renewed importance as it is intimately linked to the creation and manipulation of the gaze and to the politics of vision (Foster 1988, 107).

The crucial question here is what is made visible and why (Gazi 2019). Iconic monuments in particular, such as the Acropolis monuments, 'tend to be viewed and "consumed" in terms of their (partly real, partly constructed and partly imagined) visual exaltation' (Gazi 2019, 249). Indeed, the museum needs to be understood as a 'material intervention within the politics of vision' by which the 'management of gaze is the primary concern of its archaeological and museographic apparatus' (Hamilakis 2011, 626). By 'management of gaze', Hamilakis refers to how the glass architecture of the new museum not only enables visual contact of the museum with the Acropolis Hill; it also shows how blinds can be used strategically in order to hide 'ugly' modern blocks of flats and buildings directing the gaze towards the Acropolis Hill (Hamilakis 2011, 626; see also Plantzos 2011). By doing so, 'standing in the gallery should feel almost like standing at the top of Acropolis' (Rutten and B. Tschumi Architects 2009, 141). Controlling what is allowed to be seen or what is deemed appropriate to be seen is an inherently political act. However, such control does not imply that alternative expressions and voices are not expressed (Hamilakis 2011, 628).

The 'uninterrupted view' towards the Acropolis Hill has been a key concern in the modern Greek era. However, the key milestone in consolidating the prioritisation of maintaining a 'visual contact' between the museum and the Acropolis was set by Melina Mercouri in the 1980s (Lending 2018). The initial claim for the 'restitution' and 'repatriation' of the 'Parthenon Sculptures' evolved into a 'reunification' argument, according to which the 'Sculptures' would return to the original monument of which they constitute integral members (Fouseki 2014). Given that the actual relocation of the sculptures on the monument itself was not feasible, the nearest solution to this could be the relocation of the Marbles in a gallery that resembled the dimensions of the Parthenon Temple while maintaining direct visual contact with the Acropolis Hill.

As the first international architectural competition for the New Acropolis Museum in 1989 noted:

> the envisaged return of the Parthenon pediment marbles (the so-called 'Elgin Marbles') necessitates the creation of corresponding areas for their display.

The design programme went on to add:

> Since the repatriation of the original Parthenon sculptures is envisaged, room must be provided to facilitate their display together

> with the remaining architectural members and sculptures which are found in Greece. (Lending 2009, 571)

The competition programme made reference to the local climate and to 'Attic' light:

> The mild climate and Attic sky, famous for its clarity of crystal clear 'Attic Light', complemented the natural harmony of the area. (Lending 2018, 809)

The rhetoric of the competition echoes Mercouri, who at the World Conference on Cultural Politics in 1982 quoted the words of the Greek poet Yannis Ritsos: 'These stones cannot make do with less sky'. She further stated that

> time has come for these Marbles to come back to the blue sky of Attica, to their natural space, to the place where they will be a structural and functional part of a unique whole. (Mercouri 1982, in Lending 2018, 812)

It is of no surprise, therefore, to see the significance that 'natural light' has for the new museum.

Bernard Tschumi contended that the 'light of Attica is different from the light anywhere else in the world' (Tsiros 2009, 20). For Bernard Tschumi, light became an additional material with which to work.

> Floating above these many challenges were the demands of the Attic light, at once serene and implacable, which had to be incorporated both as a defining element and an architectural material ... alongside marble, concrete and glass, light became a fourth material as well as a design requirement. (Tschumi 2009, 82, 84)

For the Director of the new museum, light is the museum's 'most thrilling asset' – so much so that

> I've been thinking of having it managed, of having someone keep track of the light all day long! What I mean is that I've been thinking of putting a staff member in charge of the light. (Pandermalis 2010, 485–6)

The significance of viewing the 'Marbles' under the natural 'Attic' light is so great that the provision of information about history of the 'Marbles' is not perceived essential (Plantzos 2011, 619).

It is worth pointing out here that discourse on the significance of the 'Attic light' is not new. In 1811 Lord Byron started his poem, 'The Curse of Minerva" by stating:

> Not, as in northern climes, obscurely bright/ But one unclouded blaze of living light.

Three years later François-René de Chateaubriand stressed the necessity of Attic light in enhancing the beauty of the 'Marbles':

> The monuments of Athens, torn from places to which they were adapted, will not only lose part of their relative beauty, but their intrinsic beauty will be materially diminished. It is nothing but the light that sets off the delicacy of certain lines and certain colours: consequently, as this light is not to be found beneath an English sky, these lines and these colours will disappear or become invisible. (Chateaubriand 1814, 149 in Beresford 2017, 62; see also Beresford 2016)

It is therefore of no surprise why the 'Marbles' displayed in the British Museum have often been described as 'inhabiting a "cold and dark prison" and longing for the "light of Attica"' (Hamilakis 2007, 279).

The over-emphasis on the 'Parthenon Sculptures' meant that, although the museum attempts to achieve a dialogue between the archaeological ruins, the main Museum space and the Parthenon (Tschumi 2009; Loukaki 2016), it neglects, intentionally or unintentionally, the contemporary urban landscape. The indifference or even hostility displayed towards urban surroundings created many problems and protests against the realisation of the building.

To sum up, four main phases can be detected in the history of conflict surrounding the museum construction since its materialisation in 1991. During the first phase (1990–5), the controversy revolved around the Hellenic Ministry of Culture, later replaced by the Organisation of the Construction of the New Acropolis Museum (OANMA), and the Greek Association of Architects. What linked the involved parties in this complex network was initially the symbolic significance of the historic landscape marked by the presence of the Acropolis Hill and the Parthenon. Many of the claims and objectives were based on the extent to which the modern building would disrupt the aesthetics of the 'sacred' classical monuments of the Acropolis Hill. This network of actors was gradually enlarged with the participation of more parties after the discovery of the archaeological site, which provoked further disputes and reactions. The first opposing parties were the British Museum, archaeologists (mainly academics), the Citizens' Movement and the local inhabitants whose houses had to be compulsorily purchased(1997–8).

While the disputing reactions were becoming more intensive, third parties (such as the Central Archaeological Council) endeavoured to achieve a compromise by the suggestion of the creation of an in-situ museum (1999–2000). This solution not only failed to be accepted by all parties, but also generated further reactions, including those by ICOMOS. Within this negative climate and close to the national elections of 2004 (and the Olympic Games), the opposing political parties began to accuse the museum of destroying the archaeological site (2003–5).

The parties involved in the disputing discourses around the museum construction can be grouped into 'supporters' and 'opponents'. The values assigned to the Acropolis and the museum may have been the same, but the ways in which they were used differed, as did the ultimate goals. Indeed, the 'values' on which the arguments from both sides are based reflect the Greek 'authorised heritage discourse' (Smith 2006), which prioritises the 'sacred aesthetics' and 'national values' of the classical era. The heritage organisations that supported the museum construction were two independent private organisations (Melina Mercouri Foundation and the Organisation for the Construction of the New Acropolis Museum (OANMA)) that had been created to facilitate and carry forward the construction of the museum, a scheme initially started by the Hellenic Ministry of Culture.

The Central Archaeological Council is mainly a governmental body and therefore its decisions on archaeological issues of major importance are strongly affected by the political party in power at the time. However, the British Museum at an international level and the Hellenic ICOMOS at a national level denounced the destruction of the archaeological site. Certainly the archaeological site's destruction provided an additional reason for the British Museum to justify their refusal to repatriate the Parthenon Marbles. A group of architects and archaeologists not working for OANMA and the Makriyianni excavations also opposed the construction of the New Acropolis Museum (NAM), each group for completely different reasons. The local voice was represented mainly by the local inhabitants whose houses had to be compulsorily purchased and the Citizens' Movement.

When the 'modern' clashes with the 'classical'

It was not only the 1950s blocks of flats that were targeted for demolition in order to enhance the aesthetics of the museum's surroundings while allowing an undisrupted view towards the Acropolis Hill. An Art Deco listed building, dating back to the 1930s and located next to the museum building, was de-listed so that it could be demolished. This decision once again provoked a public outcry at national and international level. The executive committee of the World Archaeological Congress urged the then Minister of Culture, Georgios Voulgarakis

> not to consent to removing the designation of 17 Dionysiou Areopagitou Street, Athens, as a building-monument. It is an important example of 1930s Art Deco architecture, and a testament to the recent material and cultural memory of Greece. (Zimmerman 2007)

The building had been declared as a scheduled monument by the Ministry of Urban Development (YPECHODE) in 1978 and a 'work of art' by the Hellenic Ministry of Culture in 1988. Zimmerman further stated that

> one of the most important features of the landscape of the Athenian Acropolis is its **character as a palimpsest of human activity from ancient times to the present. It is this multi-temporal material culture** that is valued by archaeologists and the public the world over. The demolition of this building, a monument of high aesthetic, historical and mnemonic value, will harm and degrade this sense of diachronic cultural development, and will devalue the Acropolis and its New Museum, as well as the Athenian Cultural Heritage as a whole. (author's emphasis) (YPECHODE; see also Fouseki 2007)

Zimmerman's contention nicely summarises a 'deep cities' approach for sustainable urban transformations that I have advocated with colleagues on the European CURBATHERI project (Fouseki, Guttormsen and Swensen 2020; see also website of the European project www.deepcities.eu). A 'deep cities' approach advocates for the incorporation of temporal layers of the city into its multiple and complex socio-spatial dimensions' (Fouseki, Guttormsen and Swensen 2020, 3). It challenges

> a traditional aesthetic approach in the heritage discourse on perspectives on the protection and uses of the past by emphasising the long-term historical changes and the *longue durée* of changing memories of cities. (Fouseki, Guttormsen and Swensen 2020, 6)

As such, it connotes a shift to preservation based on the history of change and today's uses of the past, including

> perspectives on the intangible, relict or fragmented, ruin-like and many-layered heritage produced as the result of how the present cityscape is the historic product of the risings and falls of many cities with place continuity over time, in other words, viewing the city as the product of both continuity and change. (Fouseki, Guttormsen and Swensen 2020, 6)

While the integration of the archaeological remains into the new museum building complied with the principles of a 'deep cities' framework which values 'fragmented' remains, the expropriation, de-listing and demolition of later structures is contradictory to a 'deep cities' approach. However, as is clearly shown above by the construction of the New Acropolis Museum, lack of a transtemporal approach towards the integration of the past, present and future will threaten the sustainability of a project.

Unpacking the mechanisms of 'heritage dissonance'

This section aims to address the following questions: How does 'heritage dissonance' as a social practice work? In other words, how does 'heritage dissonance' emerge, evolve and shift over time? Furthermore, how is heritage transformed during a process of dissonance? Finally why, and for whom, are insights into the mechanisms of 'heritage dissonance' important?

The case of the New Acropolis Museum serves graphically to illustrate the complex interplay between museums and historic urban landscapes. A historic urban landscape is a complex and dynamic heritage assemblage; it consists not only of what we 'see' in the present, but also of what lies beneath the surface (what we cannot see) and what is planned in the future (what we may foresee). In such a context, a new museum building related to the 'past' history of an area functions architecturally and conceptually as the bridge between past, present and future. However, as each museum project is a political project, only certain aspects of past, present and future are selected to be visible; others are overshadowed and salient. Controversies in highly imbued symbolic spaces are inevitable.

The Acropolis Museum united a group of different 'supporters' and different 'opponents'. Each group advocated for the protection of specific values, even if the driving goals themselves were different. The museum acted in its early stages as a projection of the Acropolis Hill and its monuments (especially the Parthenon Temple); in later stages it needed to incorporate the archaeological remains currently in its basements. For its supporters, the values with which the Acropolis and Parthenon are attributed were also invested in the museum; they were indeed enhanced by the museum's presence. For the museum's opponents, the opposite was the case. The values assigned to the Acropolis and the Parthenon Marbles (as well as the discovered archaeological site) were placed under threat as a result of the museum construction.

The museum as a national and international emblem

For its supporters, the museum became a symbol of national pride and prestige, as well as a tool for ruling political parties to strengthen their power and influence. Construction of the museum was unavoidably associated with the Athens 2004 Olympic Games, the revival of which – alongside the potential return of the 'Parthenon Sculptures' – would symbolise the restitution of Hellenism in its fullness (Yalouri 2001, 86). On an international level, the museum constituted a response to doubts raised by the British Museum about Greece's ability to fulfil its role as a guardian of its cultural heritage, a doubt reinforced after the discovery of the archaeological site and its partial destruction (Fouseki 2008). On the other hand, the authorities of the museum and the Greek state politicians, by suggesting the construction of the in-situ museum, sought to emphasise not only Greece's ability to safeguard its heritage but also its status as a modern and developed state. It is another example of recurring attempts by the Greek nation to stress their 'honourable profile' (Mouliou 1996) and to counter any patronising attitude of foreign powers as expressed through the ownership of national heritage (Yalouri 2001, 83).

For the museum's supporters, the construction project was almost synonymous from its beginnings with raising the local claim for repatriation of the Parthenon Marbles into a global issue (Fouseki 2008). The museum acquired further symbolic significance when the Olympic Games returned to Athens in 2004. The completion of two projects was meant to signify the 'celebration of Hellenism in its complete restitution' (Yalouri 2001, 86). It was also meant to celebrate the rebirth of a modern state and its remarkable progress and development. Indeed, the innovative integration of the in-situ conserved archaeological remains was phrased within this rhetoric. The integration provided additional evidence of Greece's 'honourable profile' and of the country's ability to safeguard its national and international heritage (Boniface and Fowler 2002). The promotion of the 'new' museum as a symbol of development is inseparable from the general development of public projects that took place in Greece, especially in Athens, in the last decades. These include the Acropolis Metro Station, the Unification of Archaeological Sites in Athens and the extensive conservation and restoration works on the Acropolis Hill (Fouseki 2006; 2015).

For the museum's opponents, discovery of the archaeological remains and their partial destruction – as well as the construction of a high, modern building close to the 'sacred' rock – were perceived as threats to the national vision, which includes the repatriation of the Parthenon Marbles. Since this national vision is also a 'sacred' one, both the destruction of the archaeological site and the museum building itself were characterised as acts of national sacrilege. The 'Citizens' Movement' opposed the construction of the museum at the Makriyianni area, for instance, arguing that its construction would lead to destruction of the archaeological finds. They stressed that

> it is unbelievable that the CAC and the Ministry of Culture act in such an authoritarian manner, causing the Greek as well as the global reaction against the construction of the New Acropolis Museum and spoiling greatly these significant elements of our cultural heritage. (*Kathimerini,* 4/04/2002)

Furthermore, the 'Citizens' Movement' claimed,

> we will have the paradox of having a museum which, even though it is intended to preserve and present the ancient relics, will however be constructed over them, leading to their destruction. (*To Vema,* 20/05/2001)

Another newspaper expressed concern that destruction of the archaeological site could serve to frustrate the ultimate goal.

> This will constitute a powerful argument for the British Museum to refuse the repatriation of the Parthenon Marbles. (*Eleftherotypia,* 03/08/2001)

According to these arguments, the role of the museum seems paradoxical. The main aim of such an institution should be the conservation and presentation of the archaeological finds rather than their destruction. Moreover, opponents of the museum emphasised the negative impact that such actions might have at international level regarding the national claim for the repatriation of the Parthenon Marbles. The national profile and image in the global arena thus constitutes an issue that raises concern among Greek people.

The New Acropolis Museum – an act of 'sacredness' or 'sacrilege'?

For its opponents, the museum was perceived as disrupting the aesthetics of the 'sacred rock' of Acropolis (sacrilege of aesthetics) because of its size and the modern materials of which it is built. Destruction of the archaeological remains was also characterised as 'sacrilege', mainly by archaeologists and the Citizens' Movement (archaeological sacrilege). The decision to build a museum of that type on the slopes of the Acropolis Hill while endangering the underground antiquities was regarded a 'national sacrilege' which placed the national claim for the repatriation of the Parthenon Marbles in jeopardy.

For museum supporters, on the other hand, the building was perceived as a means of enhancing the 'sacredness of aesthetics' through allowing visual contact of the Parthenon Marbles with the Acropolis Hill and the Parthenon. It was promoted as an innovative structure that successfully integrated the discovered archaeological remains in the form of an in-situ museum, thus enhancing the 'sacredness' of archaeology. The museum was perceived by supporters as an effective means of achieving the local demand for repatriation of the Parthenon Marbles, constituting a proof of Greece's ability properly to safeguard its cultural heritage ('national sacredness').

How did the Acropolis transform into a 'sacred' place? After the establishment of the Greek state in 1830, the Acropolis was imbued with a sense of sacredness; its purity and aesthetics had to be protected. The aesthetics refer to the surrounding landscape, marked by the presence of the Parthenon and the Acropolis monuments, as well as to the characterisation of the Acropolis Hill as a work of high art (Yalouri 2001,149). The 'purification' of the Acropolis by the removal of recent, vernacular buildings and buildings later than the Classical period of Athens started as early as in 1835, transforming the Acropolis and its landscape into a monumental place in time and space (Yalouri 2001, 153). This process is associated with 'perceptions of purity and pollution, which characterise many religious systems of thought' (Hamilakis and Yalouri 1999, 118). A similar act of 'purification' took place in the case of the museum, where surrounding blocks of flats had to be demolished in order to plant trees. For opponents of the museum's construction on the Makriyianni plot, the erection of a modern high building in the proximity of the Acropolis Hill was viewed by both the architects and the 'Citizens' Movement' as aesthetic sacrilege; it disrupted the view to the Acropolis that had to remain dominant, while also spoiling the character of the landscape (*Eleftherotypia* 19/02/2002). Words such as 'desecration' or 'sacrilege' were often used by protestors to oppose the construction of the building on the slopes of the Acropolis Hill. A characteristic event, revealing this contention, occurred during the presentation of the design of the NAM by Bernard Tschumi at the Hellenic Ministry. On that occasion two individuals raised panels with the following text written in English and Greek:

> (A) Museum in Makriyianni (is) sacrilege (hybris). It destroys antiquities (and) antagonises the massiveness of the Parthenon. (*Eleftherotypia* 19/02/2002)

The use of the word sacrilege [*hybris* in Greek] indicates the sacredness with which the Acropolis monuments are associated. Any building close to them is thus considered profane.

The notion of aesthetics results not only from the sacred connotations with which the Acropolis monuments are imbued, but also from the perception of these monuments as works of high art. On this basis, a debate regarding the appropriate display of the Marbles in the museum context arose between the British Museum and the NAM as sacrilege in terms of aesthetics. The supporters of the NAM argue that the Duveen Gallery of the British Museum is confusing; it gives a misleading idea of the size, shape and colour of the Parthenon and its sculptures by rearranging them in a false symmetry and using coloured spotlights which exaggerate the shadows (Fouseki 2006, 34). In contrast, they claim, the Parthenon Hall of the NAM, which has the dimensions of the Parthenon frieze and allows Attic light to enter through transparent walls, made of different types of glass, is the only place that constitutes an 'appropriate place' for the 'Parthenon Sculptures'. This will permit the promotion of the aesthetic value of 'whiteness' that is attributed to the Acropolis monuments. For the museum's supporters such a move legitimises their ownership of the Parthenon Marbles, the real 'whiteness' of which can only be found under the 'Greek sun' and in the Attic landscape (Yalouri 2001, 184). In view of this, their display at the British Museum makes the sculptures inauthentic.

Two further notions are associated with the notion of aesthetics here. Authenticity, original context and 'whiteness' are closely linked to the notion of aesthetics. These concepts in turn are indirectly related to the notion of sacredness, since if 'whiteness' and 'authenticity' are considered by NAM supporters to be essential prerequisites of aesthetics, and aesthetics a prerequisite of sacredness, then the intermix of the above elements affects perceptions. In reply, the British Museum emphasises a further dimension that is related to the aesthetics, that of integral and comparative art. Representatives from the British Museum argue that the Parthenon Marbles are an integral part of the museum because only as a whole do they allow a comparative study with the rest of the collections. In view of this, their sense of aesthetics can be revealed and understood wholly, giving scholars the chance to compare and recognise their unique value through this comparison (see Fouseki 2006; 2008).

An additional notion associated with aesthetics is that of 'original context'. This partly relates to the notion of authenticity, but also has a more spatial meaning, in addition to a conceptual one. In detail, the museum's supporters claim that the location of the NAM in the vicinity of the Acropolis rock as a central part of the Unification of the Archaeological Sites could provide 'a true sense of the aesthetics' of the Parthenon Marbles that can be understood only in their original historical and cultural context. The argument that the Parthenon Marbles will regain their 'true sense of aesthetics' if they are exhibited at the NAM implies that the British Museum presents an inauthentic view of the Parthenon Marbles since they are isolated from their historic context. Here the role of the museum in creating a cultural context is obvious. The NAM not only constitutes part of the historical context in which the Parthenon Marbles were created, but also creates a contemporary context in which the sculptures' authenticity and meaning will be presented.

The above debate reveals the subjectivity of the notion of 'aesthetics' and 'sacredness', both of which have been employed for specific purposes. In any case, the important element in this debate is to examine how heritage managers can assess subjective perceptions (not excluding their own) and how if necessary they can modify and manage them.

The concept of sacredness is also related to the national symbolism that the Acropolis has for the Greek nation (Yalouri 2001, 142). Similarities between nationalist imagining and religious ideology have been pointed out by various authors (Yalouri 2001, 142). If the NAM as a national symbol is imbued with these notions of sacredness or sacrilege, then the discovered archaeological heritage is consequently attributed with similar connotations.

The values and meanings analysed above are inseparable from economic profits derived mainly from tourism and the financial support of the European Union. Indeed, tourism constitutes one of the most important financial resources for Greece, while at the same time contributing to the financial support of the Archaeological Receipts Fund, responsible for the conservation of Greek archaeological sites. In view of this, it seems that the commodification of antiquities is a necessary evil (Tunbridge and Ashworth 1996, 59; Yalouri 2001, 103).

The association of the NAM with tourism development was, however, viewed from two contradictory perspectives. Despite the fact that tourism could potentially constitute a meeting point of the local–global relationship through the immediate and personal contact of local people with tourists (Clifford 1997, 213–19), it is often criticised by Greeks. Tourism is often viewed by local communities as a threat to the local–national identity; it is negatively associated with the homogenisation, consumption and commodification linked to the phenomenon of globalisation. On the other hand, tourism is considered to be the 'ambassador' of Greek heritage, particularly by the Greek state. It thus serves to accomplish the national mission of promoting Greek heritage internationally (Yalouri 2001, 135).

The association of the NAM with the Athens 2004 Olympic Games evoked mixed responses. On the one hand it was considered a 'touristic fiesta' (*Eleftherotypia,* 07/04/2002); on the other hand it was thought to provide a unique opportunity to promote Greek heritage internationally. Representatives of the 'Citizens' Movement' stressed that:

> The Ministry of Culture must decide if it desires (or is able) to link the New Acropolis Museum with the Olympic Games of 2004. It has to be clarified that the New Acropolis Museum constitutes a building that will exist for us ... **a building that we do not construct for the tourists but for ourselves**, our city, [our] Athens and the Parthenon Sculptures.... (author's emphasis) (*To Vema* 30/07/2000)

In this statement commodified associations of both the NAM and the Olympic Games are implied. The reference to 'tourists' represent the tourists–travellers as consumers rather than as pilgrims (Yalouri 2001, 135). The tourists visiting the country for the Olympic Games – and who would possibly visit the NAM – are not accepted by Greeks as consumers of culture. The appropriation of cultural symbols of national significance – such as the New Acropolis Museum and the Olympic Games – by tourists is perceived by Greeks as an appropriation of a national identity.

The presence of archaeological remains within a surrounding historic context can function as a link between an absent, unfamiliar and remote past with a more recent, familiar historic past. If it is accepted that recent historic events and the surviving buildings with which they are associated engender memories and feelings of familiarity then the archaeological past, as a link to the recent past, can also be familiar, arousing opposition to its destruction. In addition, the ancient past is evidence of the continuity of history. It therefore contributes unavoidably and unconsciously to the reinforcement of national identity in Greece as well as the wider world.

Conclusion

'Heritage dissonance' or 'dissonant heritage' is a social, systemic and dynamic practice. Its emergence and continuation depends on the dynamic interlinkages between values, materials, space/place, senses/emotions, skills/competencies, resources and time. These elements obviously do not stand alone, but are performed by a wide array of 'agents', who as a matter of fact are omnipresent. Each agent or group of agents determines the linkages based on their values, aspirations, needs and goals.

In the case of the New Acropolis Museum construction, the contestation was implanted as soon as the Makriyianni area – a narrow plot located in the densely inhabited centre of Athens beneath the slopes of the Acropolis Hill – was selected as the site for the 'new museum'. Here, we see the contested interplay between the 'present' place of the Makriyianni area and the Acropolis Hill and the 'future' space of the museum. Initial conflict was fed by the interrelationship between 'space/place' and 'values'. It proceeded to evolve when the museum design was announced in 1991, following two unsuccessful national competitions in the 1970s. The museum proposal made a strong linkage with the repatriation of the 'Parthenon Sculptures', turning the project itself into a 'claim for the repatriation of the Parthenon Marbles': in other words, the claim was materialised through the museum. The emphasis upon the museum's uninterrupted 'visual contact' with the Parthenon Temple and the display of the 'Parthenon Sculptures' in the 'Attic light', although already acknowledged in the previous competitions, had now become more pertinent than ever. The dispute was consequently fed by an antagonistic interrelationship between 'place/space', 'values' and 'materials', as evidenced in the museum design.

Both aesthetics and pride have proved to be essential elements in this process. Although in theory the design proposal of the first international architectural competition could alleviate the dispute, the discovery of the archaeological remains provided a catalyst for further conflict, alongside the expropriation and demolition of the surrounding blocks of flats from the 1950s, as well as the de-listing of the Art Deco building. There is here a contested relationship between 'materials' that represent different historic periods. Remains or buildings associated with 'more ancient' layers in the city are prioritised over buildings linked to 'more modern' phases.

In addition, I demonstrated how the museum evolved into a 'supreme object' similar to the Acropolis – anything in between was an obstacle. The second and final international architectural competition, which intended to incorporate the archaeological remains into the museum structure, sought unsuccessfully to resolve the conflict. In court, the 'modern' listed building was, in the end, saved from demolition. However, the blocks of flats were demolished and 150 households relocated.

This case study has demonstrated, more vividly than the examples analysed in previous chapters, the fluidity of the elements of 'heritage dynamics'. The 'visual contact' and 'Attic light', for instance, evolved from a 'sensual' and 'spatial element' into a 'material' element, at least for the lead architect. The diagram below (Fig. 6.4) summarises the dynamics of 'heritage dissonance' as manifested in the construction of the New Acropolis Museum. Segments of the diagram that illustrates this case have been shown and discussed above.

The conditions that marked a significant shift in the historic urban landscape and the museum construction development are marked in red. The 'sacredness' with which the Acropolis Hill, the Parthenon and its Sculptures are valued proved to act as the frame around which arguments were formulated. The densely inhabited area of Makriyianni posed constraints from early on in the project. The relationships that tend to be 'negative' and 'balancing' for the opponents of the museum and 'positive' and 'reinforcing' for the supporters are highlighted in purple. This shows that, based on the perspective of each group of stakeholders, the relationships will have a different outcome. It is therefore imperative to identify the diversity of opinions at stake. Even if they are not depicted in the model (although they could be), the diversity of responses needs to be highlighted in the diagram.

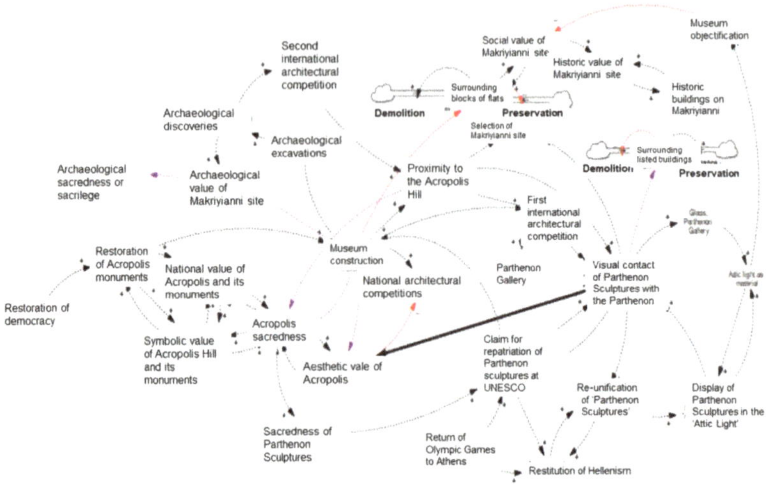

Fig. 6.4 The dynamics of 'heritage disonnance' at the New Acropolis Museum.

How is this analysis significant? This case study constitutes a characteristic example of lack of consultation, participation and negotiation which resulted in huge project delays. Identifying – and more importantly working with – the various stakeholders is critical for the sustainability of a heritage project. The New Acropolis Museum, despite the huge delays, compromised the architectural, archaeological, interpretation, political and aesthetic challenges – but the 'social' challenges were less effectively met. The 1950s blocks of flats (and consequently their inhabitants) were simply not viewed as equally important – in contrast to the surrounding listed building (and its famous inhabitants), which was saved in the end. There is thus not only a practical (project management) dilemma here, but also an ethical, moral duty that calls for multivocality, dialogue, participation and negotiation.

7
When performing arts meet heritage

Introduction

In the previous chapters I delved into the dynamics of heritage in disparate contexts from the lens of a researcher who aspires to retain, as much as possible, personal distance from the object of study. In this chapter I opt for an alternative research approach as I intend to ponder the dynamics of art and heritage creation through auto-ethnography. I do so by unravelling the dynamics of the creation of a flamenco choreographic fusion with my 'Flamenco Heritage Artists' group (Flamenco Heritage Artists facebook.com).

Flamenco was inscribed on UNESCO's 'Representative List of the Intangible Cultural Heritage of Humanity' in 2010 and as such it is an internationally recognised form of 'intangible heritage'. Flamenco is also a form of performing art and tradition, but primarily it 'is a living art which represents a way of perceiving and interpreting life' (Cuellar-Moreno 2016, 6).

In order to unfold the complex nature of flamenco as heritage, art, tradition and way of life, I will use auto-ethnography. I will do so by drawing upon my personal experience, using my dual identity as flamenco dancer and heritage researcher for the development of contemporary flamenco choreographic fusions, inspired by the multiple historic and cultural influences that flamenco has received since its emergence in the nineteenth century (see Nomination File no. 0036 for Inscription on the Representative List of the Intangible Cultural Heritage in 2010, https://ich.unesco.org/doc/src/07533-EN.pdf).

Auto-ethnography emerged in postmodern philosophy as a method 'in which the dominance of traditional science and research is questioned and many ways of knowing and inquiring are legitimated', with auto-ethnography offering 'a way of giving voice to personal experience to advance sociological understanding' (Wall 2008, 39). Auto-ethnography is used for the systematic analysis of personal experience, a process that in turn enables our understanding of cultural experience (Ellis et al. 2011, 273). Such an approach regards research as a 'political, socially-just and socially-conscious act' (Ellis et al. 2011, 273).

According to Adams, the term auto-ethnography invokes the *self* (auto), *culture* (ethno) and *writing* (graphy)' (Adams et al. 2015, 46). In other words, auto-ethnography is the 'ethnography of the self' and as such 'it combines characteristics of autobiography and ethnography' (Ellis et al. 2011, 275). In following this process, auto-ethnographers 'confront the tension between insider and outsider perspectives, between social practice and social constraint' (Reed-Danahay 2009, 32). When we undertake auto-ethnography we look inward – into our identities, thoughts, feelings and experiences – and outward into our relationships, communities and cultures (Adams et al. 2015, 46; see also Adams et al. 2017). Auto-ethnography consequently allows an in-depth, critical, reflective process to the emotions, beliefs and experiences. An auto-ethnographer writes retroactively and selectively about past experiences, assembled using hindsight (Ellis et al. 2011, 275).

Although auto-ethnographers describe and analyse personal experiences, they do so in such a way that they depict 'facets of cultural experience', making 'characteristics of a culture familiar for insiders and outsiders' (Ellis et al. 2011, 276). Auto-ethnographers do not therefore rely only on the analysis of their personal experiences, but they also juxtapose those with existing research or with collections of complementary data, such as interviews (Ellis et al. 2011, 276). As such, auto-ethnographies are necessarily trans-cultural communications, articulated in relation to self and a wider social field that includes an audience of 'others' (Butz and Besio 2009).

My auto-ethnographic work revolves around the dynamic interactions between materials, values, space/place, senses/effect, time, competencies/skills and resources that occurred during the creation of a flamenco choreographic fusion. I will argue that it is imperative that the elements above are examined through the theoretical lens of 'embodiment', since the performativity, action and continuity of flamenco – as with any form of performance art – is conveyed through the dancers' bodies. Accordingly, I will manifest that the continuity of flamenco as a form of heritage surmises the unceasing interaction of embodied artefacts/materials, embodied meanings, embodied time, embodied space and place, embodied senses and embodied skills.

This hypothesis was abruptly tested during the Covid-19 pandemic. The introduction of lengthy lockdowns and the consequent closure of dance studios and performance venues paused precipitously live art productions. Digital technologies, such as Zoom, proved inadequate in replacing live performances, signalling the limitations of digital technologies in sustaining forms of living performance art listed as 'heritage'. Indeed, the 'embodied place' that allows the congregation of performers and audiences was revealed to be one of the most critical elements for the continuity and sustainability of 'performing art heritage'.

Flamenco as 'intangible heritage'

As mentioned above, flamenco was inscribed on UNESCO's 'Representative List of the Intangible Cultural Heritage of Humanity' in 2010. Article 16 of the 2003 UNESCO Convention on Intangible Heritage specifies the need for a 'representative list of the intangible cultural heritage of humanity', in order 'to ensure better visibility of the intangible cultural heritage and awareness of its significance, and to encourage dialogue which respects cultural diversity' (Article 16.1). The 2003 UNESCO Convention on Intangible Heritage expands UNESCO's previous 1972 Convention on World Heritage to include

> practices, representations, expressions, knowledge, skills – as well as the instruments, objects, artefacts and cultural spaces associated therewith – that communities, groups and, in some cases, individuals recognize as part of their cultural heritage. (Article 2.1)

The convention stressed that

> This intangible cultural heritage, transmitted from generation to generation, is constantly recreated by communities and groups in response to their environment, their interaction with nature and their history, and provides them with a sense of identity and continuity, thus promoting respect for cultural diversity and human creativity. (Article 2.1)

The 'safeguarding' role of the convention and its associated instruments is emphatic as with previous conventions. However, the means of 'safeguarding' are different. Indeed, the 2003 convention marks a shift to the conceptualisation of heritage from an essentialist, static paradigm that focuses on preserving what needs to be transmitted from one generation to another to a dialogical one by which heritage is questioned and recreated by individuals who bring life to it (Bodo 2012, 182).

The 'safeguarding' is achieved not necessarily through traditional ways of preservation and documentation, but mainly through constant creation and re-creation. This approach constitutes a significant shift regarding the ways in which heritage is perceived. The focus of the 2003 UNESCO Convention is now centred on the dynamic nature of culture and on the performing and continuous re-creation of cultural expressions.

> This new approach aims at conceiving of heritage not only as a consecrated masterpiece of the past to be venerated and preserved, but also as a symbolic and living space to be appropriated by local communities who are the bearers of a collective and active memory. (Bortolotto 2007, 21)

Despite this shift, it should be noted that the inscription of a 'heritage element' into the Representative List requires the demonstration of

> urgent need of safeguarding because its viability is at risk despite the efforts of the community, group or, if applicable, individuals and State(s) Party(ies) concerned.

Alternatively, insertion into the List may be required for an element that

> is in extremely urgent need of safeguarding because it is facing grave threats as a result of which it cannot be expected to survive without immediate safeguarding. (https://ich.unesco.org/en/procedure-of-inscription-00809#criteria)

However, as flamenco has been thriving prior to its recognition as 'intangible heritage', one may wonder how the nomination was justified. Before reviewing the history of flamenco's nomination, it is worth pinpointing here that, while the convention prompts a rethinking of heritage as a dynamic and constantly evolving process, the continuity of which depends on re-creation and change, the problematic binary distinction between 'tangible' and 'intangible' can have the opposite effect.

The distinction between 'tangible' and 'intangible' heritage has already been extensively critiqued (see, for instance, Iacono and Brown 2016; Naguib 2013; Smith and Akagawa 2008) as all heritage, in effect, is intangible. Moreover, 'intangible' heritage has tangible dimensions (also acknowledged by the convention itself, which refers to the objects and artefacts associated with intangible heritage). Indeed, a distinction between 'intangible' and 'tangible' heritage stands in contradiction to the core argument of this book. According to this argument, heritage is a systemic and dynamic social practice, the continuation and change of which depends on multiple, non-linear interconnections of varied elements, both tangible and intangible. In the context of dance in particular, the term 'intangible' proves even more problematic. This is due to

> the central role that the human body has in the practice of dance, and because the phenomenon of dance is simultaneously emergent from, and constitutive of, culture and society. (Iacono and Brown 2016, 85)

Furthermore, if the rhetoric adopted for 'tangible' heritage is fundamentally different from the discourse on 'intangible' heritage, the shift that we would hope to see ensuing in heritage conceptualisation will not be materialised. In other words, if the rhetoric for 'tangible' heritage is that preservation is achieved through preventing or managing change while preservation for 'intangible' heritage is sustained through re-creation and change, then heritage management practices will remain practices of 'managing' instead of 'adapting' to change. In addition, if the fundamental conceptualisation of heritage does not alter, the 'heritagisation' of arts, or other forms of traditions, may freeze living arts and traditions in time and space. The 'heritagisation' here relates to the provision of 'state protection' without which 'the existence of this cultural phenomenon would be endangered' (Krüger 2011, 146). The heritagisation thus signifies a new life cycle for that object, practice or site, as protection always creates 'something new' (Kirshenblatt-Gimblett 1995, 370ff).

Here flamenco provides a good case in point. The protection of flamenco – and consequently its 'heritagisation' – occurred prior to the final inscription of flamenco into UNESCO'S List of Representative Intangible Heritage in 2010. In fact, the heritagisation and patrimonialisation of flamenco has been taking place over the past 150 years, nurtured by local governments' concept of 'heritage-transmitted-from-the-past' (Washabaugh 2012, 10).

The 'heritagisation' of flamenco has been a contentious process. A controversial legal framework for protecting flamenco was introduced in 2007 by the then Andalusian regional government. It defined flamenco as Andalusian cultural property (Article 68) and declared the 'research, diffusion and promotion of flamenco as exclusive competences of the Junta de Andaluciá' (Krüger 2011, 147). Efforts to promote flamenco at regional and international level have since intensified, with the catalyst being the inscription of flamenco into the UNESCO list in 2010.

The nomination of flamenco was preceded by two rejections in 2004 and 2005. All three attempts to include flamenco in UNESCO's list of intangible heritage formed a top-down procedure that aimed to boost regional identity and tourism in Andalusia (Debarbieux et al. 2021, 9). Indeed, those practising flamenco were not involved in the application process. Their support was sought at a later stage, just before the submission of the nomination file. The 'cultural practitioners' emphatically stressed in UNESCO's Convention on Intangible Heritage did not play a central role in the nomination process.

Interestingly, the 'authenticity' and 'purity' of the 'flamenco' originating from Andalusia (concepts intentionally excluded in the 2003 UNESCO Convention) were featured in the nomination file (Nomination File no 00363: https://ich.unesco.org/en/RL/flamenco-00363. Here it was acknowledged that 'Andalusia is the heartland of flamenco' and Andalusia is its 'place of origin'. The worldwide spread of flamenco is accepted, but its variants found abroad are said to be different; they are 'open to new trends' but are deemed non-pure forms despite 'clear cultural and musical ties to flamenco'. Thus, driven by the desire of the Junta de Andalucía to assert and display a regional identity, flamenco was inscribed in the name of Spain alone.

The nomination file continues with the observation:

> Andalusia is the heartland of flamenco. The vast majority of names behind the art form's creations and interpretations, the highest standards and quality of contributions to the worlds of flamenco song, music and dance are Andalusian. Many of the styles and musical forms of flamenco likewise reveal their place of origin in Andalusia: malagueña, alegrías de Cádiz, bulerías de jerez, granaína, sevillanas, fandangos de Huelva, verdiales de los montes de Málaga, rondeña, tangos de Triana, cantiñas de Córdoba, Taranta de Linares and Taranto de Almería. (https://ich.unesco.org/en/RL/flamenco-00363)

This statement indicates that the 'real', the 'pure', the 'authentic' forms of flamenco emanate from Andalusia, as can be evidenced by the names of flamenco dances. Inevitably this list excludes a wide range of flamenco dances that do not have a local association, such as 'seguidillas' and 'guajiras'. Some of these have traces and origins beyond Andalusia (in Cuba, for instance).

However, the nomination file states also that

> Flamenco does, though, have roots in other bordering regions of Spain (for example, Extremadura, with its jaleos and tangos, and Murcia, with its cartageneras and cantes de minas), and has expanded into the central and northern regions of the country, such as Madrid and Catalonia, partly as a result of the emigration of people from Andalusia, Extremadura and Murcia.

The file acknowledges the fact that flamenco is nowadays a 'worldwide, cross-border phenomenon, open to new trends, at the centre of an intercultural dialogue without which it would be inconceivable'. However, although the national and transnational influence and presence of flamenco is mentioned, the Andalusian origins of flamenco are accentuated.

The nomination file underscores the regional and national nature of flamenco in Spain by making special reference to the flamenco clubs, or '*peñas*', and associations. The nomination file notes that

> They [flamenco clubs and *peñas*] constitute a distinct social fabric. Such organisations are to be found throughout Spain. They share a sense of the preservation and dissemination of flamenco culture.

This statement excludes references to the flamenco clubs and *peñas* that operate beyond Spain. By doing so it excludes the diaspora associated with those associations.

Despite the flaws, UNESCO approved the third application. The approval of the third nomination file affirms that 'authenticity' still constitutes an underpinning value for UNESCO. It also asserts that regionalism as a method of protecting from 'cultural standardisation' exacerbated by globalisation is approved by the convention, despite the transnationality and fluidity of living traditions.

The nomination introduces new mechanisms to comply with UNESCO's 'Operational Directives for the Implementation of the

Convention for the Safeguarding of the Intangible Cultural Heritage', aimed at avoiding over-commercialisation (Article 102) and respecting the conventional practices of the cultural heritage (Article 13) (Krüger, 2011, 148). However, none of these is necessarily a concern when flamenco is practised by artists and the general public as a form of creative and artistic expression. The means of protecting flamenco from 'cultural standardisation' still allow for constant re-creation and creativity, opening up new forms of expression. 'Cultural standardisation' may result more from regionalism than from openness.

By understanding the dynamics of flamenco, our comprehension of regional tensions (East and West Andalusia) may be enhanced, due to the powerful role played by flamenco in the construction of a unified regional identity (Machin-Autenrieth 2016). The 'unified regional identity' effort is important for Andalusia, which is known for its multicultural history (Machin-Autenrieth 2016, 10). Flamenco dancing is the result of centuries of exchange and intermixing between multiple cultural groups. The 'multicultural' nature of flamenco was used as a response to the twentieth-century theory that flamenco originated in *gitano* families between 1800 and 1860 (Machin-Autenrieth 2016, 11). The process of nomination is thus another political act in the long history of competing theories around the origin and influences of flamenco – when, in reality, flamenco is a hybrid patchwork of different styles that emerged from a plethora of cultural influences in and outside southern Spain (Washabaugh 2012, 27–52).

I would like to argue that it is not just the appropriation or nomination of flamenco as 'world heritage' that constitutes a 'political act'. Performing flamenco is also political – something that I came to realise while co-creating the choreographic fusion merging 'seguidillas' with dance movements inspired by 'Byzantine' manuscripts. My acceptance that practising heritage (especially through performing acts) is inevitably political was an unintended consequence of what initially looked like a fun, creative activity. While conducting research on the 'Byzantine' influences, I soon realised that the theory according to which certain forms were influenced by 'Byzantine music' was not as 'innocent' as our original intention to create a choreographic fusion was. The connection of flamenco with 'Byzantine music' constituted an attempt to glorify or 'purify' flamenco in the 1920s. In so doing, proponents sought to render flamenco a prestigious form of art performance, disassociating it from its dominant identification with '*gitanos*' (Christoforidis 2007).

Embodied heritage

The underpinning premise of this book – that heritage is a dynamic, socio-cultural practice, the continuity of which depends on the interactions of materials, values/meanings, senses/feelings, place/space, skills/competencies, time and resources – is evidently manifested in dance heritage. This premise confirms the proposition of Iacono and Brown (2016) for a 'living cultural heritage' model for dance heritage in which

> the cultural, embodied, practical, spatial, temporal and artefactual elements of cultural heritage are retained as each contributes to an emergent process of exchange and dialogue resulting in cultural heritage. (Iacono and Brown 2016, 84)

Their argument besets the heritage dynamic elements outlined in this book – that is, 'materials' (artefactual), 'values/meanings' (cultural), 'space/place' (spatial), 'practical' (skills, resources), 'time' (temporal) and 'senses' (embodied). The exploration of this argument in the context of performing arts as heritage bolsters the thesis that embodiment is essential for performing an art heritage practice. In this chapter I will thus be referring to embodied materials, embodied values, embodied space, embodied skills, embodied time and embodied feelings/senses. This is because all the 'heritage dynamic elements' in dancing are mediated via the body.

In order better to fathom the embodiment process in 'dance heritage', I will briefly review a few key, theoretical ideas on 'body' and 'embodiment'. It has been claimed that the body is a social actor's vehicle, tool and instrument of 'being' in the world (e.g. Merleau-Ponty 2011). Dancers use their bodies constantly to build their identities and to construct their position inside the group. Indeed, body 'is crucial in this social role, as this is the only way through which a dancer may be judged' (Byczkowska 2009, 102). For dancers, the body is not only the main 'tool' for identity construction; it is also their 'interactional partner' and 'material', something that 'needs to be changed according to the needs of the social group' (Byczkowska 2009, 103).

One of the most influential works on 'embodiment' is that of the French philosopher Maurice Merleau-Ponty (2011). His 1962 study on the 'Phenomenology of Perception' (republished in 2010) in particular uses a phenomenological perspective to investigate the body (Iwakuma 2002, 78). For Merleau-Ponty the body extends an object so that it literally becomes part of the body (Merleau-Ponty 2011). As a process of embodiment, an object becomes part of the identity of the person to whom it belongs.

The body also embodies time. Embodiment of time ties temporality as a stream of time, the past, present and future (Merleau Ponty 2011. The body itself is, for Merleau-Ponty, a point of view upon the world, as well as one of the objects that constitutes the world. The distinction between abstract and concrete movement is thereby clarified: the background of concrete movement is the given world while the background of abstract movement is, on the contrary, constructed.

What does this approach imply for dance heritage? How does the 'heritagisation' of dance practices impact on the 'concrete' and 'abstract' movements? If the background of a 'concrete movement' is the 'given world', does this then entail the actual, physical space in which a dance performance is displayed? Is the 'abstract movement' one that superimposes a virtual or human space over a physical space through dance movements?

> The normal function that makes abstract movement possible is a function of 'projection' by which the subject of movement organises before himself a free space in which things that do not exist naturally can take on a semblance of existence. (Merleau-Ponty 2011, 142)

The relationship between the observer (human actor) and the observed (heritage) is consequently embodied (Kearney 2008, 211). It is for this reason that any distinction between tangible and intangible becomes redundant

> as the only imperative status of tangible is held by the human actor and agent, as physical embodiment of culture and heritage. Through this 'being', human heritage is always and at once tangible and intangible. (Kearney 2008, 211)

Similarly to Merleau-Ponty's contention on how an object becomes the extension of the body,

> heritage as an embedded concept cannot be disengaged from the world and people around it, while establishing distinguishing links between the perceptual subject and their distinct and owned perceptual objects. (Kearney 2008, 211)

In a way, all heritage is embodied because the presence of 'practitioners' (i.e. those who practise heritage) is a prerequisite for its existence and sustainability.

The sustainability of heritage, and even more so the so-called 'intangible heritage', depends on its embodiment. This hints that heritage can remain alive if it is enacted by those who practise it. As Blake contends, the nature of 'intangible' cultural heritage (as with any form of heritage, I would argue) 'is such that it is people acting as the communities, groups or individuals of the 2003 Convention on whom its very existence is predicated' (2009, 65). Blake continues by stating that unlike

> a site, a monument or artefact that has a material existence beyond the individual or society that created it … it is only through its enactment by cultural practitioners that ICH has any current existence and by their active transmission that it can have any future existence. (Blake 2009, 65)

Although it could be counterargued that practising heritage (visiting a site or volunteering in the conservation of a monument, for instance) is a form of enactment that characterises both 'tangible' and 'intangible' heritage, Blake's contention reiterates the need for embodied enactment as a prerequisite for the continuity of 'performing heritage'. In other words, 'intangible heritage' (especially heritage that links to performances such as dance) can only be sustained if people practise it with their bodies. The embodied enactment of 'intangible heritage' unavoidably cultivates constant re-creation, as acknowledged by the World Heritage Convention, and constant reinvigoration of voices, movements and histories that may have been underrepresented or undervalued within 'source' or 'bearer communities', or within the dominant cultures that surround them (Kosmala and Beall 2019, 351). A new potential for heritage to be inclusive is created through the connection of 'distinct' or 'disparate' communities through embodied action (Kosmala and Beall 2019, 352).

Embodied senses, embodied identity

January 2018. I am celebrating the viva of one of my PhD students at a Greek-Cypriot restaurant in North London. George, one of my former PhD students and founder of the art-café 'Artfix', is also participating in the celebrations. During our conversation on flamenco, he invited me to perform a flamenco piece as part of a series of art events he was planning to host – an invitation that I happily accepted without much thought. Indeed, a few months later, in June, George asked me to perform a 'short', 'pop-up' flamenco dance during the break of an event where Greek artists living in London were showcasing their work (music, singing, etc.). I spontaneously responded 'yes', again without giving much thought, despite the short notice; creating art requires time for inspiration, for creation and for practice. Due to the emphasis of the event on 'Greece' I embarked upon what seemed at the time a 'bizarre creative inquiry'. How might I be able to connect flamenco – a dance associated with Andalusia – with an event dedicated to Greece?

While pondering how to bring the two together, I recollected a reference in a book by Leblon and Shuinear, *Gypsies and flamenco: The emergence of the art of flamenco in Andalusia* (2003), to a 1920s theory that stressed the influence of 'Byzantine' ecclesiastical music on certain forms of flamenco, such as seguidillas. This reference triggered my exploration of dance movements as depicted in 'Byzantine manuscripts', which I hoped to incorporate into a choreographic fusion of seguidillas and 'Byzantine' dance. This attempt constituted the foundation of the formation of the 'Flamenco Heritage Artists', a group that consisted of four flamenco dancers, all of whom met at the 'Ilusion Flamenca' dance school. The 'Flamenco Heritage Artists' group is a multicultural group; it includes an Andalusian dancer (Ana), an Asturian dancer (Paloma), a French dancer (Julie) and a Greek dancer (myself). While reflecting on the different identities we represent, I realised that our choreographic choices are a means of negotiating our identities and expressing the ways in which we connect with flamenco.

While reflecting on this 'epiphanic hindsight', I discerned that I, unconsciously, specified the local origin of our two Spanish dancers in the group while the 'identification' of Julie and myself was given in terms of our national origins. My unconscious specification of the local origin of my Spanish flamenco friends derives from discussions and readings implying that the 'authentic', 'pure' flamenco can only link to Andalusia. A similar contention implicitly underpins the nomination file for the inscription of flamenco into the representative list, as discussed above. And yet our different origins did not prevent the four of us from coming together as a group, since what united us is our shared passion for flamenco and creativity.

Interestingly, very few authors have researched the topic of flamenco as a marker of personal identity (Krüger 2011, 150). Chuse reaffirms our journeys in which we construct our personal identities while creating the choreography by stating that 'according to the requirements of the moment national, regional, local or sub-local identities are salient' (Chuse 2003, 284). Therefore I have argued that identity is the 'foundation feeling' in creating and dancing flamenco – a feeling of belonging to a certain group sharing similar values and meanings. However, 'identity' is not singular. In fact, multiple identities unfolded during the grouping/ coming together at regional and national level. And yet, as we all embarked into a collective process of co-creation, our multiple and distinct identities dissolved over time, regrouping as one 'identity' – that of 'flamenco heritage dancers'. There is thus fluidity in how multiple identities are performed, especially in the early stages of creation, which eventually amalgamate into one. The 'geographical' or 'national' boundaries that may have delineated our identities at the early stages of our choreographic creation were gradually interwoven and blurred.

Identity –no matter in what form – is an essential expedient for heritage to emerge and be sustained. In a social context, such as that of a performance, it is the bonding glue between performers and audience. From a social constructionism perspective, 'every collective becomes a social artifact – an entity molded, refabricated, and mobilized in accord with reigning cultural scripts and centers of power' (Cerulo 1997, 388). This makes me question what is the identification process that we go through as a group? What are the mechanisms by which we create a collective identity? By doing so, do we create 'symbolic boundaries' which exclude certain audiences or is there an opportunity to open up the boundaries and include more audiences (Lamont and Fournier 1992)? Equivalently, is there is a risk of creating exclusive, 'symbolic boundaries' by officially recognising a form of performing art that is transnational and multicultural, of global significance as heritage while, at the same time, attaching it to a specific region?

The dynamics thus in the performance of 'dance heritage' begin as a 'personal identity journey' and evolve as a 'collective identity journey'. During this process, 'physical' and 'symbolic' boundaries among the dancers, or between the dancers and audiences or dancers and 'heritage managers', may be created. It is well known that identities are fluid, in a continual state of becoming. In other words,

> identities are about questions of using the resources of history, language and culture in the process of becoming rather than being: not 'who we are' or 'where we came from', so much as what we become. (Hall and Du Gay 1996, 4)

In my personal case, the performativity began as a journey that emerged from my need to identify 'nationally' – a need that constituted the form of inspiration for a rather unique and unexpected fusion. This project triggered conversations on future fusions associated partially with countries of origin, for example a fusion of Celtic and Flamenco dancing. Our conversations initially reflected our need to locate our legitimate place in an Andalusian tradition. It soon became apparent that what renders Andalusian culture distinct is its multiculturalism (Machin-Autenrieth 2016).

So far I have focused on the dynamics of identity. I outlined that a 'personal identity journey' evolved into a 'collective, co-creative process' during which all dancers were united though their shared passion for dance and heritage. At this early phase, the core elements interconnected in a dynamic manner include 'identity' and 'dancing skills' embodied through 'dancers'. Although the relationship does not change, the scale of identity does. Below I will manifest how the 'value' of 'authenticity' influences the dynamic interconnection of 'identity' and 'dance skills'.

Embodied authenticity

In our attempt to create the 'Byzantine flamenco' choreographic fusion, we delved into historical research. This endeavour generated questions around 'authenticity' and 'historical accuracy' and their potential tension with creativity and innovation. Although the term 'authenticity' is not explicitly stated in the 2003 UNESCO Convention on Intangible Heritage, nor consequently in the nomination, I ended up battling with two dimensions of authenticity. One dimension relates to 'what makes flamenco' authentic in terms of its regional identity (as discussed above). I concluded that it is the cultural diversity of Andalusia that makes the region unique and as such flamenco should reflect this. However, cultural diversity can be jeopardised by the institutionalisation of heritage.

The second dimension, with which this section deals, is how the constant re-creation and innovation moves beyond 'authenticity' or contributes to the 'authenticity' in the sense that flamenco has always been re-created. When it comes to the use of history as a source of inspiration, I navigated between my two identities: that of an academic researcher who researches the 'objective truth' (if there is such a thing) based on available sources and that of the artist who creates liberally without restrictions imposed by academic research. Indeed I used the academic research as a source of inspiration, a point of departure and creativity rather than an end in itself. Authenticity was certainly not what I was looking for – it was innovation, something unique inspired by the past but belonging to the present, or, to phrase it better, something being a product of the present. In the process of developing the choreography, I experienced how my understanding of 'authenticity' changed from searching for historical accuracy to accepting that my academic research inquiry could not be completely fulfilled. In so doing we created a new form of choreography inspired by the past.

What is authenticity? Authenticity often invokes something being genuine or 'faithfully reconstructed' and 'represented' (Van Leeuwen 2001, 393–4). It is not a 'static entity' but a cultural, dynamic construct of the Western ideology (Handler 1986). Although the term has been used in non-Western contexts (see, for instance, the 'Nara document on Authenticity'), it has been done so in order that the Western approach to 'authenticity', which prioritises the originality of the material fabric, is deconstructed and shifted towards a more holistic approach to authenticity – one that merits tradition, skills and the 'practice of doing', rather than the object or site itself. In my personal auto-ethnographic experience, a pursuit for 'authenticity' was initially a quest for historic accuracy. As a deduction, the development of the choreography was transformed into a negotiation process between historical accuracy and authenticity, creativity and imagination (see also Dean 2017).

When did this negotiation start? I highlighted in the previous section that the 'heritage choreographing' commenced as a journey of 'personal identity', which soon evolved into a process of 'collective identity'. In this section I remarked that my 'personal identity' journey was driven, on the one hand, by my need to identify a transnational connection between the 'Andalusian' flamenco and Greece. On the other hand, it was prompted by 'disciplinary identity' as a historian and heritage researcher, as well as by my 'artistic identity' as a dancer. While developing the choreography, I was negotiating my various identities with that of the researcher becoming less dominant over time. Accordingly, the need to be 'historically accurate' and 'authentic' was overshadowed by the demands of my 'artistic identity' to get inspired, create and innovate. As a result, my approach to 'authenticity' shifted in a similar manner to what is construed by Macdonald (2013, 118). Macdonald expounds that

> accuracy and authenticity are matters of negotiation and the faithful reproduction of an original does not necessarily lead to an authentic representation. (Macdonald 2013, 118)

In other words, 'historical authenticity' in our dance performances can be accomplished even if we diverge 'from strict adherence to historical accuracy': what ultimately matters is 'the honesty with which we proceed, and whether what results is convincing for others' (Macdonald 2013, 118). Authenticity is thus not so much about origins or provenance, but rather about the 'truth to a disposition and to the story – and vantage point – that deserves to be told' (Macdonald 2013, 118). Interestingly, the World Heritage Convention on Intangible Cultural Heritage dismisses the concept of authenticity (Jokilehto 2006), as such a reference would contrast the very nature of intangible cultural heritage as dynamic, constantly changing and fluid. However, by doing so the convention 'rendered a gap in the understanding of authenticity' in intangible cultural heritage (Su 2018, 919).

To sum up, the dynamics of 'authenticity' in our choreography unfolded as below. We began with a focus on being 'historically accurate', based on 'evidence' provided by the 'Byzantine' manuscripts. Over time we deviated from this approach, instead using the historical sources only as a means of inspiration, creativity and innovation, rather than as a means of reproducing the past. This venture made us realise that what makes flamenco 'authentic' (as any form of heritage, intangible or tangible) is its constant creation and re-creation.

Our experience as 'art practitioners of intangible heritage' is an experience of what Su calls the subjective authenticity (or existential authenticity). Su defines 'subjective authenticity' as the ability of 'intangible cultural heritage' practitioners to convey their intangible cultural heritage values spontaneously through cultural practices with their knowledge, skills, society (for example, other people and community) and the natural environment (for example, tangible heritage and place) (Su 2018, 924). By doing so, 'cultural heritage practitioners … feel authentic because they realise their intrapersonal and inter-personal subjective wellbeing, or the values of ICH [existential authenticity]' (Su 2018, 924).

Artefactual embodiment

The embodiment of dance movements emboldened by the 'flamenco' and 'Byzantine' traditions was complemented by golden and red accessories reminiscent of these traditions. A 'Byzantine-looking' dress was enriched with 'Byzantine-looking', 'fake golden' earrings, bracelets and necklaces. Flamenco red flowers were used for styling hair. The use of the 'golden' bracelets became 'functional' as they afforded an additional 'sound-making' device which we incorporated into the dancing. During our pursuit of accessories, the significance of the tangibility of flamenco became evident to us. Most objects, traditionally handmade in the past, are nowadays mass-produced and can be ordered online (as we also did). The quality of the manufacturing and materials is poor. The craftsmanship skills associated with making flamenco accessories are almost extinct – yet these skills are barely referenced in the nomination file.

In addition to the embodiment of the various accessories, our body developed into a 'dance device'. Arms, hands and head movements had to be combined with flamenco footwork in such a way that the 'Byzantine-flamenco' fusion could be realised. In the process of embodiment, you are neither Greek, French nor Andalusian, but a member of a group of dancers who co-creates collectively.

Byczkowska (2009, 103) reaffirms our personal experience of embodiment:

> What is very interesting about own body perception among ballroom dancers is that they incorporate their partner's body into the notion of 'my body'.

The body in group dancing is a social creation and as such its physicality is socially constructed (Byczkowska 2009, 101). Moreover, the object, as highlighted by Merleau-Ponty (2011), becomes the extension of the body. For instance, if a dancer practises with an object, such as bracelets and flowers in our case, the objects become part of the dancer's embodiment, as he or she learns to use them like they use their own body (Byczkowska 2009, 101). Dancers claim that before you perform with something on stage you have to learn to use it outside from your mind. The object has to be incorporated into your body and to become a part of it (Merleau-Ponty 2011).

The phenomenon of embodiment of artefacts and objects experienced in dancing occurs in several heritage practices. To some extent

> practices and the artefacts that surround them are embodied heritage, internal to all human beings and affecting us at physical and emotional levels. (Iacono and Brown 2016, 86)

The interrelationship of body and artefacts is so close that the body is objectified and the artefacts embodied. Indeed, artefacts are inseparable from 'the society and culture that creates them and the bodies that manipulate them' (Iacono and Brown 20016, 97). An artefact embodies human action as well as enabling the embodiment of an action (such as in dance). Our way of 'being in the world', of acting, knowing and thinking, is thus largely dependent on artefacts and how they re-form embodiment (Burkitt 1999, 36).

Artefacts are thus an integral part of performing or practising 'intangible' heritage. The tangibility of intangible heritage should therefore be considered when examining the dynamic evolution of a practice. While the World Heritage Convention includes 'objects' in the definition of 'intangible heritage', the operational Directive 109 (c) on raising awareness on intangible cultural heritage calls for

> focus on the continuous recreation and transmission of knowledge and skills necessary for safeguarding intangible cultural heritage, rather than on the objects that are associated with it (https://ich.unesco.org/en/Decisions/4.COM/6)

This call excludes 'objects' from the performance 'equation'. In addition, it neglects the fact that in 'performing arts', in particular, the body of the 'cultural practitioners' is the main, 'multisensory object' which

> seems to obey our will, has the ability to interact with other objects, can incorporate them, and can be perceived and understood from the inside. (Blanke 2012 in Schettler et al. 2019, 4)

Dancers are in the position to embody artefacts into their 'body schema', thereby enlarging their body schema (Heersmink 2012, 122). As these artefacts are embodied, they are experienced as part of the human and social system, rather than in isolation. The perceptual focal point is thus at the artefact–environment interface rather than at the agent–artefact interface, with artefacts performing 'their function only when we bodily interact with them' (Heersmink 2021, 577). To do so, the dancers have to learn how to embody the artefact (skill, knowledge). The flamenco *guajiras*, for instance, requires practice of the technique of dancing with a flamenco fan. Practice necessitates time. The 'embodied skill' of dancing with a fan thus contains 'embodied time'.

Time, knowledge and skills are required so that artefacts are 'absorbed in the body schema' (Heersmink 2021). In view of this, the embodiment of objects may be defined as the sense that those objects have become 'part of us', in a similar way that our limbs or our fingers are parts of us (Schettler et al. 2019). The appropriative embodiment of a 'performative object' cultivates a sense of 'affective embodiment' by which the performers demonstrate 'the same affective reactions for the object as for their own body' (de Vignemont 2011, 85).

Embodied place and space

March 2020. A few days before the inauguration of a lengthy lockdown during the Covid-19 pandemic, we were about to perform our choreographic fusion at one of London's regular *peñas*. A yellow warning for wind and rain meant that we did not manage to reach the venue. At that time it did not seem like a 'disaster'. After all, we knew that plenty of opportunities for performances would appear in the near future. Little did we know that the performance venues were to remain closed for more than a year. As soon as the lockdown started, we endeavoured to explore alternative forms of performing using digital technologies. However, we soon gave up this idea. In what we do the face-to-face connection with the audiences is a vital component of the choreographic experience. The Covid-19 pandemic revealed how decisive a physical place is for the continuation of a 'dance heritage' practice.

'Space and place are always "lived" through bodies' (McCormack 2008, 1829). The Covid-19 pandemic exposed the critical role of 'place' and 'space' in the continuity of a heritage practice, especially of 'performing art heritage'. As with objects, 'place and performance are bound together through the human body' (Ruggles and Silverman 2009, 11). Embodied space and place thus become 'the location where human experience and consciousness takes on material and spatial form' (Low 2003, 9). However, while the absence of *objects* may not have such a detrimental effect threatening the continuation of performing arts (and consequently of art heritage), the absence of physical, performative *space* can endanger the continuation of 'art heritage'. The role of digital technologies is limited. Digital technologies can be instrumental for the preservation of 'art heritage'. However, digital technologies cannot replicate the experiences of audiences and performers gained through watching or performing events on stage.

What makes the 'physical' space that imperative? The fact that

> bodies move in more ways than one (spatio-temporally, kinaesthetically, affectively, collectively, politically and imaginatively) and that this movement is potentially generative of different kinds of spaces. (McCormack 2008, 1822)

In 'dance heritage' the physical space permits dancers to connect with each other; while they do so, they also connect with the audiences. The physical space mediates the sensory experience of both dancers and audiences. Moreover, a place embodies certain values and meanings, which they may not necessarily relate to the physical location or to events that happened in the past (Bleam 2018, 79). The art-café 'Artfix', our place of rehearsals and performance, signifies for us creativity and socialising, this 'being together' moment, a value associative with the particular space.

Of course, the 'art nature' of the space, decorated with constantly renewed art paintings or other 'art work', contributed to its sense of creativity and inspiration. All these senses were embodied in the physical space. An embodied place is the existential and phenomenological reality of place experienced through its smell, feel, colour and other sensory dimensions (Low 2003). An 'embodied place' thus connotes the idea 'of being there' and 'doing something together' or the idea of 'being-in-the-world' (see, for instance, Richardson 1982), a sense that was violently removed from our everyday life during the pandemic. A 'place' becomes embedded when it is converted from a 'static space' to an 'action' (Schiller and Rubidge 2014).

Embodied skills

Article 2 of the World Heritage Convention on Intangible Heritage defines 'intangible cultural heritage' as

> the practices, representations, expressions, knowledge, skills – as well as the instruments, objects, artefacts and cultural spaces associated therewith – that communities, groups and, in some cases, individuals recognize as part of their cultural heritage.

The convention also observes that 'intangible heritage' is manifested inter alia in various domains including performing arts and traditional craftsmanship, among others.

Iacono and Brown have noted that the skills and artefacts mentioned in the UNESCO definition

> are allocative resources connected to each other and are also, in turn, embodied in the individuals that form part of the fields which produce those skills and artefacts. (Iacono and Brown 2016, 98)

Skills associated with 'intangible heritage' are embodied in a person and as such are integral to the sustainability of intangible heritage (Akagawa 2016, 70). Therefore, 'intangible heritage' 'consists of cultural manifestations (knowledge, skills, performance) that are inextricably linked to persons' (Kirshenblatt-Gimblett 2014, 171). Consequently the bodies of the 'performers', the 'practitioners' of the skills, become inseparable from the skills themselves. As Kirshenblatt-Gimblett argues:

> It is not possible – or it is not as easy – to treat such manifestations as proxies for persons, even with recording technologies that can separate performances from performers and consign the repertoire to the archive. (2014, 171)

Those practising the skills are the bearers and transmitters of heritage.

Would it be possible for the practice of 'performing art heritage' to continue without 'skills' and 'knowledge'? In other words, how critical are 'skills' and 'knowledge' for the existence and continuation of 'performing art heritage'? Skills constitute a form of 'intangible heritage'. At the same time, 'skills' are also the medium for sustaining 'tangible' and 'intangible' dimensions of heritage. A reciprocal relationship exists between the material fabric of heritage and the craft skills required for performing this heritage (Djabarouti 2021, 400). Moreover, do 'skills' and 'knowledge' disappear completely or do they stay 'dormant' for certain periods before they revive? Shove et al. (2012) have argued 'that competences can lie dormant, persisting in the memory for years without being activated, or being at least partly preserved in written form – in recipes, manuals and instructions'. However, they also note that 'as things fall out of use, the know-how associated with them tends to disappear as well' (Shove et al. 2012, 48).

In the example of flamenco, the skills linked to the craftsmanship of handmade fans or other related objects have largely disappeared, to be replaced by machine production. However, the extinction of craftsmanship skills did not, in this instance, imperil the flourishing of flamenco. The dance, art and heritage of flamenco adjusts to the new era and obtains new forms, as it has always done.

Embodied time

The notion of 'time' is embodied in multiple ways in 'dance heritage'. Firstly, our choreographic journey is a journey of 'time' that aims to transcend the present and merge it with the past. Although we explore 'historic' cultural influences on flamenco, our final choreographic product aligns more with the principles of 'contemporary flamenco'. By looking at the nomination file, 'contemporary flamenco' may not be regarded by dancers or scholars as 'heritage' since it differs from 'traditional' or 'pure' flamenco. On the other hand, the fact that 'contemporary flamenco' is constantly created and re-created renders the classification of 'contemporary flamenco' under heritage more appropriate than 'tradition'. This is because

> the concept of tradition expresses temporal continuity, marking a phenomenon or a hereditary custom that is transmitted from generation to generation. (Kuutma and Kästik 2014, 284–5)

Intergeneration transmission is also an 'attribute' of heritage. However, according to contemporary theoretical strands of heritage, the continuity of heritage depends on constant creation and re-creation, rather than on the replication of 'original', 'authentic' and 'pure' forms of heritage from the past. There is a 'time dimension' that needs to be considered in this discussion. Tradition connotes something 'old' and possibly something 'authentic' and 'pure'. Heritage, on the other hand, connotes 'something' made in the present even if it is associated or inspired by the past. Tradition also has a present temporal dimension, but it implies closer alignment with the past.

Time is also embodied through our dance movements. Merleau-Ponty (2011, 117) contends that a body's movement inhabits space and time: 'because it is not limited to submitting passively to space and time, it actively assumes them'. In our choreographic fusion, the past is merged with the present through our dance movements as 'ways of thinking that embody different cultures' (Sklar 2001, 92).

Other ways in which time is embodied during a dance performance is when dance movements synchronise with music (Iacono and Brown 2016, 93). Additional elements such as sound and light can be critical in the embodiment process of time and effect (see, for instance, Adshead 1988). Indeed, our choreographic fusion utilised bells, cymbals, jewellery, all echoing the time of 'Byzantium' with the ultimate goal to evoke feelings in the 'present'. In other words our bodies, accessories and surrounding environment acted as the mediating device between past and present. Embodied time is thus 'a notional way of capturing the past as it is in the lived present' (Dewsbury 2002, 149).

As with any form of art, the performing arts have the ability to create the experience of 'vertical time' for audiences 'by plunging a stake or dropping an anchor into the endless flow of time, thereby creating a sense of eternity in the human body' (Bogart 2019, 4). The vertical time reflects the performer's spiritual experience, an experience that includes layers of the past into the present (Marievskaya 2015, 38–9). The sense of eternity is communicated through the combination of 'tempo, duration or rhythm'; it also 'traffics in the semantics of space, encompassing architecture, shape or spatial relationship' (Bogart 2019, 4).

Bresnahan has commented that

> Dancing is a thinking-while-doing process that involves the sort of temporal consciousness that is itself either both thoroughly embodied and spatial in an integrated way or in which embodied and spatial experiences occur concurrently. (Bresnahan 2017, 339)

Sondra Horton Fraleigh points out that for the dancer, 'movement, space, and time are only abstractions until they are embodied' (1987, 182). Thus, as Bresnahan observes,

> the dancer's consciousness of time and space arises with and is influenced by his dynamic and embodied experience, and this is one of interacting with the world outside of himself. (Bresnahan 2017, 339)

Embodied resources

The core element of 'resources', in the context of 'performing art heritage', moves beyond the resources needed to produce a performance encompassing 'language, gesture, gaze, head movement, facial expression, body posture and body movement, as well as object manipulation, technology and body movement within space' (Douglah, 2020). In other words, embodied resources can include anything that lives in a performer's body (Markakis 2016, 1). As a result, 'when analysing an activity that is centred around the body (e.g., budo or dancing), and where embodied resources are as necessary as verbal conduct, it is vital to bear in mind that certain embodied resources can serve the same function as words' (Markakis 2016, 1). In our case, all 'objects' used for the choreography, including our own bodies, constituted embodied resources – in the sense that without them we would have not been able to develop the choreography. The central element in dance heritage is therefore the 'body' and the 'process of embodiment' of the space, place, affect and materials.

Conclusion

In this chapter I embraced an auto-ethnographic approach, mustering my personal experience as a 'flamenco heritage' choreographer and researcher. Although a certain element of auto-ethnography underpins the entire book, in this chapter auto-ethnography drives the analysis of how the 'heritage dynamic elements' (materials, values, time, resources, senses, space/place and skills) are sustained or broken over time in the context of 'dance heritage'.

I argued that the 'heritage dynamic elements' in 'dance heritage', or 'performing art heritage' more generally, are fused together through the dancers' bodies. Subsequently the heritage dynamic elements in the dance context are transformed into embodied components of the dynamic practice of performance creation. In addition to the 'body' – a prerequisite for 'dance heritage' – I stressed that for 'performing art heritage' the availability of 'physical space' is one of the most critical elements for the continuation and sustainability of a dance practice. From a 'heritage dynamics' perspective, I illustrated how the identity of dancers evolves from a 'personal identity' journey into a collective identity formation, transcending any cultural or national boundaries that may have initially been in place. I also demonstrated how the individual 'material' elements merged together through the 'embodiment' process in order to generate an 'affect' for dancers and audiences. Furthermore, I unveiled how different times, represented by culturally different dances, also merge and create a new product in the present.

To conclude, the notion of 'fusion' is of interest here. Since our intention was to create a 'fusion' of what initially seemed to be two fundamentally different traditions and dances, by fusing the various individual elements we created a 'product' that is both timeless (that is, it does not belong to a specific temporal moment) and 'placeless' (that is, it can belong to everywhere). This fusing process has potential implications for providing the platform for different communities and cultural groups to work together creatively, synthesising their own personal experiences and traditions in such a way as to convey contemporary messages.

For future research, it would be interesting to unpack the dynamics of the inscription of flamenco to the World Heritage List, as well as considering the impact of this inscription on the 'art' and 'heritage' dimensions of flamenco and the potential of flamenco and 'performing arts heritage' as community engagement strategies. Comprehending the dynamic mechanisms of 'performing art heritage' can re-orientate traditional thinking on 'tangible heritage' by shifting attention to the 'materiality', 'authenticity', 'originality' and 'integrity' towards 'fluidity', 'embodiment', 're-creation through co-creation' and 'adaptability'.

Conclusion

This book has proposed a fresh approach to the study and practice of heritage which it refers to as 'heritage dynamics'. I argued that heritage as a 'thing' and as a 'process' is a dynamic, complex 'system'. I have used the term 'system' to denote the non-linear, dynamic interrelationships between 'materials', 'values/meanings', 'place/space', 'senses/emotions', 'time', 'resources' and 'skills/competencies' that underpin the ways in which heritage emerges, shifts, declines and revives over time. I contended that the continuation and transformation of heritage will depend on how these interconnections evolve or break. If broken, a heritage object, site, or practice may disappear but also re-appear in a new form.

In view of this, I highlighted the 'renewable' nature of heritage. In contrast to heritage management discourses (especially in the context of sustainable development) which stress that heritage is a 'non-renewable resource' (Blagojević and Tufegdžić, 2016; Brattli 2009; CofEU 2014; Comer 2014; Rukavina et al. 2018), I demonstrated that heritage is 'renewable'. As a 'renewable resource', heritage in all its forms is characterised by circular life cycles, with each end of a life cycle marking a new beginning. The idea of heritage as a 'renewable resource' opens up novel and creative ways for heritage to drive rather than deter sustainable development.

This concept of heritage guided the elaboration of the 'heritage dynamics' framework – a framework developed through the 'meta-interpretation' of several case studies representing diverse heritage contexts. I argued that heritage is a socio-cultural dynamic practice, the continuation and transformation of which depends on how links between 'values', 'materials', 'senses and feelings', 'place, space, environment', 'skills/competencies', 'resources' and 'time' are maintained or broken. Although I have previously explored in depth some of the examples discussed here as individual case studies, drawing on a vast amount of qualitative data that has been collected and analysed over the last 17 years, my approach in this book was rather different. In *Heritage Dynamics* I endeavoured to conduct a meta-interpretation analysis of the rather diverse case studies through the theoretical lens of 'heritage dynamics' (Chapter 1). By drawing on such a diverse array of examples, I was able to refine and apply the proposed 'heritage dynamics' framework more widely.

Chapter 2 advanced the 'heritage dynamics' framework introduced in Chapter 1 by presenting a preliminary 'urban heritage dynamics' theory in the context of urban heritage and urban regeneration. The focal point of the chapter was the regeneration of the Royal Arsenal site in Woolwich, a project that has been transforming the area over the last 20 years. I attempted to unpack the underpinning forces that drive 'sustainable' or 'unsustainable' social and cultural change in this case. By doing so, I enhanced my initial 'heritage dynamics' framework with elements from 'urban dynamics' studies and models as a point of departure. 'Urban dynamics' are founded on 'system dynamics' – a method that can be proved particularly useful for cultivating a systems thinking approach towards heritage.

However, I also demonstrated that as much as urban dynamics models and theories offer a potentially useful tool for visualising and communicating the unintended consequences of a decision on urban growth and revitalisation, they do not apply more broadly in urban heritage areas. Since traditional urban dynamic models support revitalisation through demolition of 'deteriorated' housing stock and other 'ageing' structures, in historic cities existing built structures can formulate the basis for revitalisation and rebirth. As in subsequent chapters, it became evident that the abandonment of the Royal Arsenal in its traditional form in fact signified a new 'life cycle' for the area. Most existing structures were listed, requiring new ways of transformation that had to rely on a mixture of 'old' and 'new' structures. However, such a transformation was the catalyst for a social division between the 'old' and 'new', more affluent communities. This division was exacerbated by a physical boundary: a 1980s road and wall that disconnect the Royal Arsenal from the nearby town centre.

In the light of this, I illustrated that 'physical boundaries' can generate symbolic and social boundaries beyond the initial physical demarcation. I concluded Chapter 2 by presenting an 'urban heritage dynamics' model to show that, in the context of an urban heritage area, it is inadequate simply to observe the dynamic interconnections of the number of businesses, houses and population; more qualitative elements such as 'heritage values', 'community participation' and 'community well-being' data need also to be integrated. What remains to be completed in the future is the elaboration and further enhancement of the 'urban heritage dynamics' model. This requires equations that will allow the performance of simulations, thus facilitating the use of this model by future practitioners as a practical tool for decision-making. This work is currently ongoing as part of the JPI-JPHE CURBATHERI (Curating Urban Transformations through Heritage – Deep Cities) project, of which Woolwich is one of the four main case studies (www.deepcities.eu).

Chapter 3 focuses on smaller-scale components of the 'urban heritage system' – that is, the 'old' listed or non-listed residences. I refer to them as 'everyday heritage', meaning heritage experienced in 'everyday life', not just from the perspective of the 'viewer' but also from the angle of the 'user'. In this chapter I considered how residents' meanings and values towards 'original' features change over time, in accordance with their need to improve thermal comfort and energy efficiency, for example. Building upon previous work investigating the ways in which residents negotiate their decisions on thermal comfort improvements, energy efficiency and heritage conservation (Fouseki, Newton et al. 2020), I explored the dynamic 'interconnectedness' of 'heritage values'. I argued that 'heritage values' are dynamic processes, formulated and reshaped through interconnections of 'materials', 'values' and 'feelings'. I stressed that 'heritage values' cannot be classified or grouped into individual categories as there is a high degree of interconnectedness between 'values' and 'meanings'. By drawing on theories of 'everyday aesthetics' and 'functional beauty', I illustrated how heritage values decline over time as prioritisation over thermal comfort increases, but also revive while an area is going through 'gentrification'.

In Chapter 4 I further expanded the discussion on 'functional aesthetics' and 'everyday heritage' by examining how functional everyday objects become heritage and, ultimately, museum objects. For this purpose, I used the example of the 'old', traditional, Maltese buses which, following their replacement with modern ones, embarked on various journeys. When the buses came to the end of their original use, due to 'material' and 'environmental' challenges, new socio-cultural 'meanings' and 'values' emerged or became visible (as they may have already been inherent in the vehicles). The loss of buses from the Maltese urban landscape provoked feelings of nostalgia and sorrow; this in turn led to 'heritagisation', aimed to be achieved through collection and display. However, lack of 'space' and 'resources' did not allow protection for the full 'bus collection'. New life cycles thus opened, including the use of buses for heritage tours or souvenir shops. This example vividly demonstrates not only the 'circularity' and 'non-renewable' nature of heritage, but also the practical constraints in managing collections of large objects.

Chapter 5 moves from the context of collection acquisition to that of exhibition development. By drawing upon the 'London, Sugar and Slavery' and 'Atlantic Worlds' exhibitions, located in London at the Museum of Docklands and the National Maritime Museum respectively, I argued that a museum exhibition is also a socio-cultural, dynamic and systemic practice. The development and continuation of such a practice depends on the interconnections of materials, values/meanings, space/place, skills/competencies, resources, time and senses/feelings. By analysing evidence I revealed that 'senses/feelings' and 'space' proved to be the most critical elements in demarcating the life cycle of a museum exhibition.

Since 2007, the launch year of the exhibitions that marked the bicentenary of the abolition of the slave trade in the UK, none of the displays have remained static. The 'London, Sugar and Slavery' gallery has from its early phases incorporated a changeable exhibition space, updated periodically through co-creation with community groups. The surrounding landscape of the museum also changed substantially after the removal of the statue of Robert Milligan in 2020 as a response to the 'Black Lives Matter' movement. The 'Atlantic Worlds' exhibition is currently undergoing dramatic transformation. A 'Work in Progress' section was established in response to reactions from the local African Caribbean community. Here the exhibition's narrative style and design differ fundamentally from the 'factual', 'academic' and 'historic' style adopted for the rest of the gallery. The different exhibition styles (i.e. 'factual' for the original 'Atlantic Worlds' exhibition and 'emotional' for the 'London, Sugar and Slavery' display) reflect to some extent the degree of participation of groups from beyond the museums themselves.

This example illustrated that a museum exhibition, like any other 'system', evolves, changes and shifts in accordance with external forces, and vice versa. External forces will influence the content and style of an exhibition. This dialogical relationship is often forgotten, especially in museum practice, where a museum project has a beginning, a middle and an end before a new project begins. In fact change always occurs, even if it is not intentional.

Chapter 6 revolved around the dynamics of 'heritage dissonance' as manifested in one of the most controversial of recent museums, the New Acropolis Museum in Athens. In the case of the New Acropolis Museum, the Greek 'authorised heritage discourse' (Smith 2006) privileged the monumental, aesthetic and sacred rock of Acropolis de-appreciating and erasing layers of the 'deep history' of the area (Fouseki, Guttormsen and Swensen 2020). The process of exclusion and erasure ultimately fosters heritage dissonance. However, interestingly in this case, the rhetoric adopted by both opponents and supporters framed their argument around the values supported in an 'authorised heritage discourse', i.e. 'aesthetics of sacredness' and 'national and international emblematic' significance of the Parthenon Sculptures. 'Heritage dissonance' or 'dissonant heritage' is a social practice, the emergence and continuation of which depends on the dynamic interlinkages between values, materials, space/place, senses/emotions, skills/competencies, resources and time. These elements do not obviously stand alone, but are rather performed by a wide array of 'agents'.

As a matter of fact, agents are omnipresent. Each agent or group of agents determines the linkages based on their values, aspirations, needs and goals. In the case of the construction of the New Acropolis Museum, the contestation was implanted when the Makriyianni area, a narrow plot located in the densely inhabited centre of Athens beneath the slopes of the Acropolis Hill, was selected as the site for the 'new museum'. This case revealed the contentious interplay between the 'present' place of the Makriyianni area, the Acropolis Hill, and the 'future' space of the museum. The conflict required an interrelationship between 'space/place' and 'values'. The contestation evolved when the museum design was announced in 1991, following two unsuccessful national competitions in the 1970s.

The museum proposal made a strong connection with the repatriation of the 'Parthenon Marbles'. As such, the museum itself became part of the 'claim for the repatriation of the Parthenon Marbles'; in other words, the claim was materialised through the museum. The need for 'visual contact' and display in the 'Attic light', although already acknowledged in the previous competitions, was now more pertinent than ever. The dispute was thus fed by the antagonistic interrelationship between 'place/space', 'values' and 'materials' as evidenced in the museum design.

Senses of aesthetics and pride are essential elements in this process. While in principle this proposal would alleviate the conflicts, the discovery of archaeological remains further triggered the conflicts alongside the compulsorily purchased homes and the de-listing of the Art Deco building surrounding the site. There is a contested relationship here between 'materials' representing different historic periods, a clash between the 'ancient', the 'modern' and the 'post-modern'. The museum evolved into a 'supreme object' similar to the Acropolis Hill – anything in between was viewed as an obstacle.

The new competition and integration of the remains aimed to resolve the conflict through a re-design of the space. In reality this did not occur, due to expropriations and the modern buildings. In court, the Art Deco building was saved from demolition, though the blocks of flats were not. The 'visual contact' and 'Attic light' evolved from a 'sensual' and 'spatial' element into a 'material' element, at least for the lead architect. So, in the end, what led to the conflict 'resolution'? The elements of 'time' and 'resources' proved significant in this project, not only in terms of posing an obstacle but also of contributing to resolution. Time and resources were added substantially for the completion of the museum project, possible only due to its 'national significance'.

In Chapter 7 I adopted an auto-ethnographic approach. Here I drew upon my personal experience as flamenco choreographer and 'heritage enthusiast' in order to comprehend how the interconnections of heritage dynamics (materials, values, time, resources, senses, space/place and skills) are sustained or broken. I argued that all elements are connected through a process of embodiment in 'performing art heritage'. I also stressed that for 'performing art heritage' the most critical element for its continuation and sustainability proved to be the 'space'. This was abruptly revealed during the Covid-19 pandemic.

The departure point for the case of choreography illustrated in the chapter was the need to 'create' and 'identify' through creation and innovation. Although our name, the 'Flamenco Heritage Artists', reveals our enthusiasm for exploring historic influences on flamenco, I came to realise that our final product aligns more with the principles of 'contemporary flamenco'. By looking at the nomination file, 'contemporary flamenco' may not be counted by some as 'heritage' as it differs from 'traditional' or 'pure' flamenco. However, the fact that it is a 'new' creation inspired by the 'past' in fact makes it more relevant as heritage, since heritage is a concept created in the present. Tradition, on the other hand, connotes something 'old' and possibly something 'authentic' and 'pure'.

'Heritage dynamics' force us to rethink and reimagine heritage objects, places and practices as dynamic, complex systems. The term also motivates us to think of 'change' in a non-linear way, prompting heritage management plans to evolve from linear progression to a circular form. Some key ideas that emerged while applying this framework are the ideas of 'non-linear change', heritage as a 'renewable resource' and the 'interconnectedness' of values. The 'non-linearity' of change and continuity will hopefully influence the way in which heritage management processes, currently linear and processual, are conceived. The idea of heritage as a 'renewable resource' will re-orientate heritage management strategies and policies, from managing change as a threat to dealing with change as a value and opportunity for renewal. Awareness of the interconnectedness of values will hopefully motivate us to use more sophisticated methods, able to capture the complex and systemic interconnections of value and to move beyond static typologies and classifications.

Ultimately, *Heritage Dynamics* is only an introduction to theorising and methodologically exploring the dynamic nature of various forms of heritage and heritage processes. These range from collections to historic cities and buildings, and from participatory museums and exhibitions to performing arts. Hopefully the book will encourage future in-depth studies into the dynamic and systemic nature of heritage, as well as complement the growing studies that revolve around 'future heritage' and 'heritage futures' (Holtorf and Högberg, 2021) by offering a trans-temporal approach that merges the past ('deep heritage', see for instance Fouseki, Guttormsen and Swensen 2020), the present and the future.

References

Abbott, A. 1995. 'Things of boundaries', *Social Research* 62(4): 857–82.

Adams, T. E., S. H. Jones and C. Ellis. 2015. *Autoethnography*. Oxford: Oxford University Press.

Adams, T. E., C. Ellis and S. H. Jones. 2017. 'Autoethnography'. In *The International Encyclopedia of Communication Research Methods*, edited by J. Matthes, C. Davis and R. Potter, 1–11. Hoboken, NJ: Wiley.

Adshead, J. 1988. 'An introduction to dance analysis: Its nature and place in the study of dance'. In *Dance Analysis: Theory and practice*, edited by V. Briginshaw, P. Hodgens and M. Huxley, 4–20. Binsted, Hampshire, UK: Dance Books Limited.

Ahmer, C. 2020. 'Riegl's "Modern Cult of Monuments" as a theory underpinning practical conservation and restoration work', *Journal of Architectural Conservation* 26(2): 150–65.

Akagawa, N. 2016. 'Intangible heritage and embodiment: Japan's influence on global heritage discourse'. In *A Companion to Heritage Studies*, edited by W. Logan, M. N. Craith and U. Kockel, 69–86. Hoboken, NJ: John Wiley & Sons.

Alfeld, L. E. and A. K. Graham. 1976. *Introduction to Urban Dynamics*. Waltham, MA: Pegasus Communications.

Alfeld, L. E. 1995. 'Urban dynamics—the first fifty years', *System Dynamics Review* 11(3): 199–217.

Alfeld, L. E. 2009. 'Urban dynamics in system dynamics'. In *System Dynamics*, edited by Y. Barlas, vol. 1, 69–84. Oxford: UNESCO in partnership with Eolss publishers (Encyclopedia of Life support systems).

Ameen, J. 2012. 'You can own an old "iconic" bus', *Times of Malta*, 13 February 2012. https://timesofmalta.com/articles/view/You-can-own-an-old-iconic-bus.406486.

Anderson, B. 2008. 'For Space (2005): Doreen Massey'. In *Key Texts in Human Geography*, edited by P. Hubbard, R. Kitchin and G. Valentine, 227–35. New York: Sage.

Anderson, B. and P. Harrison. 2010. *The Promise of Non-Representational Theories*. Farnham, Surrey: Ashgate.

Anderson, B. and C. McFarlane. 2011. 'Assemblage and geography', *Area* 43(2): 124–7.

Araujo, A. L. 2012. 'Transnational memory of slave merchants: Making the perpetrators visible in the public space'. In *Politics of Memory: Making slavery visible in the public space*, edited by A. L. Araujo, 15–35. London; New York: Routledge.

Arrhenius, T. 2004. 'The cult of age in mass-society: Alois Riegl's theory of conservation', *Future Anterior: Journal of Historic Preservation, History, Theory and Criticism*, 75–81.

Ashley-Smith, J. 2013. *Risk Assessment for Object Conservation*. London; New York: Routledge.

Ashworth, G. J., B. Graham and J. E. Tunbridge. 2007. *Pluralising Pasts: Heritage, identity and place. Multicultural societies*. Wallingford, Oxfordshire: CABI Publishing.

Attard, M. and D. Hall. 2003. 'Public transport modernisation and adjustment to EU accession requirements: The case of Malta's buses', *Journal of Transport Geography* 11(1): 13–24.

Attfield, J. 2020. *Wild Things: The material culture of everyday life*, vol. 4. London: Bloomsbury.

Averch, H. and R. A. Levine. 1971. 'Two models of the urban crisis: An analytical essay on Banfield and Forrester', *Policy Sciences* 2(2): 143–58.

Avrami, E. C. 2012. *A Systems Approach to Historic Preservation in an Era of Sustainability Planning*. New Brunswick, NJ: Rutgers: The State University of New Jersey.

Bajada, T. and H. Titheridge. 2017. 'The attitudes of tourists towards a bus service: Implications for policy from a Maltese case study', *Transportation Research Procedia* 25: 4110–29.

Bakker, F. 2013. 'Shapes of "culture" and the sacred surplus: Heritage formation and Pentecostal conversion among the Pataxó Indians in Brazil', *Material Religion* 9(3): 304–27.

Bala, B. K., F. M. Arshad and K. M. Noh. 2017. 'Causal loop diagrams'. In *System Dynamics: Springer texts in business and* economics, edited by B. K. Bala, F. M. Ashad and K. M. Noh, 37–51. Singapore: Springer.

Barile, S., M. Saviano and M. Montella. 2012. 'A service-based systems view of cultural heritage', *Journal of Business Market Management* 32(3): 106–36.

Basile, G., H. R. Kaufmann and M. Savastano. 2018. 'Revisiting complexity theory to achieve strategic intelligence', *International Journal of Foresight and Innovation Policy* 13(1–2): 57–70.

Batty, M., Y. Xie and Z. Sun. 1999. 'Modeling urban dynamics through GIS-based cellular automata', *Computers, Environment and Urban Systems* 23(3): 205–33.

Batty, M. 2005. 'Agents, cells, and cities: New representational models for simulating multiscale urban dynamics', *Environment and Planning A*, 37(8): 1373–94.

Batty, M. 2009. 'Cities as complex systems: Scaling, interaction, networks, dynamics and urban morphologies'. In *Encyclopedia of Complexity and Systems Science*, edited by R. Meyers, 1041–71. New York: Springer. https://doi.org/10.1007/978-0-387-30440-3_69.

Beauregard, R. A. 1993. 'Representing urban decline: Postwar cities as narrative objects', *Urban Affairs Quarterly* 29(2): 187–202.

Bendell, J. 2018. *Deep Adaptation: A map for navigating climate tragedy*. Institute for Leadership and Sustainability. University of Cumbria, Ambleside, UK. Online: http://www.lifeworth.com/deepadaptation.pdf.

Bennett, J. 2010. *Vibrant Matter: A political ecology of things*. Durham, NC: Duke University Press.

Beresford, J. 2016. 'The Caryatids in the New Acropolis Museum: Out of sight, out of light, out of mind', *Journal of Conservation and Museum Studies* 14(1): 1–16.

Beresford, J. 2017. 'Tripping on the fantastic light: Reclaiming the Parthenon Marbles'. In *Colour and Light in Ancient and Medieval Art*, edited by S. Aulsebrook, 61–78. London; New York: Routledge.

Berlinski, D. J. 1970. 'Systems analysis', *Urban Affairs Quarterly* 6(1): 104–26.

Bertuglia, C. S. 2013. *Urban Dynamics: Designing an integrated model*. London; New York: Routledge.

Bhaskar, R. 1997. *A Realist Theory of Science*. London: Verso.

Bhaskar, R., A. Collier, T. Lawson and A. Norrie (eds). 1998. *Critical Realism: Essential readings*. London; New York: Routledge.

Bhaskar, R. 2010. 'Contexts of interdisciplinarity: Interdisciplinarity and climate change'. In *Interdisciplinarity and Climate Change: Transforming knowledge and practice for our global future*, edited by R. Bhaskar, C. Frank, K. G. Høyer, P. Naess and J. Parker, 1–24. London; New York: Routledge.

Bicchieri, M., A. Sodo, G. Piantanida and C. Coluzza. 2006. 'Analysis of degraded papers by non-destructive spectroscopic techniques', *Journal of Raman Spectroscopy: An International Journal for Original Work in all Aspects of Raman Spectroscopy, Including Higher Order Processes, and also Brillouin and Rayleigh Scattering* 37(10): 1186–92.

Bickford, A. 1981. 'The patina of nostalgia', *Australian Archaeology* 13(1): 1–7.

Bille, M. 2012. 'Assembling heritage: Investigating the UNESCO proclamation of Bedouin intangible heritage in Jordan', *International Journal of Heritage Studies* 18(2): 107–23.

Blagojević, M. R. and A. Tufegdžić. 2016. 'The new technology era requirements and sustainable approach to industrial heritage renewal', *Energy and Buildings* 115: 148–53.

Blake, J. 2009. 'UNESCO's 2003 convention on intangible cultural heritage: The implications of community involvement in "safeguarding"'. In *Intangible Heritage*, edited by L. Smith and N. Adagawa, 45–73. London; New York: Routledge.

Blanke, O. 2012. 'Multisensory brain mechanisms of bodily self-consciousness', *Nature Reviews Neuroscience* 13: 556–71. https://doi.org/10.1038/nrm3292.

Bleam, R. M. 2018. 'Unbounded place meanings and embodied place identities for conservation volunteers in Scottsdale, Arizona', *Journal of Environmental Psychology* 56: 76–83.

Blühm, A. 2016. 'Managing change at the Groninger Museum', *Museum Management and Curatorship* 31: 96–101.

Blunt, A., C. L. Ebbensgaard and O. Sheringham. 2021. 'The "living of time": Entangled temporalities of home and the city', *Transactions of the Institute of British Geographers* 46(1), 149–62.

Bodo, S. 2012. 'Museums as intercultural spaces'. In *Museums, Equality and Social Justice*, edited by R. Sandell and E. Nightingale, 181–91. London; New York: Routledge.

Bogart, A. 2019. 'Foreword: Embodied time'. In *Time and Performer Training*, edited by M. Evans, K. Thomaidis and L. Worth, 3–6. London; New York: Routledge.

Bogle, E. 2013. *Museum Exhibition Planning and Design*. Lanham, MD: AltaMira Press.

Bonnell, J. and R. I. Simon. 2007. *Difficult Exhibitions and Intimate Encounters. Museum and society* 5(2): 65–85.

Boniface, P. and P. Fowler. 2002. *Heritage and Tourism in the Global Village*. London; New York: Routledge.

Bortolotto, C. 2007. 'From objects to processes: UNESCO's intangible cultural heritage', *Journal of Museum Ethnography* 19, 21–33.

Bouquet, M. 2013. 'Heritage: Renovation, relocation, remediation and repositioning museums', *Museum Worlds* 1(1), 85–100.

Bowell, K. 2018. 'Object reincarnation: Imagining a future outside the permanent collection'. In *Active Collections*, edited by E. Wood, R. Tisdale and T. Jones, 152–61. London; New York: Routledge.

Bratasz, L., T. White, S. Butts, C. Sease, N. Utrup, R. Boardman and S. Simon. 2018. 'Toward sustainable collections management in the Yale Peabody Museum: Risk assessment, climate management and energy efficiency', *Bulletin of the Peabody Museum of Natural History* 59(2): 249–68.

Brattli, T. 2009. 'Managing the archaeological world cultural heritage: Consensus or rhetoric?', *Norwegian Archaeological Review* 42(1): 24–39.

Bresnahan, A. W. 2017. 'Dancing in time'. In *Routledge Handbook of Philosophy of Temporal Experience*, edited by I. Phillips, 339–48. London; New York: Routledge.

Bressey, C. and T. Wareham. 2010. *Reading the London, Sugar & Slavery Gallery*. London: Museum of London Docklands.

British Standards Institute. 2009. *Code of Practice for Cultural Protections Management*. PAS: 197: 2009.

Bryson, N. 1988. 'The gaze in the expanded field'. In *Vision and Visuality*, edited by H. Forster, 87–108. Seattle, WA: Bay Press.

Buchanan, I. 2017. 'Assemblage theory, or the future of an illusion', *Deleuze Studies* 11(3): 457–74.

Buchanan, I. 2020. *Assemblage Theory and Method: An introduction and guide*. London: Bloomsbury Academic.

Buchanan, I. 2015. 'Assemblage theory and its discontents', *Deleuze and Guatarri Studies* 9(3): 382–92.

Buchanan, S. A. 2019. 'The assemblage of repository and museum work in archaeological curation', *Information Research* 24(2), paper 816. Retrieved from http://InformationR.net/ir/24-2/paper816.html. Archived by WebCite® at http://www.webcitation.org/78mjUYkhj.

Burkitt, I. 1999. *Bodies of Thought: Embodiment, identity and modernity*. London: Sage.

Buskell, A., M. Enquist and F. Jansson. 2019. 'A systems approach to cultural evolution', *Palgrave Communications* 52(1): 1–15.

Butz, D. and K. Besio. 2009. 'Autoethnography', *Geography Compass* 3(5): 1660–74.

Byczkowska, D. 2009. 'What do we study studying body? Researcher's attempts to embodiment research', *Qualitative Sociology Review* 5(3): 100–12.

Byrne, D. 1997. 'Complexity theory and social research', *Social Research Update* 18 (Autumn), 1–6.

Byrne, D. and G. Callaghan. 2013. *Complexity Theory and the Social Sciences: The state of the art*. London; New York: Routledge.

Caro, R. and J. J. Sendra. 2020. 'Evaluation of indoor environment and energy performance of dwellings in heritage buildings: The case of hot summers in historic cities in Mediterranean Europe', *Sustainable Cities and Society* 52: 101798. https://doi.org/10.1016/j.scs.2019.101798.

Cassar, G. and M. Avellino. 2020. 'Negotiating a postmemory dichotomy: Nostalgia and aversion in Malta', *Politeja* 2(65): 239–56.

Cerulo, K. A. 1997. 'Identity construction: New issues, new directions', *Annual Review of Sociology* 23(1): 385–409.

Chevron. 2015. *A Graveyard for the Malta Buses*. Online: retrieved from 'Malta Buses Graveyard – The Bus Museum Malta', Chevron Air Holidays, https://www.chevron.co.uk/blog/a-graveyard-for-the-malta-buses/, 8 August 2020.

Christoforidis, M. 2007. 'Manuel de Falla, flamenco and Spanish identity'. In *Western Music and Race*, edited by J. Brown, 230–43. Cambridge: Cambridge University Press.

Chuse, L. 2003. *Cantaoras: Music, gender, and identity in flamenco song*. London; New York: Routledge.

Clark, C. 2005. 'Coming into the light: The rediscovery and reuse of naval heritage buildings', *WIT Transactions on the Built Environment* 79, 33–44.

Clifford, J. 1997. *Routes: Travel and translation in the late twentieth century*. Cambridge, MA: Harvard University Press.

Cocroft, W. D. 2006. 'First World War explosives manufacture: The British experience'. In *Frontline and Factory: Comparative perspectives on the chemical industry at war, 1914–1924*, edited by R. MacLeod and J. A. Johnson, 31–46. Dordrecht: Springer.

CofEU (The Council of the European Union). 2014. 'Council conclusions on participatory governance of cultural heritage', *Official Journal of the European Union* C 463, 1–3.

Cole, E., S. Skedd, J. Clarke and S. Newsome. 2020. *The Rotunda (former Royal Artillery Museum), Woolwich Common: History, structure and landscape*. London: London Borough of Greenwich.

Comer, D. 2014. 'Archaeological world heritage as a non-renewable resource: Threats from the laissez-faire world of tourism', *Public Archaeology* 13(1–3): 121–32.

Coppola, F., N. Brown, F. Amicucci, M. Strlič and A. Modelli. 2020. 'Non-destructive collection survey of the historical Classense Library. Part II: Conservation scenarios', *Heritage Science* 8(1): 1–10.

Cubitt, G. 2014. 'Atrocity materials and the representation of transatlantic slavery: Problems, strategies and reactions'. In *Representing Enslavement and Abolition in Museums: Ambiguous engagements*, edited by L. Smith, G. Cubitt, K. Fouseki and R. Wilson, 229–59. London; New York: Routledge.

Cuellar-Moreno, M. 2016. 'Flamenco dance: Characteristics, resources and reflections on its evolution', *Cogent Arts & Humanities* 3(1): 1260825. https://doi.org/10.1080/23311983.2016.1260825.

Danbolt, M. 2019. '5 Exhibition addresses'. In *Curatorial Challenges: Interdisciplinary perspectives on contemporary curating*, edited by M. V. Hansen, A. F. Henningsen and A. Gregersen, 65–78. London; New York: Routledge.

Dean, D. 2002. *Museum Exhibition: Theory and practice*. London; New York: Routledge.

Dean, D. 2017. 'Negotiating accuracy and authenticity in an Aboriginal King Lear', *Rethinking History* 21(2): 255–73.

Debarbieux, B., C. Bortolotto, H. Munz and C. Raziano. 2021. 'Sharing heritage? Politics and territoriality in UNESCO's heritage lists', *Territory, Politics, Governance*, 1–17. https://doi.org/10.1080/21622671.2020.1854112.

De Clercq, S.W. 2004. 'The "Dutch approach", or how to achieve a second life for abandoned geological collections', *Scripta Geologica. Special Issue* 4: 83–99.

Degen, M. 2018. 'Timescapes of urban change: The temporalities of regenerated streets', *Sociological Review* 66(5): 1074–92. https://doi.org/10.1177/0038026118771290.

Degoulet, C. B., D. Gundry, E. Pani, I. Fossé, I. S. E. Wetzel, J. Panayotou, L. Lynen, M. Rackwitz, S. Tornack and S. Wayman. 2012. *An Assessment of the Effects of Conservation Areas on Value*. London: English Heritage.

DeLanda, M. 2006a. 'Deleuzian social ontology and assemblage theory'. In *Deleuze and the Social*, edited by M. Fuglsang, 250–66. Edinburgh: Edinburgh University Press.

DeLanda, M. 2006b. *A New Philosophy of Society: Assemblage theory and social complexity*. London: Continuum.

DeLanda, M. 2016. *Assemblage Theory*. Edinburgh: Edinburgh University Press.

Deleuze, G. and F. Guattari. 1988. *A Thousand Plateaus: Capitalism and schizophrenia*. London: Bloomsbury Publishing.

Dent, E. B. 1999. 'Complexity science: A worldview shift', *Emergence* 1(4): 5–19.

Deodhar, V. 2004. *Does the Housing Market Value Heritage? Some empirical evidence* (no. 0403). Sydney: Macquarie University, Department of Economics.

DeSilvey, C. 2017. *Curated Decay: Heritage beyond saving*. Minneapolis, MN: University of Minnesota Press.

DeSilvey, C. 2020. 'Palliative curation and future persistence: Life after death'. In *Cultural Heritage and the Future*, edited by C. Holtorf and A. Högberg, 217–29. London; New York: Routledge.

DeSilvey, C. and R. Harrison. 2020. 'Anticipating loss: Rethinking endangerment in heritage futures', *International Journal for Heritage Studies* 26(1): 1–7. https://doi.org/10.1080/13527258.2019.1644530.

de Vignemont, F. 2011. 'Embodiment, ownership and disownership', *Consciousness and Cognition* 20(1): 82–93.

Dewsbury, J. D. 2002. 'Embodying time, imagined and sensed', *Time & Society* 11(1): 147–54.

Diemer, A. and C. Nedelciu. 2020. 'System dynamics for sustainable urban planning'. In *Sustainable Cities and Communities: Encyclopedia of the UN Sustainable Development Goals*, edited by W. Leal Filho, U. Azeiteiro, A. M. Azul, L. Brandli, P. Gökcin Özuyar and T. Wall, 760–73. Cham: Springer.

Dillon, C., J. Taylor, W. Lindsay and M. Strlič. 2012. 'Implicit and explicit time preferences in collections care and conservation'. In *10th International Conference Indoor Air Quality in Heritage and Historic Environments, London*, 17–20. London: University College London.

Dillon, C., W. Lindsay, J. Taylor, K. Fouseki, N. Bell and M. Strlič. 2013. 'Collections demography: Stakeholders' views on the lifetime of collections'. In *Climate for Collections Conference, Munich, Doerner Institut*, edited by J. Ashley-Smith, A. Burmester and M. Eibl, 45–58. London: Archetype.

Djabarouti, J. 2021. 'Stories of feelings and things: Intangible heritage from within the built heritage paradigm in the UK', *International Journal of Heritage Studies* 27(4): 391–406.

Dolák, J. 2018. 'Thing in museum: Museum collection as structure', *Studia Slavica et Balcanica Petropolitana* 24(2): 25–35. https://doi.org/10.21638/spbu19.2018.202.

Douglah, J. 2020. '"Use the mirror now" – Demonstrating through a mirror in show dance classes', *Multimodal Communication* 9(2). https://doi.org/10.1515/mc-2020-0002.

Dowling, C. 2010. 'The aesthetics of daily life', *The British Journal of Aesthetics* 50(3): 225–42.

Dunn Jr, E. S. 1970. 'Book Review: *Urban Dynamics*: by J.W. Forrester, Cambridge, Mass.: The MIT Press. 1969'. Review published in *Urban Studies* 7(2): 215–17.

Edwards, E. and J. Hart. 2004. 'Introduction'. In *Photographs, Objects, Histories: On the materiality of images*, edited by E. Edwards and J. Hart, 1–15. London; New York: Routledge.

Egghe, L. and R. Rousseau. 2000. 'Aging, obsolescence, impact, growth, and utilization: Definitions and relations', *Journal of the American Society for Information Science* 51(11): 1004–17.

Eleftherotypia. Greek daily newspaper.

Elliot, T., B. Rugani, J. B. Almenar and S. Niza. 2018. 'A proposal to integrate system dynamics and carbon metabolism for urban planning', *Procedia Cirp* 69, 78–82. https://doi.org/10.1016/j.procir.2017.10.003.

Ellis, C., T. E. Adams and A. P. Bochner. 2011. 'Autoethnography: An overview', *Forum Qualitative Sozialforschung / Forum: Qualitative Social Research* 12(1): Art. 10. http://nbn-resolving.de/urn:nbn:de:0114-fqs1101108.

Ezard, J. 1999. 'Empire show arouses pride and prejudice', *The Guardian*, 23 August 1999. Online: retrieved from https://www.theguardian.com/uk/1999/aug/23/johnezard.

Faubion, J. D. 2018. 'On the character of character: An immodest proposal', *Social Anthropology* 26(2): 168–81.

Ferguson, Bruce W. 1996. 'Exhibition rhetorics: Material speech and utter sense'. In *Thinking About Exhibitions*, edited by R. Greenberg, B. W. Ferguson and S. Nairne, 126–36. London; New York: Routledge.

Filippides, D. 1992. 'The urban planning issues', *Design+Art in Greece* 23: 80–1.

Flexner, J. L. 2016. 'Archaeology and ethnographic collections: Disentangling provenance, provenience and context in Vanuatu assemblages', *Museum Worlds* 4(1): 167–80.

Fluck, H. and M. Dawson. 2021. 'Climate change and the historic environment', *The Historic Environment: Policy & Practice* 12(3–4): 263–70.

Forrester, J. W. 1968. *Principles of Systems*. Waltham, MA: Pegasus Communications.

Forrester, J. W. 1969. *Urban Dynamics*. Portland, OR: Productivity Press.

Forrester, J. W. 1971. *World Dynamics*. Cambridge, MA: Wright-Allen Press, Inc.

Forrester, J. W. 1987. 'Lessons from system dynamics modelling', *System Dynamics Review* 3(2): 136–49.

Forrester, J. W. 2009. 'On the history, the present and the future of system dynamics'. In *System Dynamics*, vol. 1, edited by Y. Barlas, 223–38. Oxford: UNESCO in partnership with Eolss publishers (Encyclopedia of Life support systems).

Forss, A. M. 2014. 'The aesthetics of dwelling', *Journal of Aesthetics and Phenomenology* 1(2): 169–90.

Foster, H. 1988. *Vision and Visuality*. Seattle, WA: Bay Press.

Foucault, M. 1980. 'Nietzsche, genealogy, history'. In *Language, Counter-Memory, Practice*, edited by D. F. Bouchard, 139–64. New York: Cornell University Press.

Fouseki, K. 2006. 'Conflicting discourses on the construction of the new Acropolis Museum: Past and present', *European Review of History – Revue européenne d'Histoire* 13(4): 533–48.

Fouseki, K. 2008. *Conflict Resolution in the Management of In-Situ Museums*. PhD thesis. London: University College London.
Fouseki, K. 2010. '"Community voices, curatorial choices": Community consultation for the 1807 exhibitions', *Museum and Society* 8(3): 80–192.
Fouseki, K. and L. Smith. 2013. 'Community consultation in the museum: The 2007 bicentenary of Britain's abolition of the slave trade'. In *Museums and Communities: Curators, collections and collaboration*, edited by V. Golding and W. Modest, 232–45. London: A & C Black.
Fouseki, K. 2014. 'Claiming the Parthenon Marbles back: Whose claim and on behalf of whom?' In *Museums and Restitution: New practices, new approaches*, edited by K. Arvanitis and L. Tythacott, 161–78. Farnham, Surrey: Ashgate.
Fouseki, K. 2015. *Dispute Management in Heritage Conservation: The case of in-situ museums*. BAR International Series 2774. Oxford: British Archaeological Reports.
Fouseki, K. and Y. Bobrova. 2018. 'Understanding the change of heritage values over time and its impact on energy efficiency: Decision-making at residential historic buildings through system dynamics'. In *The 3rd International Conference on Energy Efficiency in Historic Buildings (EEHB2018), Visby, Sweden, September 26th to 27th, 2018*, 11–21. Upsalla: Uppsala University.
Fouseki, K. and M. Nicolau. 2018. 'Urban heritage dynamics in "heritage-led regeneration": Towards a sustainable lifestyles approach', *The Historic Environment: Policy & Practice* 9(3–4): 229–48.
Fouseki, K. and Y. Bobrova. 2020. 'The utility of system dynamics to heritage research: An example from a study on residents' attitudes towards energy efficiency in heritage buildings'. In *LDE Heritage Conference on heritage and the sustainable development goals, 26–28 November 2019*, edited by Uta Pottgiesser, Sandra Fatoric, Carola Hein, Erik de Maaker and Ana Pereira Roders, 345–56. Delft: TU Delft.
Fouseki, K., T. S. Guttormsen and G. Swensen. 2020. *Heritage and Sustainable Urban Transformations: A 'deep cities' approach*. London; New York: Routledge.
Fouseki, K., D. Newton, K. S. Murillo Camacho, S. Nandi and T. Koukou. 2020. 'Energy efficiency, thermal comfort and heritage conservation in residential historic buildings as dynamic and systemic socio-cultural practices', *Atmosphere* 11(6): 604. https://doi.org/10.3390/atmos11060604.
Fraleigh, S. H. 1987. *Dance and the Lived Body: A descriptive aesthetics*. Pittsburgh, PA: University of Pittsburgh Press.
Gazi, A. 2019. 'Heritage as obstacle: Or which view to the Acropolis?' In *Contested Antiquity: Archaeological heritage and social conflict in modern Greece and Cyprus*, edited by E. Solomon, 245–71. Bloomington, IN: Indiana University Press.
Geerlings, L., I. Geerts, M. Groten, S. Legêne, J. O. de Almeida Meroz and W. de Vries. 2015. 'Manifesto: Towards a historical critique of exhibitions'. Online: retrieved from https://www.historici.nl/wp-content/uploads/2019/11/2015-03-15_historical-critique-of-exhibitions_draft-for-OPG.pdf.
Ghaffarzadegan, N., J. Lyneis and G. P. Richardson. 2011. 'How small system dynamics models can help the public policy process', *System Dynamics Review* 27(1): 22–44.
Giddens, A. 1984. *The Constitution of Society*. Cambridge: Polity Press.
Giombini, L. 2020. 'Everyday heritage and place-making', *Espes* 9(2): 50–61.
Goetcheus, C. and N. Mitchell. 2014. 'The Venice Charter and cultural landscapes: Evolution of heritage concepts and conservation over time', *Change Over Time* 4(2): 338–57.
Gold, J. R. 1998. 'Creating the Charter of Athens: CIAM and the functional city, 1933–43', *The Town Planning Review* 69(3): 225–47.
Gosden, C. and Y. Marshall. 1999. 'The cultural biography of objects', *World Archaeology* 31(2): 169–78.
Gray, J. N., D. Pessel and P. P. Varaiya. 1972. 'A critique of Forrester's model of an urban area', *IEEE Transactions on Systems, Management and Cybernetics* 2: 139–44.
Greenwich Council. 2007. *Progress Estate Conservation Area. Character Appraisal*. Online: retrieved from https://www.royalgreenwich.gov.uk/info/200194/conservation_areas_and_listed_buildings/1547/conservation_area_appraisals_and_management_strategies.
Grever, M., P. de Bruijn and C. Van Boxtel. 2012. 'Negotiating historical distance: Or, how to deal with the past as a foreign country in heritage education', *Paedagogica Historica* 48(6): 873–87.
Grima, G. 2011. 'Farewell to the Xarabank', *BUSES* 63(678).

Guillery, P. (ed.). 2012. *Survey of London, Volume 48: Woolwich*. New Haven, CT; London: Yale University Press.
Haapala, A. 2005. 'On the aesthetics of the everyday: Familiarity, strangeness, and the meaning of place'. In *The Aesthetics of Everyday Life*, edited by A. Light and J. M. Smith, 39–55. New York: Columbia University Press.
Hall, S. and P. Du Gay (eds). 1996. *Questions of Cultural Identity*. New York: SAGE Publications.
Hambrecht, G. and M. Rockman. 2017. 'International approaches to climate change and cultural heritage', *American Antiquity* 82(4): 627–41.
Hamilakis, Y. and E. Yalouri. 1999. 'Sacralising the past: Cults of archaeology in modern Greece', *Archaeological Dialogues* 6(2): 115–35.
Hamilakis, Y. 2007. *The Nation and its Ruins: Antiquity, archaeology and national imagination in Greece*. Oxford: Oxford University Press.
Hamilakis, Y. 2011. 'Museums of oblivion', *Antiquity* 85(328): 625–9.
Hamilton, D. J. and R. J. Blyth (eds). 2007. *Representing Slavery: Art, artefacts and archives in the collections of the National Maritime Museum*. London: Lund Humphries.
Handler, R. 1986. 'Authenticity', *Anthropology Today* 2(1): 2–4.
Harrison, R. 2012. *Heritage: Critical approaches*. London; New York: Routledge.
Harrison, R. 2018. 'On heritage ontologies: Rethinking the material worlds of heritage', *Anthropological Quarterly* 91(4): 1365–83.
Harrison, R. 2020. 'Heritage practices as future-making practices'. In *Cultural Heritage and the Future*, edited by C. Holtorf and A. Högberg, 29–45. London; New York: Routledge.
Heaton, J. 2008. 'Secondary analysis of qualitative data: An overview', *Historical Social Research/ Historische Sozialforschung* 33(3): 33–45.
Heersmink, R. 2012. 'Defending extension theory: A response to Kiran and Verbeek', *Philosophy & Technology* 25(1): 121–8.
Heersmink, R. 2021. 'Varieties of artifacts: Embodied, perceptual, cognitive, and affective', *Topics in Cognitive Science* 13(4): 573–96.
Hemmings, C. 2005. 'Invoking affect: Cultural theory and the ontological turn', *Cultural Studies* 19(5): 548–67.
Heritage Malta. 2011. *Annual Report 2011*. Online: retrieved from https://heritagemalta.org/wp-content/uploads/2019/04/annual-report-2011.pdf.
Heritage Malta. 2016. *Annual Report 2016*. Online: retrieved from Heritage Malta Annual Report 2016 (parlament.mt).
Heritage Malta. 2017. *Annual Report 2017*. Online: retrieved from https://heritagemalta.org/wp-content/uploads/2019/04/annual-report-2017.pdf.
Heritage Malta, 2018. *Annual Report 2018*. Online: retrieved from http://heritagemalta.org/wp-content/uploads/2019/07/heritage-malta-annual-report-2018.docx.pdf.
Herzog, T. R. 1992. 'A cognitive analysis of preference for urban spaces', *Journal of Environmental Psychology* 12(3): 237–48.
Hetherington, K. 2004. 'Secondhandedness: Consumption, disposal and absent presence', *Environment and Planning D: Society and space* 22(1): 157–73.
Hill, M. J. 2018. 'Assembling the historic city: Actor networks, heritage mediation and the return of the colonial past in Post-Soviet Cuba', *Anthropological Quarterly* 91(4): 1235–68.
Historic Vehicles Malta. n.d. *The Malta Historic Vehicle Trust – About us*. Online: retrieved from http://historicvehiclesmalta.org/html/About%20Us.html.
Hogg, O. F. G. 1963. *The Royal Arsenal [Woolwich]*. Oxford: Oxford University Press.
Holder, J. 2001. 'The concept of character in old buildings', *Building Conservation Directory*. https://www.buildingconservation.com/articles/character/character.htm. Retrieved from https://onlinelibrary.wiley.com/doi/epdf/10.1111/1469-8676.12532.
Holling, C. S. 1992. 'Cross-scale morphology, geometry and dynamics of ecosystems', *Ecological Monographs* 62: 447–502.
Holtorf, C. 2006. 'Can less be more? Heritage in the age of terrorism', *Public Archaeology* 5(2): 101–9.
Holtorf, C. 2015. 'Averting loss aversion in cultural heritage', *International Journal of Heritage Studies* 21(4): 405–21.
Holtorf, C. 2017. 'Perceiving the past: from age value to pastness', *International Journal of Cultural Property* 24(4): 497–515.
Holtorf, C. 2018. 'Embracing change: How cultural resilience is increased through cultural heritage', *World Archaeology* 50(4): 639–50.

Holtorf, C. and A. Högberg. 2021. 'Final reflections: The future of heritage'. In *Cultural Heritage and the Future*, edited by C. Holtorf and A. Högberg, 264–9. London; New York: Routledge.
Hudson, B. T. and J. M. Balmer. 2013. 'Corporate heritage brands: Mead's theory of the past', *Corporate Communications: An international journal* 18(3): 347–61.
Iacono, V. L. and D. H. Brown. 2016. 'Beyond binarism: Exploring a model of living cultural heritage for dance', *Dance Research* 34(1): 84–105.
Ingold, T. 2006. 'Rethinking the animate, re-animating thought', *Ethnos* 71 (1): 1–12.
Ingold, T. 2010. *Bringing Things to Life: Creative entanglements in a world of materials*, vol. 15, 1–14. Realities working papers. Aberdeen: University of Aberdeen.
International Council of Monuments and Sites (ICOMOS). 1931. *The Athens Charter for the Restoration of Historic Monuments*. Adopted at the First International Congress of Architects and Technicians of Historic Monuments, Athens 1931. Online: https://www.icomos.org/en/167-the-athens-charter-for-the-restoration-of-historic-monuments.
International Council on Monuments and Sites (ICOMOS). 1964. International charter for the conservation and restoration of monuments and sites. Venice. Online: https://www.icomos.org/charters/venice_e.pdf.
Iwakuma, M. 2002. 'The body as embodiment: An investigation of the body by Merleau-Ponty'. In *Disability, Postmodernity, Embodying Disability Theory*, edited by M. Corker and T. Shakespeare, 76–87. London: Bloomsbury Publishing.
Jackson, M. C. 2001. 'Critical systems thinking and practice', *European Journal of Operational Research* 128(2): 233–44.
Jackson, M. C. 2019. *Critical Systems Thinking and the Management of Complexity*. Hoboken, NJ: Wiley.
Jackson, M. C. 2020. 'Critical systems practice 1: Explore – Starting a multimethodological intervention', *Systems Research and Behavioral Science* 37(5): 839–58.
Jaeckel, T. V., B. H. Aithal and D. D. Sanna. 2012. 'Insights to urban dynamics through landscape spatial pattern analysis', *International Journal of Applied Earth Observation and Geoinformation* 18: 329–43.
Jive'n, G. and P. J. Larkham. 2003. 'Sense of place, authenticity and character: A commentary', *Journal of Urban Design* 8(1): 67–81.
Jokilehto, J. 2006. 'Considerations on authenticity and integrity in world heritage context', *City & Time* 2(1). Online: retrieved from: http://www.ct.ceci-br.org.
Jones, P. and S. MacLeod. 2016. 'Museum architecture matters', *Museum and Society* 14(1): 207–19.
Jones, S. 2010. 'Negotiating authentic objects and authentic selves: Beyond the deconstruction of authenticity', *Journal of Material Culture* 15(2): 181–203.
Jones, S. and M. Mean. 2010. 'Resilient places: Character and community in everyday heritage'. London: DEMOS Report.
Jung, Y. and A. R. Love (eds). 2017a. *Systems Thinking in Museums: Theory and practice*. Lanham, MD: Rowman & Littlefield.
Jung, Y. and A. R. Love. 2017b. 'Systems thinking and museum ecosystem'. In *Systems Thinking in Museums: Theory and practice*, edited by Y. Jung and A. R. Love, 3–16. Lanham, MD: Rowman & Littlefield.
Kallis, G. and H. March. 2015. 'Imaginaries of hope: The utopianism of degrowth', *Annals of the Association of American Geographers* 105(2): 360–8.
Kathimerini. Greek daily newspaper.
Kearney, A. 2008. 'Intangible cultural heritage'. In *Intangible Heritage*, edited by L. Smith and N. Akagawa, 209–25. London; New York: Routledge.
Kennet, J. 1985. *The Eltham Hutments*. The Eltham Society. Online: retrieved from http://www.theelthamsociety.org.uk.
Khalaf, R. W. 2020. 'Authenticity or continuity in the implementation of the UNESCO World Heritage Convention? Scrutinizing statements of outstanding universal value, 1978–2019', *Heritage* 3(2): 243–74.
Kim, D. H. 1999. *Introduction to Systems Thinking*, vol. 16. Waltham, MA: Pegasus Communications.
Kirshenblatt-Gimblett, B. 1995. 'Theorising heritage', *Ethnomusicology* 39(3): 367–80.
Kirshenblatt-Gimblett, B. 2014. 'Intangible heritage as metacultural production', *Museum International* 66(1–4): 163–74.
Kontaratos, S. 1978. 'The Acropolis Museum', *Architectonika themata. Architecture in Greece* 12: 215–40.

Kontaratos, S. 1992. 'The unfortunate outcome of the competition and the responsibilities of both the Ministry and Jury', *Design+Art in Greece* 23: 78–9.
Kopytoff, I. 1986. 'The cultural biography of things: Commoditisation as process'. In *The Social Life of Things: Commodities in cultural perspective*, edited by A. Appadurai, 64–91. Cambridge: Cambridge University Press.
Korsmeyer, C. 2016. 'Real old things', *The British Journal of Aesthetics* 56(3): 219–31.
Korsmeyer, C. 2018. *Things: In touch with the past*. Oxford: Oxford University Press.
Kosmala, K. and T. S. Beall. 2019. 'Problematising silences in intangible heritage: Unsettling historical records of women in protests', *International Journal of Heritage Studies* 25(4): 348–64.
Krüger, M. 2011. 'How to purify the syncretistic – The construction of authenticity and identity in discourses, policy and practice of Andalusian flamenco', *Journal of Mediterranean Studies* 20(1): 137–62.
Kuutma, K. and H. Kästik. 2014. 'Creativity and "right singing": Aural experience and embodiment of heritage', *Journal of Folklore Research: An International Journal of Folklore and Ethnomusicology* 51(3): 277–310.
Kynourgiopoulou, V. 2011. 'National identity interrupted: The mutilation of the Parthenon Marbles and the Greek claim for repatriation'. In *Contested Cultural Heritage: Region, nationalism, erasure and exclusion in a global world*, edited by H. Silverman, 155–70. New York: Springer.
LaCapra, D. 1999. 'Trauma, absence, loss', *Critical Inquiry* 25(4): 696–727.
Lamarque, P. 2016. 'Reflections on the ethics and aesthetics of restoration and conservation', *The British Journal of Aesthetics* 56(3): 281–99.
Lamont, M. and M. Fournier (eds). 1992. *Cultivating Differences: Symbolic boundaries and the making of inequality*. Chicago: University of Chicago Press.
Lane, D. C. 2007. 'The power of the bond between cause and effect: Jay Wright Forrester and the field of system dynamics', *System Dynamics Review: The journal of the System Dynamics Society* 23(2–3): 95–118.
Lane, D. C. and J. D. Sterman. 2011. 'Jay Wright Forrester'. In *Profiles in Operations Research*, edited by A. A. Assad and S. I. Gass, 363–86. Boston, MA: Springer.
Lang, K. A. 2006. *Chaos and cosmos: On the image in aesthetics and art history*. New York: Cornell University Press.
Lang, T. 2005. *Insights in the British Debate about Urban Decline and Urban Regeneration. Working paper no 32.* Erkner: Leibniz-Institute for Regional Development and Structural Planning.
Latour, B. 1996. 'On actor–network theory: A few clarifications', *Soziale Welt* 47(4): 369–81.
Latour, B. 2007. *Reassembling the Social: An introduction to actor–network theory*. Oxford: Open University Press.
Law, J. 2004. *After Method: Mess in social science research*. London; New York: Routledge.
Leblon, B. and S. N. Shuinear. 2003. *Gypsies and Flamenco: The emergence of the art of flamenco in Andalusia*, vol. 6. Hatfield, Hertfordshire: University of Hertfordshire Press.
Leddy, T. 2015. 'Experience of awe: An expansive approach to everyday aesthetics', *Contemporary Aesthetics* 13(8). Online: retrieved from https://digitalcommons.risd.edu/liberalarts_contempaesthetics/vol13/iss1/8.
Lee, J. J. 2010. 'Home life: Cultivating a domestic aesthetic', *Contemporary Aesthetics* 8(1). Online: retrieved from http://hdl.handle.net/2027/spo.7523862.0008.015.
Lending, M. 2009. 'Negotiating absence: Bernard Tschumi's new Acropolis Museum in Athens', *The Journal of Architecture* 14(5): 567–89. https://doi.org/10.1080/13602360903119363.
Lending, M. 2018. 'Negotiating absence: Bernard Tschumi's new Acropolis Museum in Athens', *The Journal of Architecture* 23(5): 797–819.
Lewis, G. 1992. 'Attitudes to disposal from museum collections', *Museum Management and Curatorship* 11(1): 19–28.
Lewis, G. and A. Fahy. 1995. 'Legislation relating to the acquisition and disposal of museum collections in the United Kingdom'. In *Collections Management*, edited by A. Fahy, 131–41. London; New York: Routledge.
Lidchi, H. 2001. 'Exhibiting cultures. The poetics and politics of museum display'. In *Making Representations: Museums in the post-colonial era*, edited by M. H. Simpson, 151–208. London; New York: Routledge.
Lindsay, W. 2005. 'Time perspectives: What "the future" means to museum professionals in collections-care', *The Conservator* 29(1): 51–61.
Littlejohn, A. 2021. 'The potential of intangible loss: Reassembling heritage and reconstructing the social in post-disaster Japan', *Social Anthropology* 29(4): 944–59.

Littlewood, K. and B. Butler. 1998. *Of Ships and Stars: Maritime heritage and the founding of the National Maritime Museum, Greenwich*. London: Bloomsbury Publishing.

Loeve, S., X. Guchet and B. V. Bensaude. 2018. 'Is there a French philosophy of technology? General introduction'. In *French Philosophy of Technology*, edited by S. Loeve, 1–20. Cham: Springer.

Longair, S. and J. McAleer. 2013. 'Introduction: Shifting interpretations of empire', *Museum History Journal* 6(1): 3–5.

Loukaki, A. 2016. *Living Ruins, Value Conflicts*. London; New York: Routledge.

Low, S. M. 2003. 'Embodied space(s) anthropological theories of body, space and culture', *Space and Culture* 6(1): 9–18.

Lowenthal, D. 2000. 'Stewarding the past in a perplexing present'. In *Values and Heritage Conservation*, edited by E. Avrami, R. Mason and S. J. Alberti, 18–26. Los Angeles: Getty Conservation Institute.

Lynch, B. T. and S. J. Alberti. 2010. 'Legacies of prejudice: Racism, co-production and radical trust in the museum', *Museum Management and Curatorship* 25(1): 13–35.

Lynch, B. 2011. 'Collaboration, contestation, and creative conflict: On the efficacy of museum/community partnerships'. In *Redefining Museum Ethics*, edited by J. Marstine, 146–63. London; New York: Routledge.

Lynch, B. 2013. 'Reflective debate, radical transparency and trust in the museum', *Museum Management and Curatorship* 28(1): 1–13.

Lünenborg, M. and T. Maier. 2018. 'The turn to affect and emotion in media studies', *Media and Communication* 6(3): 1–4.

Macdonald, S. 2009. 'Reassembling Nuremberg, reassembling heritage', *Journal of Cultural Economy* 2(1–2): 117–34.

Macdonald, S. 2013. *Memorylands. Heritage and identity in Europe today*. London; New York: Routledge.

MacDougall, P. (ed.). 2019. *Five Hundred Years of Deptford and Woolwich Royal Dockyards: Marking the 500th anniversary of the foundation of the Thames yards by Henry VIII*. Portsmouth: Naval Dockyard Society.

MacLeod, S., L. H. Hanks and J. Hale (eds). 2012. *Museum Making: Narratives, architectures, exhibitions*. London; New York: Routledge.

McAleer, J. 2013. '"That infamous commerce in human blood": Reflections on representing slavery and empire in British museums', *Museum History Journal* 6(1): 72–86.

McBryde, I. 1997. 'The ambiguities of authenticity – rock of faith or shifting sands?', *Conservation and Management of Archaeological Sites* 2(2): 93–100.

McCormack, D. P. 2008. 'Geographies for moving bodies: Thinking, dancing, spaces', *Geography Compass* 2(6): 1822–36.

McCormick, K., S. Anderberg, L. Coenen and L. Neij. 2013. 'Advancing sustainable urban transformation', *Journal of Cleaner Production* 50: 1–11.

Machin-Autenrieth, M. 2016. *Flamenco, Regionalism and Musical Heritage in Southern Spain*. London; New York: Routledge.

Malta Independent. 2011. 'Transport. Nostalgia versus efficiency', *Malta Independent*, 28 June 2011. Online: retrieved from https://www.independent.com.mt/articles/2011-06-28/newspaper-leader/Transport:-Nostalgia-Vs-efficiency-294787.

Manson, S. M. 2001. 'Simplifying complexity: A review of complexity theory', *Geoforum* 32(3): 405–14.

Marcus, G. E. and E. Saka. 2006. 'Assemblage', *Theory, Culture & Society* 23(2–3), 101–6.

Marievskaya, N. E. 2015. 'Time in Cinema', *Russian Studies in Philosophy* 53(1): 37–53.

Markakis, N. 2016. 'Cultivating roots: A tensional-hybrid investigation of embodied resources through traditional Cretan folkloric and contemporary dance practices'. Canada: York University. Online: retrieved from https://yorkspace.library.yorku.ca/xmlui/handle/10315/35117.

Matassa, F. 2011. *Museum Collections Management*. London: Facet Publishing.

Medhurst, L. and J. P. Lewis. 1969. *Urban Decay. An analysis and a policy*. London: Macmillan.

Meerow, S., J. P. Newell and M. Stults. 2016. 'Defining urban resilience: A review', *Landscape and Urban Planning* 147: 38–49.

Melchionne, K. 2011. 'Aesthetic experience in everyday life: A reply to Dowling', *The British Journal of Aesthetics* 51(4): 437–42.

Mendoza, N. 2017. *The Mendoza Review: an independent review of museums in England*. London: Department for Digital, Culture, Media and Sport.
Merleau-Ponty, M. 2011. *Phenomenology of Perception*. London; New York: Routledge.
Merriman, N. 2008. 'Museum collections and sustainability', *Cultural Trends* 17(1): 3–21.
Messham-Muir, K. 2002. 'Here we are! National museums of postcolonial Australasia in a post-nation-state world', *Journal of Postcolonial Writing* 39(2): 71–83.
Meyer, B. and M. De Witte. 2013. 'Heritage and the sacred: Introduction', *Material Religion* 9(3), 274–80.
Mingers, J. 2014. *Systems Thinking, Critical Realism and Philosophy: A confluence of ideas*. London; New York: Routledge.
Monat, J. P. and T. F. Gannon. 2015. 'What is systems thinking? A review of selected literature plus recommendations', *American Journal of Systems Science* 4(1): 11–26. https://doi.org/10.5923/j.ajss.20150401.02.
Morgan, J. and S. Macdonald. 2020. 'De-growing museum collections for new heritage futures', *International Journal of Heritage Studies* 26(1): 56–70.
Moser, S. 2010. 'The devil is in the detail: Museum displays and the creation of knowledge', *Museum Anthropology* 33(1): 22–32.
Mosler, S. 2019. 'Everyday heritage concept as an approach to place-making process in the urban landscape', *Journal of Urban Design* 24(5): 778–93.
Mouliou, M. 1996. 'Ancient Greece, its classical heritage and the modern Greeks: Aspects of nationalism in museum exhibitions'. In *Nationalism and Archaeology*, edited by J. A. Atkinson, I. Banks and J. O'Sullivan, 174–99. Glasgow: Cruithne Press.
Munroe, L. 2016. 'Constructing affective narratives in transatlantic slavery museums in the UK'. In *Heritage, Affect and Emotion: Politics, practices and infrastructures*, edited by S. Watson, 114–31. London; New York: Routledge.
Naguib, S. A. 2013. 'Collecting moments of life. Museums and the intangible heritage of migration', *Museum International* 65(1–4): 77–86.
Naukkarinen, O. 2013. 'What is "Everyday" in Everyday Aesthetics?', *Contemporary Aesthetics* 11(1). Online: retrieved from https://digitalcommons.risd.edu/liberalarts_contempaesthetics/vol11/iss1/14/.
Ntaflou, C. 2012. 'The New Acropolis Museum and the dynamics of National Museum development in Greece'. In *Great Narratives of the Past. Traditions and Revisions in National Museums: Conference Proceedings from EuNaMus; European National Museums: Identity Politics; the Uses of the Past and the European Citizen; Paris 28 June–1 July & 25–26 November 2011*, edited by D. Poulot, F. Bodenstein and J. M. Lanzarote Guiral, no. 078, 97–111. Linköping: Linköping University Electronic Press.
Orishimo, I. 1987. 'An approach to urban dynamics', *Geographical Analysis* 19(3): 200–10.
Ozdemir, A. 2010. 'The effect of window views' openness and naturalness on the perception of rooms' spaciousness and brightness: A visual preference study', *Scientific Research and Essays* 5(16): 2275–87.
Pandermalis, D. 2010. 'A conversation with Dimitris Pandermalis: The Acropolis Museum'. In *Dialogues on the Acropolis, Athens*, edited by F. Mallouchou-Tufano, 484–507. Athens: Skai Editions.
Paisiou, S. 2012. 'Merging local concerns and global regulations. The case of the four competitions for the New Acropolis Museum'. In *Architecture Competitions and the Production of Culture, Quality and Knowledge: An international inquiry*, edited by J.-P. Chupin, C. Cucuzzella and B. Helal, 92–109. Montreal: Potential Architecture Books.
Papachristos, N. H. 2004. περίπτωση του Νέου Μουσείου Ακρόπολης. (In Greek: this author's translation: 'The case of the New Acropolis Museum'.) In πολιτιστική κληρονομιά και το δίκαιο (this author's translation: *Cultural Heritage and Law*), edited by E. Trova. Athens; Thessaloniki: Sakkoula.
Pearce, S. 2017. *Museums, Objects, and Collections: A cultural study*. Washington DC: Smithsonian Institution Press.
Pekkala, E. 2015. *Developing Sustainable Tourism on the Mediterranean Island of Malta*. Haaga Helia: University of Applied Sciences. Online: retrieved from https://www.theseus.fi/handle/10024/88579?show=full.
Pendlebury, J. 2013. 'Conservation values, the authorised heritage discourse and the conservation-planning assemblage', *International Journal of Heritage Studies* 19(7): 709–27.

Pillière, L. 2018. 'Accommodating the visitor: How museums connect with their present-day populations', *Anglophonia. French Journal of English Linguistics* 25. https://doi.org/10.4000/anglophonia.1409.

Plantzos, D. 2011. 'Behold the raking geison: The new Acropolis Museum and its context-free Archaeologies', *Antiquity* 85(328): 613–25.

Pumain, D. and R. Reuillon. 2017. *Urban Dynamics and Simulation Models*. Cham: Springer International Publishing.

Puolakka, K. 2018. 'On habits and functions in everyday aesthetics', *Contemporary Aesthetics* 16(1). Online: retrieved from https://digitalcommons.risd.edu/liberalarts_contempaesthetics/vol16/iss1/7/.

Radzikowski, S. 2011. 'At last – Malta's Yellow Buses Retiring'. Online: retrieved from http://drshem.com/2011/06/25/at-last-maltas-yellow-buses-retiring/.

Ramachandra, T. V., B. H. Aithal and D. D. Sanna. 2012. 'Insights into urban dynamics through landscape spatial pattern analysis', *International Journal of Applied Earth Observation and Geoinformation* 18: 329–43.

Ramage, M. and K. Shipp. 2009. 'C. West Churchman'. In *Systems Thinkers*, edited by K. Shipp and M. Ramage, 131–8. London: Springer.

Randers. J. (ed.). 1980. *Elements of System Dynamics Method*. Cambridge, MA: Wright-Allen Press.

Raynsford, N. 2006. 'CROOKS, Will, Woolwich'. In *Men Who Made Labour*, edited by A. Haworth and D. Hayter, 67–74. London; New York: Routledge.

Reed, A. and J. Bialecki. 2018. 'Introduction to special section 1: Anthropology and character', *Social Anthropology* 26(2): 159–67.

Reed-Danahay, D. 2009. 'Anthropologists, education and autoethnography', *Reviews in Anthropology* 38(1): 28–47.

Reeve, A. and R. Shipley. 2014. 'Heritage-based regeneration in an age of austerity: Lessons from the Townscape Heritage Initiative', *Journal of Urban Regeneration & Renewal* 7(2): 122–35.

Richardson, G. P. 1999. 'Reflections for the future of system dynamics', *The Journal of the Operational Research Society* 50(4): 440–9.

Richardson, G. P. 2011. 'Reflections on the foundations of system dynamics', *System Dynamics Review* 27(3): 219–43.

Richardson, M. 1982. 'Being-in-the-plaza versus being-in-the-market: Material culture and the construction of social reality', *American Ethnologist* 9: 421–36.

Rico, T. 2016. 'Islamophobia and the location of heritage debates in the Arabian peninsula'. In *Cultural Heritage in the Arabian Peninsula*, edited by K. Exell and T. Rico, 19–32. London; New York: Routledge.

Robbins, D. 2003. 'Public transport as a visitor attraction', *Managing Visitor Attractions: New directions*, 86–120.

Roberts, P. 2000. 'The evolution, definition and purpose of urban regeneration'. In *Urban Regeneration*, edited by P. Roberts, H. Sykes and R. Granger, 9–36. New York: SAGE.

Robinson, M. 2018. 'Talking of heritage'. In *The Routledge Handbook of Language and Superdiversity*, edited by A. Creese and A. Blackledge, 194–207. London; New York: Routledge.

Røpke, I. 2009. 'Theories of practice – new inspiration for ecological economic studies on consumption', *Ecological Economics* 68(10): 2490–7.

Roppola, T., J. Packer, D. Uzzell and R. Ballantyne. 2019. 'Nested assemblages: Migrants, war heritage, informal learning and national identities', *International Journal of Heritage Studies* 25(11): 1205–23.

Rothlind, A. C. 2021. *Assessing Breakpoint Values in Conservation Decision-Making: For stewardship ethics managing change*. Finland: Metropolia University of Applied Sciences. Online: retrieved from https://www.theseus.fi/bitstream/handle/10024/499884/Rothlind_Ann-Cathrin.pdf?sequence=2.

Rowlands, T., N. Waddell and B. McKenna. 2016. 'Are we there yet? A technique to determine theoretical saturation', *Journal of Computer Information Systems* 56(1): 40–7.

Roy, A. 2016. 'What is urban about critical urban theory?', *Urban Geography* 37(6): 810–23.

Royal Borough of Greenwich (n.d.). *Woolwich as a Major Cultural Destination*. Online: retrieved from https://www.royalgreenwich.gov.uk/info/200224/arts_and_culture/1912/woolwich_works.

Ruggles, D. F. and H. Silverman. 2009. 'From tangible to intangible heritage'. In *Intangible Heritage Embodied*, edited by H. Silverman and D. Ruggles, 1–14. New York: Springer.

Rukavina, M., M. O. Šćitaroci and T. Lolić. 2018. 'Integrating archaeological heritage into towns and settlements', *Conservation and Management of Archaeological Sites* 20(5–6), 340–63.

Ruskin, J. 1903 [1849]. *The Works of John Ruskin. Seven Lamps of Architecture,* edited by E. Cook and A. Wedderburn. London: George Allen.
Rutten, J. and B. T. Architects. 2009. 'An architectural chronology of the New Acropolis Museum'. In *The New Acropolis Museum*, edited by B. Tschumi Architects, 136–63. New York: Skira Rizzoli.
Saeed, K. 2010. 'Economic development, creative destruction and urban dynamics: A proposal for rethinking developmental agendas'. Online: retrieved from https://papers.ssrn.com/sol3/papers.cfm?abstract_id=1724816.
Saito, Y. 2007. *Everyday Aesthetics*. Oxford: Oxford University Press.
Sanders, P. and F. M. Sanders. 2004. 'Spatial urban dynamics – A vision on the future of urban dynamics: Forrester revisited'. In *22nd International Conference on System Dynamics 2004, Oxford, UK*, 1–32. Oxford: Keble College.
Sauchelli, A. 2013. 'Functional beauty, perception and aesthetic judgements', *The British Journal of Aesthetics* 53(1): 41–53.
Saunders, J. M. 2014. 'Conservation in museums and inclusion of the non-professional', *Journal of Conservation and Museum Studies* 12(1): p.Art 6. http://doi.org/10.5334/jcms.1021215.
Schatzki, T. R. 2005. 'Practice mind-ed orders'. In *The Practice Turn in Contemporary Theory*, edited by E. von Savigny, 50–63. 2nd edition. London; New York: Routledge.
Schatzki, T. R., K. Knorr-Cetina and E. von Savigny (eds). 2001. *The Practice Turn in Contemporary Theory*, vol. 44. London; New York: Routledge.
Schembri, D. 2011a. 'The yellow buses. Latest addition to Maltese heritage', *Times of Malta*, 17 October 2011. Online: retrieved from https://timesofmalta.com/articles/view/Latest-addition-to-Maltese-heritage.389465.
Schembri, D. 2011b. 'Old buses salvaged by Heritage Malta', *Times of Malta*, 28 August 2011. Online: retrieved from https://timesofmalta.com/articles/view/Old-buses-salvaged-by-Heritage-Malta.382092.
Schettler, A., R. Vicente and M. L. Anderson. 2019. 'The embodiment of objects: Review, analysis, and future directions', *Frontiers in Neuroscience* 13: 1332. https://doi.org/10.3389/fnins.2019.01332.
Schiller, G. and S. Rubidge. 2014. 'Practising place'. In *Choreographic Dwellings*, edited by G. Schiller and S. Rubidge, 11–26. London: Palgrave Macmillan.
Scruton, R. 2007. 'In search of the aesthetic', *The British Journal of Aesthetics* 47(3): 232–50.
Sharpe, C. A. 2006. 'House prices in a heritage area: the case of St. John's, Newfoundland', *Canadian Journal of Urban Research* 15(2):175–201.
Shipley, R. 2000. 'Heritage designation and property values: Is there an effect?', *International Journal of Heritage Studies* 6(1): 83–100.
Shove, E., M. Pantzar and M. Watson. 2012. *The Dynamics of Social Practice: Everyday life and how it changes*. New York: Sage.
Silverman, H. and D. F. Ruggles. 2007. 'Cultural heritage and human rights'. In *Cultural Heritage and Human Rights*, edited by H. Silverman and D. F. Ruggles, 3–29. New York: Springer.
Simmons, J. E. and Y. Muñoz-Saba. 2003. 'The theoretical bases of collections management'. In *Collection Forum*, vol. 18, no. 1–2, 38–49.
Singh, S. 2020. 'Time, tourism area " life-cycle", evolution and heritage', *Journal of Heritage Tourism* 16(2): 218–29.
Sklar, D. 2001. 'Toward cross-cultural conversation on bodily knowledge', *Dance Research Journal* 33(1): 91–2.
Skrede, J. and H. Hølleland. 2018. 'Uses of heritage and beyond: Heritage studies viewed through the lens of critical discourse analysis and critical realism', *Journal of Social Archaeology* 18(1): 77–96.
Smith, L. 2006. *Uses of Heritage*. London; New York: Routledge.
Smith, L. and N. Akagawa (eds). 2008. *Intangible Heritage*. London; New York: Routledge.
Smith, L., G. Cubitt, K. Fouseki and R. Wilson (eds). 2014. *Representing Enslavement and Abolition in Museums: Ambiguous engagements*. London; New York: Routledge.
Smith, L., M. Wetherell and G. Campbell (eds). 2018. *Emotion, Affective Practices and the Past in the Present*. London; New York: Routledge.
Spence, D. 2007. Interview. https://archives.history.ac.uk/1807commemorated/interviews/spence.html.
Spence, D. 2011. 'Making the London, Sugar and Slavery Gallery at the Museum of London Docklands'. In *Representing Enslavement and Abolition in Museums. Ambiguous engagements*, edited by L. Smith, G. Cubitt, K. Fouseki and R. Watson, 149–63. London; New York: Routledge.

Srnicek, N. 2007. 'Assemblage theory, complexity and contentious politics: The political ontology of Gilles Deleuze'. Unpublished Master's thesis, University of Western Ontario, Ontario, Canada. Online: retrieved from http://www.urbanlab.org/articles/AssemblageTheoryComplexityandContent.pdf.

Staniforth, S. 2014. 'Environmental conditions for the safeguarding of collections: Future trends', *Studies in Conservation* 59(4): 213–17.

Sterman, J. 2002. *System Dynamics: Systems thinking and modeling for a complex world*. Cambridge, MA: Massachusetts Institute of Technology.

Stevens, S. 2016. 'Firepower museum to leave London home. Collection moving to a heritage centre in Wiltshire', *News. Museum Association*. Online: https://www.museumsassociation.org/museums-journal/news/2016/03/01032016-firepower-museum-to-leave-london-home/#.

Stevenson, W. 2007. *Spymistress: The life of Vera Atkins, the greatest female secret agent of World War II*. New York: MacDougall Arcade Publishing.

Stirling, C. 2020. 'Critical heritage and the posthumanities: Problems and prospects', *International Journal of Heritage Studies* 26(11): 1029–46.

Stovel, H. 2008. 'Origins and influence of the Nara document on authenticity', *APT Bulletin 39* (2–3): 9–17.

Strlič, M., D. Thickett, J. Taylor and M. Cassar. 2013. 'Damage functions in heritage science', *Studies in Conservation* 58(2): 80–7.

Strlič, M., C. M. Grossi, C. Dillon, N. Bell, K. Fouseki, P. Brimblecombe, E. Menart, K. Ntanos, W. Lindsay, D. Thickett and F. France. 2015. 'Damage function for historic paper. Part I: Fitness for use'. *Heritage Science* 3(1): 1–12.

Su, J. 2018. 'Conceptualising the subjective authenticity of intangible cultural heritage', *International Journal of Heritage Studies* 24(9): 919–37.

Suri, H. 2011. 'Purposeful sampling in qualitative research synthesis', *Qualitative Research Journal* 11(2): 63–75.

Sutter, G. 2006. 'Thinking like a system: Are museums up to the challenge?', *Museums and Social Issues* 1(2): 203–18.

Ta Nea. Greek daily newspaper.

Teague, S. 2020. *Royal Arsenal, Building 10 (Southern Blocks)*. Client Report, unpublished. Online: retrieved from https://library.oxfordarchaeology.com/5757/1/RYA99_%20B_10_Southern_Blocks_WB_%20March2020.pdf.

Thomsen, A. and K. Van der Flier. 2011. 'Understanding obsolescence: A conceptual model for buildings', *Building Research & Information* 39(4): 352–62.

Tobey, M. B., R. B. Binder, T. Yoshida and Y. Yamagata. 2019. 'Urban systems design case study: Tokyo's sumida ward', *Smart Cities* 2(4): 453–70.

Tolia-Kelly, D. P., E. Waterton and S. Watson. 2017. *Heritage, Affect and Emotion: Politics, practices and infrastructures*. London; New York: Routledge.

To Vema. Greek daily newspaper.

Tschumi, B. 2009. 'Conceptualising context'. In *The New Acropolis Museum*, edited by Bernard Tschumi Architects, 82–9. Athens: Aktor.

Tsiros, G. 2009. Μουσείο Ακρόπολης. Οι χώροι, τα εκθέματα, οι συντελεστές. (In Greek. This author's translation: 'The Acropolis Museum. The space, the exhibits, the contributors'), *Kathimerini* (Greek newspaper), 26 July 2009.

Tunbridge, J. E. and G. J. Ashworth. 1996. *Dissonant Heritage: The management of the past as a resource in conflict*. Chichester: Wiley.

Urland, A. 2016. 'Visual impact, colour and aesthetics in built heritage conservation and restoration'. In *Conservation of Cultural Heritage in the Arab Region*, edited by Z. Aslan, 112–16. Italy: ICCROM.

Van de Port, M. P. J. and B. Meyer. 2018. 'Introduction: Heritage dynamics politics of authentication, aesthetics of persuasion and the cultural production of the real'. In *Sense and Essence. Heritage and the Cultural Production of the Real*, edited by B. Meyer and M. van de Port, 1–39. New York: Berghahn Books. http://www.berghahnbooks.com/downloads/intros/MeyerSense_intro.pdf.

Van Leeuwen, T. 2001. 'What is authenticity?', *Discourse Studies* 3(4): 392–7.

Verticchio, E., F. Frasca, C. Bertolin and A. M. Siani. 2021. 'Climate-induced risk for the preservation of paper collections: Comparative study among three historic libraries in Italy', *Building and Environment* 206: 108394. https://doi.org/10.1016/j.buildenv.2021.108394.

Von Bertalanffy, L. 1972. 'The history and status of general systems theory', *Academy of Management Journal* 15(4): 407–26.
Waldrop, M. M. 1993. *Complexity: The emerging science at the edge of order and chaos*. New York: Simon and Schuster.
Wall, S. 2008. 'Easier said, than done: Writing an autoethnography', *International Journal of Qualitative Methods* 7(1). http://ejournals.library.ualberta.ca/index.php/IJQM/article/view/1621/1144.
Warde, A. 2005. 'Consumption and theories of practice', *Journal of Consumer Culture* 5(2): 131–53.
Wareham, T. 2007. Interview. https://archives.history.ac.uk/1807commemorated/interviews/wareham.html.
Washabaugh, W. 2012. *Flamenco Music and National Identity in Spain*. London; New York: Routledge.
Waterton, E., L. Smith and G. Campbell. 2006. 'The utility of discourse analysis to heritage studies: The Burra Charter and social inclusion', *International Journal of Heritage Studies* 12(4): 339–55.
Waterton, E. and S. Watson (eds). 2010. *Culture, Heritage and Representation: Perspectives on visuality and the past*. Farnham, Surrey: Ashgate.
Waterton, E. and S. Watson. 2013. 'Framing theory: Towards a critical imagination in heritage studies', *International Journal of Heritage Studies* 19(6): 546–61.
Waterton, E. 2014. 'A more-than-representational understanding of heritage? The "past" and the politics of affect', *Geography Compass* 8(11): 823–33.
Webb, P. Taylor. 2009. *Teacher Assemblage*. Leiden: Brill.
Weed, M. 2005. '"Meta Interpretation": A method for the interpretive synthesis of qualitative research', *Forum Qualitative Sozialforschung/Forum: Qualitative social research* 6(1). https://doi.org/10.17169/fqs-6.1.508.
Weed, M. 2008. 'A potential method for the interpretive synthesis of qualitative research: Issues in the development of "meta-interpretation"', *International Journal of Social Research Methodology* 11(1): 13–28.
Wemyss, G. 2009. *The Invisible Empire: White discourse, tolerance and belonging*. Farnham, Surrey and Burlington, VT: Ashgate.
Wetherell, M. 2013. 'Affect and discourse–What's the problem? From affect as excess to affective/discursive practice', *Subjectivity* 6(4): 349–68. https://doi.org/10.17169/fqs-6.1.508.
Whalley, R. 2004. *The Royal Arsenal, Woolwich Building 22 Car park Zone 10 Archaeological Observation and Recording*. Oxford: Oxford Archaeology South.
White, J. 2014. 'London in the First World War', *Cahiers Bruxellois Brusselse Cahiers*, 46(1E): 139–57.
Willems, W. 2020. *Rich History: Race, space and the sanitisation of colonial heritage*. London: Department of Media and Communications, London School of Economics and Political Science. Online: retrieved from https://www.lse.ac.uk/media-and-communications/research/research-projects/MediaLSE-Virtual-Research-Exhibition.
Wilson, R. 2011. 'The curatorial complex: Marking the bicentenary of the abolition of the slave trade'. In *Representing Enslavement and Abolition in Museums: Ambiguous engagements*, edited by L. Smith, G. Cubitt, K. Fouseki and R. Wilson, 131–46. London; New York: Routledge.
Wingfield, C. 2017. 'Collection as (Re) assemblage: Refreshing museum archaeology', *World Archaeology* 49(5): 594–607.
Witcomb, A. 2013. 'Understanding the role of affect in producing a critical pedagogy for history museums', *Museum Management and Curatorship* 28(3): 255–71.
Woodcraft, S. 2015. 'Understanding and measuring social sustainability', *Journal of Urban Regeneration & Renewal* 8(2): 133–44.
Woolwich Exchange, 2020. *Woolwich Exchange*. Online: retrieved from https://www.woolwichexchange.co.uk/downloads/woolwich-exchange-our-plans.pdf.
Xu, H. and S. Dai. 2012. 'A system dynamics approach to explore sustainable policies for Xidi, the world heritage village', *Current Issues in Tourism* 15(5): 441–59.
Xuereb, M. 2016. 'Vintage bus sale approaches final stop. Tuesday deadline to own a slice of Maltese history', *Times of Malta*, 9 October 2016. Online: retrieved from https://timesofmalta.com/articles/view/vintage-bus-sale-approaches-final-stop.627375.
Yalouri, E. 2001. *The Acropolis: Global fame, local claim*. Oxford; New York: Berg.
Yarrow, T. 2016. 'Negotiating heritage and energy conservation: An ethnography of domestic renovation', *The Historic Environment: Policy and practice* 7(4): 340–51.

Yarrow, T. 2018. ‘Retaining character: Heritage conservation and the logic of continuity’, *Social Anthropology* 26(3): 330–44.

Yarrow, T. 2019. ‘How conservation matters: Ethnographic explorations of historic building renovation’, *Journal of Material Culture* 24(1): 3–21.

Zimmermann, L. J. 2007. ‘Submission – Dionysiou Areopagitou Street, Athens’. Online: retrieved from https://worldarch.org/blog/submission-dionysiou-areopagitou-st-athens/.

Index

www.ingramcontent.com/pod-product-compliance
Lightning Source LLC
LaVergne TN
LVHW052017300826
846742LV00020B/82
9781787358348